PENGUIN BOOKS

PARADIGMS LOST

John Simon is a major critic of the arts. In addition to being the drama critic for *New York* magazine and the *Hudson Review*, he is the film critic for *National Review* and a frequent book reviewer for the *New Leader* and other publications. He writes about fine arts, opera, and ballet. His most recent books are *Ingmar Bergman Directs*, *Movies into Film*, *Uneasy Stages*, and *Singularities*.

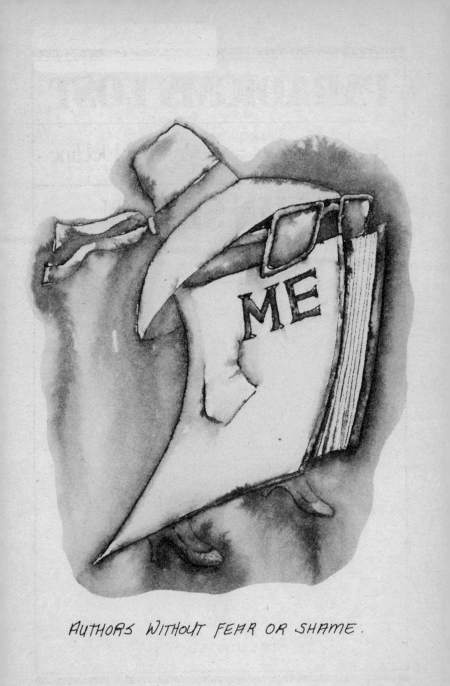

AUTHORS WITHOUT FEAR OR SHAME.

# PARADIGMS LOST

Reflections on Literacy and Its Decline

## JOHN SIMON

ILLUSTRATED BY MICHELE CHESSARE

PENGUIN BOOKS

Penguin Books Ltd, Harmondsworth,
Middlesex, England
Penguin Books, 40 West 23rd Street,
New York, New York 10010, U.S.A.
Penguin Books Australia Ltd, Ringwood,
Victoria, Australia
Penguin Books Canada Limited, 2801 John Street,
Markham, Ontario, Canada L3R 1B4
Penguin Books (N.Z.) Ltd, 182–190 Wairau Road,
Auckland 10. New Zealand

First published in the United States of America by
Clarkson N. Potter, Inc., 1980
First published in Canada by
General Publishing Company Limited 1980
Published in Penguin Books 1981
Reprinted 1981 (twice), 1984

LIBRARY OF CONGRESS CATALOGING IN PUBLICATION DATA
Simon, John Ivan.
Paradigms lost.
Reprint. Originally published: New York: C. N. Potter, 1980.
Includes index.
1. English language—Addresses, essays, lectures.
2. English language—Anecdotes, facetiae, satire, etc.
3. English language—United States—Addresses, essays, lectures. I. Title.
[PE1072.S57 1981] 401'.9 81-2095
ISBN 0 14 00.5921 0 AACR2

Printed in the United States of America by
Offset Paperback Mfrs., Inc., Dallas, Pennsylvania
Set in Palatino

The essays in this book have appeared in the following publications. *Esquire:* May 1977, June 1977, July 1977, August 1977, September 1977, October 1977, January 1978, February 1978, March 1978, April 1978, May 1978, June 1978, August 1978, September 1978, October 1978, November 1978, December 1978, January 1979, February 1979, March 1979, April 1979, May 1979, June 1979, August 1979, September 1979, October 1979. *More:* September 1976, October 1976, December 1976, February 1977, March 1977.

"Pressure from Below" and "Pressure from Above" are reprinted in *The State of the Language,* edited by Leonard Michaels and Christopher Ricks. Berkeley, California: University of California Press, 1980.

To Alexandra
Before whom words fail me

## Author's Note

The pieces in this book are not reprinted in chronological order but in thematic groupings. As a result, certain deliberate reiterations, which were separated by time, may here look like inadvertent duplication. I have allowed these recurrences to remain in the belief that a good point can stand some repetition.

## Acknowledgments

*The author wishes to thank Nancy Novogrod, his editor, for her invaluable, more than ordinary editorial contributions and Michele Chessare, for illustrations that will amuse him long after he has forgotten this book.*

# Contents

# AN EDUCATION IN LOVE

**W**hen Michael Kramer, the editor of *More* magazine, approached me about doing a column on language for him (the time was 1976), I was astounded. "Why me?" I was going to ask, but promptly checked myself so as to emend my query to "Why I?" Yet whereas the first sounded ungrammatical, the second struck me as unnatural. It occurred to me that if such a simple matter could give one pause, a problem did exist. So I said, "Why not?"— which was both idiomatic and grammatical, but rather quixotic.

But what kind of column, exactly, and was I the right person for it? Kramer and Ron Rosenbaum, his aide-de-camp, assured me that there was no time to waste on self-doubt; the English language was in critical condition, and they had spotted me as someone who cared. Perhaps the fact that I had long since given up being a teacher of English and had never been a scholar of linguistics was actually an advantage. After all, when you are inquiring into a scandal in the automotive industry, it is best not to appoint Henry Ford as investigator.

Four years later, I am still asking myself what you might ask me: Why did I do it, and what were my qualifications? Well, I had always been interested in words, in language. My father taught me the alphabet a couple of years before I started elementary school in Belgrade, Yugoslavia. Reading immediately became my favorite activity and writing followed apace. By the time I was going to elementary school, I was fluent in three languages: Serbo-Croatian, Hungarian, and German. It may be that this had a lasting effect on my attitude toward language: that I became playful with words, rattling them around in my pockets in triplicate, pulling out now one, now another version of the same thing. It may be that having three different ways of saying *cloud* or *horse* made each term more interesting. But this is merely a supposition; the only thing I remember clearly is my grandmother's astonishment when I described, in German, a lot of beetles I came across in a park as a *multitude (Menge)*. This was considered rather fancy for a four-year-old.

I am not quite sure how I discovered poetry, but I had by the time I was six, at which point I also encountered romance: somewhere around then I wrote my first love poem to an older woman of thirteen or fourteen who lived on a floor above ours ("closer to heaven") and sometimes came down to play with me. The poem, though most likely inferior to the early *canzoni* and sonnets of Dante, proved equally efficacious: like his Beatrice, my Gabriela gave me a cold shoulder. But even the most passionate love poem is a bit unfaithful to the beloved: it is also enamored of its language, of the words that intoxicate anyone who gets close enough to them to experience their sensuousness and aroma. I went on writing what I took to be poetry in Serbo-Croatian, German, Hungarian, and French before I could write English verse. My first poetic effort in my fifth language was a love lyric to a beautiful Swedish opera singer who sat across the aisle from me on a flight from Rome to Madrid (a leg of my journey to America). It enabled me to become her friend; for a lover, she preferred to an unknown fifteen-year-old the famous Italian soccer referee who sat on her right.

But let us backtrack for a moment. I began my secondary schooling in Yugoslavia, where English was not part of the curriculum. Before being sent to boarding school in England at thirteen, I got some crash tutoring in English at home; still, I remember my puzzlement at the first dinner at Leys School, Cambridge, when the boy next to me asked me to pass the milk. "Mək" did not suggest "milllk," which is what I called it. Hardly had I learned my English properly before Britain was in the war. It had not yet reached Yugoslavia, however, so my father returned me to school in Belgrade, where I promptly forgot most of my English; I recall the mirth of a sophisticated older girl I tried to impress when I referred to "a famous poetist."

On the eve of my departure for the United States I had to relearn my English in another crash course at home from the Dickensianly named Mr. Foggit, an odd-looking, whimsical tutor who may have been a British secret agent. I picked Edgar Rice Burroughs's Martian novels for us to read, partly because I was in love with their shocking-pink heroine, Princess Dejah Thoris, the color of whose skin matched that of her planet. My fiercely hatchet-faced yet gently balding tutor supplemented our reading with tales of his love life, including episodes involving a small, delicate redhead named Madge, who liked making love in the shower where her skin was as pink, I assume, as that of Dejah Thoris. No wonder English became eroticized for me, what with a rutilant princess and a dainty redhead with a steamily rubescent epidermis.

At my first American school in Pennsylvania, I had the good fortune to have for my English teacher a brilliant and unorthodox fellow named Homer Nearing, who was collaborating with his fiancée on a novel for which he solicited chapters from his more exotic students. The novel was called *The Gentle Debate*; in it, a young man and woman stranded on a desert isle took turns telling stories, mostly folk tales. His were celebrations of sexual indulgence, supposed to make the heroine sleep with him; hers were paeans to chastity, meant to make the hero accept a platonic relationship. Various Latin-American students had already contributed chapters from folk tales of their respective countries; could I come up with a suitably aphrodisiac or anaphrodisiac story from Yugoslavia? I couldn't, but I was impressed by Nearing's coinage for the heroine, whom he referred to as a "chastitute." So neologisms were possible: language could grow new shoots.

Although I never wrote that story, contemplating it made me again confound poetics with erotics, as did the verses I wrote to a pretty waitress at the local soda parlor, who would go out only with older boys but, to their annoyance, cherished my poetic outpourings. "Flo wouldn't give Simon the time of day," I overheard one of her lovers tell another (she was free with her favors), "but she knows all of his poems by heart." Language had won, even if I lost.

It was, I recall, at this time that I became sensitive to problems of pronunciation—oddly enough, not over an English word but over a Russian name. Homer Nearing insisted that the accent in Borodin fell on the second syllable, whereas I plunked for the first. I cannot now remember what authorities we consulted, but we discovered that we were both wrong, though I was less so: I had merely overlooked a secondary accent on the last syllable. Since that day, looking up things in dictionaries became important to me; strange that I should owe it to a composer I do not particularly like. Call it kismet.

To my love of words and correct pronunciation was added a recognition of the seductive power of style. In Maxwell Anderson's *High Tor*, the graduation play at Horace Mann in New York, my last high school, Julian Beck was starred and I was featured as the blind old Indian, John, who gets to deliver most of Anderson's vaporous blank-verse soliloquies. Thus John sets the scene with a lengthy recital of the seasonal activities of High Tor's birds and beasts—an effusion so long, cumbrous, and boring that Mr. Clausen, our drama coach, appropriately cut it by a third. On opening night, I forgot my lines midway, and had to improvise until I could reconnect with the text. So I desperately spun out absurd activities for fictitious fauna until I repossessed the right thread. Meanwhile, in the wings, Mr. Clausen and Julian were cursing me for "restoring the cut lines." I realized that in reproducing a man's style—even if it was only Slapsie Maxie Anderson's all too blank verse—one could capture his essence.

At the time I came to Harvard I began to write ardent verses to a number of Radcliffe girls; some of these poems were duly printed in the appropriate magazines, but my poetry ran dry before there was enough of it for a volume; by then, however, my prose had begun. It, too, was a love affair with words, although perhaps a little less mystical, more down-to-earth than poetry. And it had a by-product: watching my own prose made me start noticing what others were doing to theirs, both in speech and in writing.

I suppose I must credit my coming to English relatively late with my especially analytical, exploratory, adventurous approach to it. I am always surprised when people marvel at the way some foreigners—Joseph Conrad, Karen Blixen, alias Isak Dinesen, Vladimir Nabokov—wrote English. If you have a sufficient feeling for and facility with language, coming to a specific tongue later rather than earlier can prove a distinct advantage. One approaches that language with better credentials—linguistic (one's previous languages), cultural (one's awareness of language as the interpreter of a society), and emotional (one's ability to appreciate and love, which grows with the years). There is a sense in which one is both an insider and an outsider in that language, and the interplay between the two becomes creative play.

In the 1940s, when I became a graduate student, people were not going around saying "Come to dinner with Bill and I" or "Hopefully, it won't rain tomorrow"; they were not accentuating the penult in *influence* or using *disinterested* as a synonym for *unin-*

*terested.* Some things were causing trouble even then: for example, that the substantive *precedent* rhymes with "less a dent," whereas *precedence* rhymes with *credence;* or that *less* refers to quantity (less sugar) and *fewer* to number (fewer diabetics). But these were, so to speak, more sophisticated errors that might bring a tear to an angel's eye, but would not make heaven weep.

Why—if I am not merely a *laudator temporis acti,* and I am reasonably sure I am not—was language better in those days? And what started it on its downhill course? For one thing, standards in the schools were higher because education had not yet been dealt the four great body blows: (1) the student rebellion of 1968, which, in essence, meant that students themselves became the arbiters of what subjects were to be taught, and grammar, by jingo (or Ringo), was not one of them; (2) the notion that in a democratic society language must accommodate itself to the whims, idiosyncrasies, dialects, and sheer ignorance of underprivileged minorities, especially if these happened to be black, Hispanic, and, later on, female or homosexual; (3) the introduction by more and more incompetent English teachers, products of the new system (see items 1 and 2, above), of ever fancier techniques of *not* teaching English, for which, if the methods involved new technologies and were couched in the appropriately impenetrable jargon, grants could readily be obtained; and (4) television—the nonlanguage and aboriginal grammar of commercials, commentators, sports announcers, athletes, assorted celebrities, and just about everyone on that word-mongering and word-mangling medium that sucks in victims far more perniciously than radio ever did.

But in my graduate-school days there were still relatively prescriptive dictionaries, i.e., ones that distinguished between the incorrect and correct use of words based on established practice, cultural tradition, the way of good writers; between preferred and suspect, or even unacceptable, pronunciations. Descriptive (or structural) linguistics had not yet arrived—that statistical, populist, sociological approach, whose adherents claimed to be merely recording and describing the language as it was used by anyone and everyone, without imposing elitist judgments on it. Whatever came out of the untutored mouths and unsharpened pencil stubs of the people—sorry, The People—was held legitimate if not sacrosanct by these new lexicon artists.

Oh, for the times when we tended to go by the second edition of *Webster's International Dictionary* and its derivatives, the pre-seventh-edition *Collegiates*, and other lexical authorities that, although not totally prescriptive, nevertheless indicated preferences and exercised a certain selectivity. With the coming of *Webster's Third* in 1961, descriptive linguistics had its resounding victory. As Dwight Macdonald succinctly put it in "The String Untuned," * his magisterial critique of that seminally sinister dictionary, "Scientific revolution has meshed gears with a trend toward permissiveness, in the name of democracy, that is debasing our language by rendering it less precise and thus less effective as literature and less efficient as communication. It is felt that it is snobbish to insist on making discriminations—the very word has acquired a Jim Crow flavor—about usage. And it is assumed that the majority is right. This feeling seems to me sentimental and this assumption unfounded."

And Macdonald explains: "The objection is not to recording the facts of actual usage. It is to failing to give the information that would enable the reader to decide which usage he wants to adopt." More recently, Kingsley Amis, in "Getting It Wrong," ** after noting with approbation that the *Concise Oxford Dictionary* will use "(joc.)" or "(vulg.)" to indicate that a term is jocular or vulgar, continues: "What about '(illit.): illiterate, used only by those who have no wish to write accurately or vigorously'? A dictionary records usage impartially, agreed, but whatever anybody says or does . . . *when consulted it is taken as prescriptive too* by almost everybody who is not a lexicographer or a linguist, and prescription is partiality. It seems harsh to deny guidance to the lonely and diminishing minority who may genuinely need and want it."

This book—or the essays that follow—must be recognized as the work of an amateur. Yet an amateur, I trust, in the good sense of the word: a lover of his subject, but one who writes about his love scrupulously and disinterestedly. It seems to me that the new scientism or sciolism of the structural linguists is not truly disinterested. As Dwight Macdonald compellingly argues in his al-

* In *Against the American Grain*, New York, Random House, 1962.
** In *The State of the Language*, Leonard Michaels and Christopher Ricks, editors. Berkeley, University of California Press, 1980.

ready quoted essay, to accept *infer* as a synonym for *imply* and *bimonthly* as meaning both "once every two months" and "twice a month" is also a form of prescriptiveness and dogmatism. It stems, I would say, from some sort of populism, Marxism, bad social conscience, demagoguery, inverted snobbery, or even moral cowardice. It is significant, I think, that when a linguist like Noam Chomsky—a committed leftist—makes statements about history, they can be shown to be tendentious and unfactual.

And, apropos Chomsky, at a recent symposium on the state of the English language held in San Francisco, Randolph Quirk, Quain Professor of English Language and Literature at University College, London, accused me of letting my needle get stuck in the linguistics of the fifties; we now have, said Quain Professor Quirk, Chomsky and generative and transformational grammar; structural linguistics is passé. But it isn't, really. Chomsky is certainly not prescriptive—to the extent that he bothers his august head with such comprehensible lexical concepts—and he doesn't compile dictionaries. The rulers of the roost are *Webster's Third* and the equally descriptive *Random House Dictionary*. Even the *Supplements* to the majestic *Oxford English Dictionary* are amazingly permissive under Robert Burchfield's editorship. A young correspondent of mine from the University of Texas, Bryan Garner, having attended a lecture of Burchfield's at Oxford, put some questions to the eminent lexicographer. Here is Garner's account: "I also asked Mr. Burchfield about the status of *prioritize* and *containerize* in the *Supplements.* Yes, they appear, along with *privatize.* I find it interesting that Mr. Burchfield accepts these -ize neologisms with such equanimity, without bristling—that he (it seems) disdains those who fight against them, while, as he admits, he would never use the words himself."

"Change," writes David B. Guralnik, editor-in-chief of *Webster's New World Dictionary,* "even change through error, has been a natural process in our language from its very beginnings, and nature is not to be denied." * There is the structuralist or permissive mania at its most virulent: ignorance is natural and must not be interfered with. One is reminded of Wilde's Lady Bracknell: "I do not approve of anything that tampers with natural ignorance. Ignorance is like a delicate exotic fruit; touch it and the bloom is

* The *New York Times Magazine,* August 26, 1977.

gone." Even more revealingly, Guralnik concludes: "The language in any period accurately reflects the culture in which it is used. Let's not try to treat a fever by tampering with the thermometer." If Guralnik's analogy means anything, it is that our culture is a sickness (fever), and that we must not take it out on the language (thermometer) if we don't like what it registers. But suppose that the thermometer has become infected by mouths diseased with ignorance; should we stick it into every other mouth as well, including our own, and so have all of us sicken?

What worthies like Quirk, Guralnik, and the rest do not understand is that we need a standard written English (or normative grapholect, to give it its technical name) because, as Professor E. D. Hirsch, Jr.—with whom I disagree about other matters—persuasively argues in *The Philosophy of Composition:* "Without a normative grapholect, a classless society could not be plausibly imagined." * And without a writer's—and speaker's—ability to use the grapholect imaginatively, occasionally taking calculated liberties with it, elegant or racy speech and writing could not plausibly be imagined.

In the essays that follow I have tried to touch upon some major and minor abuses of the English language. I have also offered little disquisitions on correct usage and how it might be achieved. I have suggested, too, what can and what cannot be done to improve, protect, and save the language. My treatment is brief and suggestive rather than academic and exhaustive. But it is not afraid of being prescriptive, aggressive, and optimistic. We can fight, I say, even for things some fairly conservative linguists would abandon as lost causes. I return once more to that San Francisco symposium, at which Dwight Bolinger reproved me for trying to save the word *disinterested* from becoming synonymous with *uninterested.* The emeritus professor of Romance languages and literatures at Harvard argued that since all words with the prefix *dis-* have negative connotations, we cannot expect people to grasp a single exception. *Disinterested* has to be sacrificed; the battle lines must be drawn elsewhere. To which I responded by saying that, my eye having just caught in the audience the woman I love, I could affirm the word *disrobe* to be one of the most beautiful, poetic, and positive words in the English language. So much

* Chicago, The University of Chicago Press, 1977. P. 46.

for aberrant theories that beg to be (another often positive word) disproved.

But there is more to this. As long as there exists an active minority that knows how to distinguish between *disinterested* and *uninterested,* it is not too late to fight for such discriminating usage. The important thing is the willingness to fight, and *Paradigms Lost* makes some proposals about where and how to do it. It also stresses that strategy and tactics are less important than sheer resolve and persistence.

# WHAT IS WORTH DEFENDING

# It's Nice to Be Right

**G**rammar is a tricky, inconsistent thing. Being the backbone of speech and writing, it should, we think, be eminently logical, make perfect sense, like the human skeleton. But, of course, the skeleton is arbitrary, too. Why twelve pairs of ribs rather than eleven or thirteen? Why thirty-two teeth? It has something to do with evolution and functionalism—but only sometimes, not always. So there are aspects of grammar that make good, logical sense, and others that do not.

For example: it makes perfect sense that correct English should demand agreement; "no one," "someone," "everyone," "anyone" should be followed by singular verbs because the "one" is a clear indication that English thinks of "everyone" and "everybody" as being a singular one or body—many people acting as one. Similarly, "no one" means "not any one," and since the "one" is there (if only to be denied in actuality), it is nonsense to say "No one knew *their* American history" or "Everyone returned to *their* seats." Observe that even the most cloddish speaker would unhesitantly say "Everyone *was* happy" and would not dream of uttering "No one *were* there."

Unfortunately, it takes only one or two intruding words for agreement—and logic—to vanish. Moreover, the nearness of a plural object (in my second example, "seats") fools people into assuming that the pronoun in the possessive depends on this plural. But it depends on the subject, which is palpably singular, so that it clearly and democratically has to be one seat to one body or to one person.

There are, then, many instances where grammar is manifestly logical and where application of simple logic could spare us a good many errors. Take the absurd "overly," which has gained widespread acceptance in this country, though it is still sensibly frowned on in England. Consider that "over" is an adverb (among its several uses) and so too would be "overly," which does nothing more than add an extra syllable to turn something into what it has been all along. Why, then, say "overly complicated," "overly qualified," or "overly fond," et cetera, when "overcomplicated," "overqualified," "overfond," and so on are shorter, neater, more euphonious? The argument that we need "overly" for the negative statement "not overly" is otiose; we have "overmuch," "excessively," "very," and several others to choose from. So let the -ly serve where it logically belongs: in converting an adjective into an adverb, as in, say, "keenly," "sensibly," and the like. The gratuitous -ly is on the march, however: already we have the redundancy "firstly," the abomination "thusly," and soon, for all I know, we may get "soonly."

Thus, concision, which is a form of common sense, is another logical guiding principle. But, unfortunately, grammar is as often arbitrary as it is logical. There is, for instance, no logical reason that I can detect for "She is as beautiful as you" becoming, in a negative construction, "She is not so beautiful as you." Nevertheless, Eric Partridge, in *Usage and Abusage* (citing *Webster's*—the second edition, doubtless, not the third), records that "[not] so . . . as" is "preferred by many writers and authorities." In that very useful book *Modern American Usage*, which Wilson Follett regrettably did not live to finish, we read that in America (as opposed to England) even "workaday writers" and casual speakers will say: *"This summer is not so hot as last"* rather than "not as . . . as." A conversation with Jacques Barzun makes me suspect this entry to be one of his addenda to Follett's book as published; and it is one of the rare instances where I disagree with him: I see and hear "not as . . . as" all around me. Still, *Modern American Usage* makes a good stab at explaining this curiosity: "Perhaps *as . . . as* suggests equality so strongly that a denial of it must be signalized by *not so.*"

This would be a case of emphasis for the sake of clarity, which, along with logic and concision, must guide our use of language. But when language can be correctly inconsistent, it surely is not logical. Yet English, which clearly prefers "You are better than I" to "than me," also possesses the idiom "than whom no one is wiser." This reflects the inconsistency from which our present language arose: a bit of discrepancy in a surviving locution that points back to the initial chaos. The solution seems to be to respect the idiom as it has reached us, but in all other constructions to stick with "than" plus the nominative.

Besides logic, concision, and clarity, there is also the matter of authority. I wrote in one of these columns that you do not begin a sentence with "too" in the sense of "also," as in "Too, he was very old by then." Instead, you should write "By then, too, he was very old" or "Also, he was very old by then." Many readers wrote in asking on what authority I asserted this. Partly, of course, it is a matter of clarity, so that the "too" not be confused even for a second with "to" or with "two," either of which is apt to appear at the beginning of a sentence. But there is also the fact that good writers of the English language have not used the initial "too." This is the argument from authority, and with this kind of argument we must be extremely careful.

The two most common failures here are, one, adducing a good writer from the distant past, such as Shakespeare, who wrote before the language had become sufficiently codified; and, two, assuming that because the *Oxford English Dictionary* cites a couple of famous writers who committed a certain grammatical faux pas, the error has become legitimized. This brings me to the matter of dictionaries: quite a few readers have asked me to recommend a dictionary that speaks with full authority about what is right or wrong.

Alas, even the best dictionaries tend to abrogate that authority. In the biography of James Murray, the man behind the *Oxford English Dictionary*, K. M. Elisabeth Murray writes, "The one thing of which he was certain was that it was not the function of the Dictionary to establish a standard of 'right' or 'wrong,' " and she quotes her famous grandfather: "We do not all think alike, walk alike, dress alike, write alike, or dine alike: why should not we use our liberty in speech also, so long as the purpose of speech, to be intelligible, and its grace are not interfered with?"

This is, to me, a very disappointing position from a great dictionary maker, and it is most fortunate that his practice (and that of his collaborators) was better than his preachment. We get a rather confused statement that, on the one hand, promises considerable, if not total, freedom and, on the other, demands intelligibility and grace.

These are fine words, but what do they mean? At what point does intelligibility cease, and for whom? Some people can decipher the thickest foreign accents and the grossest mispronunciations; others cannot. On whose level of comprehension do we draw the line between intelligibility and gibberish? And what about the time factor? Is having to stop for several seconds while one unscrambles a meaning a legitimate or an illegitimate loss of time?

Yet if "intelligibility" is a somewhat elusive criterion, "grace" is as slippery as an Oriental-rug dealer. Graceful to whom, by what standards, and to what end? Is it more graceful to tell something horrible with appropriate horror or to tone it down for polite company? With grace we enter into the domain of taste, and taste is beyond the legislation of any dictionary. Here, clearly, we need expert opinion, but where, exactly, do we go looking for that?

Nevertheless, as I said before, the *Oxford English Dictionary* is a great—*the* great—dictionary, but it has to be used with discrimination. We must, each of us for himself, decide what in it represents the best in usage—and what is merely a corruption that has become more or less widespread or is, indeed, a mere hapax legomenon (a word recorded only once in a particular language). Someday I hope to write more fully about how one arrives at such distinctions, but obviously logic, concision, and clarity have much to do with it.

Another fine achievement is the *American Heritage Dictionary.* It is perhaps a trifle too short, too selective a tome, but at least it stands for something better than near total permissiveness. After all, if a dictionary does not lay down the law about what is right and what is wrong, then, *pace* Dr. Murray, who will? Yet rules do exist—in spelling, pronunciation, and definition—and it is absurd for today's dictionaries to enforce some of them while being latitudinarian about others. The *American Heritage Dictionary* has solved the problem with a usage panel—well over a hundred experts who are frequently polled by the editors about what they consider correct usage and whose votes for or against a certain usage are tabulated and reported—for example, 60 percent of the usage panel approve of this usage in spoken English, but only 45 percent in written English.

This is, of course, the creation of an ad hoc academy and makes sense—except that the names, as you look at them on pages x to xii of the dictionary, may strike you as a catholic but not consistently compelling lot. Especially startling is the paucity of literary notables (other than critics and editors, though these, too, are a mixed bunch), but this may simply mean that great novelists, poets, et cetera are too busy (or greedy) to bother with such unpaid work. Still, the membership ranges from some persons of impeccable credentials to others from whom you would not want to buy a used car (or a misused word). But it is in this direction that salvation must lie: the eventual creation of an Academy of the Anglo-American Language.

# A Pointed Discussion of Punctuation

In the writing, and even in the speaking, of good English, there is a silent partner: punctuation. Except as a pause, it is not audible (save when Victor Borge does a number on it), but it makes for basic clarity and can provide interesting shades of meaning in the form of undertones. In its first capacity, then, it is a traffic policeman averting chaos in the flow of prose; in its second, a good stage director supplementing the playwright's text with the weight of implication. And it is today in as bad a shape as any other aspect of the English language—possibly worse.

Ignorance about punctuation flourishes everywhere. Have you noticed, for example, how many letters nowadays begin with "Dear X;" when "Dear X," or "Dear Mr. X:" would be correct? Time was when people knew that a semicolon partly closes the movement of a sentence and is out of place where someone is summoned to attend to a message; some people even knew that the vocative is followed by a comma, although the colon provides, at the beginning of a more formal communication, the required

*A POINTED DISCUSSION OF PUNCTUATION*

annunciatory, or more solemn, touch. It is, in fact, usually safe not to continue reading a letter that follows up the addressee's invocation with a semicolon: nothing intelligent is likely to be contained therein.

Take a peculiarly chilling example of ignorance coupled with moral cowardice, which was communicated to me by Mr. Ray Russell, of Beverly Hills. He was fairly regularly catching out the *Los Angeles Times* in erroneously substituting single open quotation marks for apostrophes. Thus, on June 30, 1977, he found the headline SOUP 'N' SALAD, which should, of course, have read SOUP 'N' SALAD. Another headline, on August 25, 1977, read A QUICK 'N' EASY EXOTIC-STYLE MEAL, in which, by the way, "exotic-style" is rather questionable, too. What the *Times*'s editors did not seem to understand was that the apostrophe, among other things, replaces omitted letters; though the single quotation mark resembles the apostrophe in looks, it can do no such thing. Thus it is QUICK 'N' EASY that would have properly indicated the colloquial omission of the "a" and "d."

When Mr. Russell politely wrote to various editors of the paper, some of them did not even have the courtesy to answer. Finally, a reply came from the executive news editor of the View section, which had been conspicuously guilty of the particular malpractice. The editor, Don Alpert, began by dragging in an ancient and feeble joke (about not knowing one's apostrophe from one's asterisk) and went on to declare that Russell's complaint was "not one of usage but of type." He stated that the *Times*'s typeface was Bodoni and that "the way it [the apostrophe] is designed, as a single quote, may lead to some confusion." Then, rather patronizingly, he explained that Bodoni was a respectable typeface, concluding with another irrelevant, doddering joke: "Please forgive us our typefaces as we forgive others their typos."

As Russell pointed out in his rejoinder to Alpert, neither in Bodoni nor in any other established typeface are the apostrophe and single open quotation mark identical. He further noted that the mistake was not ubiquitous at the *Times:* the same issue that sported the offending SOUP 'N' SALAD also displayed a correct FISH 'N' CHIPS. And he added, "All of these typefaces provide both single quotes *and* apostrophes, the catch being to find, in this lax epoch, copy editors and proofreaders who know the difference between them and their distinctly different functions." I do not wish to press the moral point too far, but it gives one—besides soup 'n' salad—food for thought to realize that editors who commit such egregious errors are the very ones who slough off their responsibilities with silence or double-talk.

Do not commit the costly error of considering punctuation unimportant: your life may depend on it. Certainly the life of King Edward II hung by a comma. Mortimer, his enemy, sent Edward's jailers an ambiguous letter—but let me tell it in Kit Marlowe's words:

> *This letter, written by a friend of ours,*
> *Contains his death, yet bids them save his life:*
> Edwardum occidere nolite timere, bonum est—
> *"Fear not to kill the king, 'tis good he die."*
> *But read it thus and that's another sense:*
> Edwardum occidere nolite, timere bonum est—
> *"Kill not the king, 'tis good to fear the worst."*
> *Unpointed as it is, thus shall it go . . .*

"Unpointed," i.e., unpunctuated, it went—and with it Edward's life. The jailer assumed the fell interpretation to be correct.

The problem today is not only poor teaching of punctuation, et cetera, but also active opposition to the thorough teaching of it. An article in the Spring/Fall, 1974, issue of the *Florida FL Reporter* cites a syllabus for teachers of freshman composition stating that persistent "ignoring of the niceties of punctuation, spelling, and sentence construction" should be penalized. Comments the writer: "Is it any wonder that H.E.W. is currently investigating the University of Texas because of allegations of institutionalized discrimination against minorities?" Demanding that a student write correctly so as to be readily understood is in danger of becoming illegal!

Everyone can adduce examples of more or less disastrous misunderstandings stemming from mispunctuation. In a recent booklet, *Stalking the Wild Semicolon* (Thresh Publications, $1.25), William Myatt cites half a dozen ways in which the sentence "You have poison ivy so don't do anything rash" can be punctuated, yielding six very different meanings. Myatt's pamphlet, subtitled "Easy Guide to Punctuation" (which should read, "An Easy Guide . . ."), seems to be quite a seller among students; a laudatory review in the *Atlantic Monthly* recommends it to children and poets, as well. Yet, upon examination, it proves to be a pathetic little pamphlet, afflicted with an illness akin to that of the students it proposes to cure.

As for the level of instruction in it, we read, for instance, that commas are "real toughies." The precepts about their application do not amount to much more than that the comma tells the reader "when to pause within a sentence," and that the confused student should write his paper without commas, then read it aloud and stick in a comma wherever his ear tells him a pause is needed. It's a mighty tame comma that allows itself to be stalked that easily.

So this is what a popular, contemporary book on punctuation, recommended by the *Atlantic* to children and poets as well, looks like. There is nothing in it even about so basic a matter as where periods, commas, colons, and semicolons go in relation to quotation marks. In American usage, commas and periods always go inside, colons and semicolons (like exclamation points and question marks) outside the quotation marks, except when they are part of the quoted matter. In England, however, periods and commas go outside the quotation marks. Arbitrary, I concede, but not unimportant. One man, now a distinguished British scholar and critic, wrote a doctoral thesis that was rejected some years ago by the English department of a leading American university because the periods and commas were sticking out, in the British manner, instead of being tucked in, as in ours. The whole thesis had to be retyped before it was accepted. "How silly of them," we all commiserated; but they were right. Some aspects of punctuation, like some aspects of grammar, have nothing to do with logic and everything to do with consistency. The mind's eye—like the eye's mind—gets used to seeing a certain order; it becomes needlessly dislocated and unnerved by deviations.

Now, it is true that some good writers punctuate perversely. In some cases, their editors (in the days when editors still knew about such matters) silently corrected their vagaries. In other cases—especially when a writer's punctuational idiosyncrasies are tightly interwoven with his racily quirky personality and when one is reproducing letters to friends, where informality and irregularity contribute to the intimacy—such peculiarities are best left uncorrected. For example, when E. E. Cummings writes in a letter to Hildegarde Watson about the qualities of his just-deceased mother, he concludes with the following one-sentence paragraph: "such things I find wonderful: and, feeling that you love what is wonderful, I want to share my admiration with you [no period]"

There is no justification for the lowercase "such" and the absence of the final period, even though this was the style of Cummings's poetry. Yet those are harmless quirks; the colon after "wonderful," however, which promises and then denies some kind of enumeration, seems perversely misleading. Still, it may have been a calculated risk, meant to jar the reader into stopping to consider the full weight of that "wonderful." However that may be, Cummings was Cummings, and we are only we. *"Quod licet Jovi, non decet bovi"*: "What's fitting for Jove is indecent for an ox." But why go on to such esoterica when there is trouble much nearer home: just look at the posters that surround you and you will observe that differentiation between "its" and "it's" is fast becoming a lost art.

Take, for example, a poster that was recently prominent around town; it advertised a certain Vickie Sue Robinson record and read: THE NEW ALBUM FROM THE LADY THAT'S TURNED EVERYONES [*sic*] HEAD AROUND. I do not believe that this can be a mere misprint: in such a short text, and in letters as large as a boxer's fist, "they" do not perpetrate misprints—not even *they*. The curious thing, then, is that they can recognize the contraction of "that has" and punctuate correctly "that's," but that they cannot comprehend the genitive in "everyone's"—so this apostrophe goes by the board.

Clearly, knowledge of punctuation does not exist apart from a rudimentary understanding of grammar. Yet there exist more mysterious cases, where it is impossible to tell just how a particular species of ignorance operates—ignorance, like the heart, having its own inscrutable reasons.

Now consider an advertisement in the November 7, 1977, issue of *New York* magazine by the "proud owners of Sparks Steak House," noted not only for their pride but also for their illiteracy. Even the name Sparks Steak House seems to lack an apostrophe, and previous ads of theirs have been monuments to the analphabetic. This particular one begins, in huge print, YOU'RE WRONG MIMI SHERATON (no punctuation). Soon thereafter, in this answer to an unfavorable notice, we read: "One erroneous review out of you, is not going to hurt Sparks Steak House." What, we ask, is that comma after "you" doing there? How can one possibly separate the subject ("review") from the predicate ("is") by a comma? Even according to the simpleminded instructions of William Myatt's guide (the comma tells the reader when to pause within a sentence), no pause is conceivable after that "you"—barring the possibility, of course, that the author is so choked up with rage at the mere thought of Mimi Sheraton (the "you" in question) that he must pause to regain his breath.

It may also be that some errors of punctuation appearing in the public prints are directly related to the widespread inability to read proof competently. Proofreading has always been a difficult task, requiring the kind of minute attention to detail that seems to be ever harder to come by—it may even be that human nature is changing toward greater basic inattentiveness, that there is a kind of endemic loss of concentration. It is certainly extraordinary, however, to come across a flagrant lapse—in this case, of spelling—in the *New York Times*, in a headline set in what, to my untutored eyes, looks like two-line great-primer (thirty-six-point) type. In an early edition of the Sunday, October 23, 1977, "Week in Review," we read: SOUTH AFRICA HAS ALWAYS KEPT THE PRESS RAINED IN. To turn "reined" into "rained" would look bad in any type size, but writ that large, it truly hurts. In the article, we read that "editors and reporters must constantly resort to legal advice to determine who [*sic*] they can quote," which is worse still, but at least it's in much smaller type.

Punctuation, spelling, grammar—how much longer will they be with us at all? Or will there be a backlash, sweeping them in again with renewed stringency? I doubt that—unless, as several readers have suggested, we were to have an academy on the model of the French Academy. But that is highly unlikely: such academies, even if instituted long ago by royal fiat, have a hard time surviving in this permissive age of the common man; to create one now, over the hue and cry of the linguistic levelers, would be nearly impossible. But necessary.

## Sibling Rivalry

**M**ankind has difficulties with fine discriminations. Even perceiving major differences can be a problem, but when the distinction is less than deafening or blinding, it has been known to escape speakers and writers with frightening ease. Even halfway

MASTERLY

MASTERFUL

educated people tend by now to have caught on to the difference between *lie* and *lay,* but this enlightenment was probably brought on by the embarrassment caused by the slang meaning of *lay.* Other similarities, however, continue to throw people, as witness the Republican National Committee's "Critical Issues Survey," forwarded to me by Joe B. Whisler, of Kansas City, Missouri. Question six reads: "Do you believe that continued U.S. Federal Budget deficits are a principle cause of inflation?" If you did not blanch as you read this, you too fail to differentiate between *principal* and *principle* and need to consult your dictionary forthwith.

Some readers have sent in an ad that states: "Let Arnie and I cater it for you." The real confusion comes in when two words are more similar than *I* and *me.* Thus the ever-watchful Rabbi Lyle Kamlet upbraids me for having written in a review: "Tennessee Williams backs away even farther from honest self-revelation." *Farther,* argues Rabbi Kamlet, "should be restricted to convey literal distance," whereas *further* refers to "the figurative sense of degree, quantity, etc." I agree, but insist that *backing away,* even when used metaphorically, is an image of space and distance to which the spatial *farther* is perfectly suited. But this is a fine point open to debate; the following matters are not.

In the same communication, Rabbi Kamlet quotes Richard Eder of the *New York Times* as having written in a drama review "among all the floundering" instead of *"amid." Among* clearly presupposes a number of surrounding but separate entities, for example, "among those countless hungry children"; whereas *amid* denotes a position in the middle of something larger but of a piece and not divisible, for example, "amid all that bustle" or "chaos," or, as in Eder's phrase, "floundering." This is an example of what I would call verbal sibling rivalry: pairs of almost but not really twin words getting into each other's hair. And while I am on *each other,* let me remind you that it is correct for relationships involving two elements; where there are three or more, *one another* is required, for reasons that will appear to you if you stop to think.

But who, nowadays, stops to think? Time, wrote Aldous Huxley, must have a stop; but not, apparently, *Time* magazine, which when a reader wrote in to point out a grammatical error answered with a two-line note beginning, "Yes indeed, tsk, tsk." This condescending response is a clear indication of the tsk-tsk fly at work, spreading the dreadful (but insufficiently dreaded) sleeping

sickness of the mind. Not to stray from today's topic, however, let
me return to some prime examples of sibling rivalry.

One of the more offensive and widespread specimens is the
confusion of *most* and *almost*. Almost any day you will hear someone say "most any day." But *most* is the superlative of *many* or
*much* or refers to what is greatest in amount, size, or degree. *Almost*, on the other hand, is a synonym for *nearly*. Thus "most
people" is correct, being the superlative of "many people"; but
"most everybody" is incorrect, the proper synonym for "nearly
everybody" being "almost everybody." One difficulty, obviously,
lies in the similarity in sound between *most* and *almost*. The other
stems from faulty analogy, one of the most insidious linguistic
pitfalls. It is assumed that if *though* and *although* are synonyms, the
same must be true of *most* and *almost*. Similarity of sound or faulty
analogy gives rise to most sibling rivalry.

Take, for instance, *flout* and *flaunt*. The meanings are as dissimi-
lar as can be. The former means "to defy"; the latter, "to show
off." But the fl . . . t sequence the two words have in common is
enough to get them less and less extricably mixed up. That the
confusion was relatively rare until recently only goes to show the
alarming loss of literacy in our time.

If the foregoing is an example of sibling rivalry based on close-
ness of sound, the confounding of *enormity* and *enormousness* is
based on faulty analogy. Usually, abstract nouns that can take
both Latin and Anglo-Saxon endings maintain the same meaning.
*Anxiety* and *anxiousness, pomposity* and *pompousness, credulity* and *cred-
ulousness* are hardly, if at all, distinguishable from each other—are,
in fact, twins. But *enormousness* and *enormity* are merely siblings: the
former refers to immensity of size; the latter, to immensity of
indecency or immorality. It is "the enormousness of the task," but
"the enormity of the crime."

There are rules that govern sibling rivalry. Take the pair *fortunate* and *fortuitous*. The former means something like "happy,"
"lucky," or "felicitous"; the latter, "chance" or "accidental." They
have the same etymological root but have branched out in different directions. Alas, in our more permissive, nonprescriptive dictionaries, they have become accepted as synonyms. Yet it would
be imbecile (not, by the way, *imbecilic,* a substandard adjective
derived by faulty analogy) to say, "This fortuitous event was carefully planned in advance." If the event was fortuitous (accidental),

it could not have been planned. (Sometimes, to be sure, the two can overlap: finding a diamond ring in the street is both fortuitous and fortunate.) Note, however, that whereas people will say *fortuitous* when they mean *fortunate*, the reverse is almost never the case. That is because *fortunate* is the easier word, more common and learned earlier; you might say that it is the older and stronger sibling that beats out the younger and weaker one.

Consider, next, the case of *imply* and *infer*. The former means "to hint" or "to suggest"; the latter, "to deduce" or "to conclude." Both words designate relatively subtle mental activities; therein, more than in their sounds, lies the similarity. But these activities are not merely different: they are, at best, complementary; at worst, antithetical. And still people confuse them, but it is only *infer* that gets misused, not *imply*. Again it is the more familiar word—the older, stronger sibling—that comes out unscathed.

Sometimes, however, two such kindred words seem to be, or ought to be, equally familiar—siblings with a negligible difference in age. Such a pair is *masterful* and *masterly*, and they get steadily confused, even though the first means "powerful," "command-ing," or "domineering"; whereas the second means "with the skill (or knowledge) of a master." I regret to say that here even the *American Heritage Dictionary*—the only current American dictionary *of any size* that I can countenance—is at fault: its third and fourth definitions of *masterful* are inadmissible. "Disregard of [the dis-tinction]" says Fowler, "is so obviously inconvenient that it can only be put down to ignorance." Yet even though *masterly* is en-countered by people as early in their lives as *masterful*, it is the latter that keeps wrongly supplanting the former, never the other way round. To some extent, it is the greater number of everyday adjectives ending in *-ful* than in *-ly* that is behind this error; more important, I believe, is the fact that our society admires power more than it does knowledge or skill. Here, most likely, it is pop-ularity or prestige that makes one sibling more masterful (*not* mas-terly) than the other.

Consider a similar pair: *uninterested* and *disinterested*. The former designates lack of intellectual or emotional involvement; the lat-ter, absence of a profit motive or of some other motive involving personal advantage or bias. Yet *disinterested*, which, I assume, en-ters a person's vocabulary later than *uninterested*, has almost totally usurped the place reserved for the latter. Here I imagine the reason to be laziness. Because we can say both *disinterestedness* and *disinterest* but have no shorter variant of *uninterestedness*, the shorter form wins out across the board and smuggles in its corresponding adjective, *disinterested*. The fact that *dis* and *in* constitute an assonance pleasing to the ear may add to the greater popularity of the *dis-* forms. That *uninteresting* has not yet been superseded by *disinteresting* is due only to the fact that the latter word does not exist. But such a trifle, I fear, will not keep the illiterates at bay much longer.

Sometimes siblings do not even sound alike: for example, *verbal* and *oral*. The first denotes anything having to do with words, written or spoken; the second refers to spoken words only. Yet *verbal* has well-nigh dislodged *oral* in the sense of a statement or agreement made by word of mouth. This may be so because *oral* also designates nonspeaking functions of the mouth, as in *oral hygiene* or *oral sex*, and so begets the ignorant assumption that the spoken word must be covered by that other adjective, *verbal*.

Finally, there are cases in which, even without the existence of a specific sibling, people are misled by the sound of a word. Thus *fulsome*, merely because its first syllable suggests fullness, a good thing, is taken to mean something positive related to fullness, such as "abundant" or "unstinting." Actually, it means "objectionably overdone" or "insincerely excessive" and is bad news indeed.

Keep those unruly siblings in their places! There are others I have overlooked, but if this article has the right effect, it will affect your future dealings with all of them.

## Just Between Us

**W**hy does language keep changing? Because it is a living thing, people will tell you. Something that you cannot press forever, like a dead flower, between the pages of a dictionary. Rather, it is a living organism that, like a live plant, sprouts new leaves and flowers. Alas, this lovely albeit trite image is—as I have said before and wish now to say with even greater emphasis—largely nonsense. Language, for the most part, changes out of ignorance.

Certainly new words can become needed, and a happy invention or slang can sometimes supply useful, though usually perishable, synonyms. But by and large, linguistic changes are caused by the ignorance of speakers and writers, and in the last few centuries—given our schools, dictionaries, and books on grammar—such ignorance could have been, like the live nettle or poison ivy it is, uprooted. It is, or ought to be, possible to stop—or at least considerably delay—unnecessary change, of which one of the most preposterous and nefarious examples is the recently proliferating but still weedable *between you and I.*

To get back, however, to our initial botanical analogy: let us concede that language is indeed a living plant—a rhododendron, say. Well, a rhododendron can be depended on to sprout rhododendron leaves and rhododendron flowers as long as there is life in it. At no point will it start sprouting petunia blooms or *Ficus* leaves. Then why in the name of the living plant, or the living God, should we, after centuries of *between you and me,* switch to *between you and I?*

Let me explain, first of all, what drove home to me the need to devote an entire column to this single heinous error. Several readers sent me Harry Stein's interview with Tennessee Williams from the June 5, 1979, issue of *Esquire* magazine. There was Williams comparing himself to Tom, the hero of *The Glass Menagerie,* but adding: "The principal difference between he and I is stamina." I couldn't believe my eyes, so I immediately asked Stein whether Williams had actually said "between he and I," and Harry solemnly confirmed the melancholy fact. The man who after Eugene O'Neill was our best playwright—I say *was* because his later plays have been pitiful travesties of his beautiful early ones—had committed a grammatical error of *unsurpassable* grossness. I would like to think, in fact, that the author of *The Glass Menagerie* and *A Streetcar Named Desire* could not have uttered that abomination, but even from the heartbreaking old square who concocted *Vieux Carré* and *Crève Coeur,* I would have expected better.

What is this *between you and I*—to take its most frequently heard form—and where does it come from? It is the flouting of a very simple, basic rule; not so long ago, any halfway self-respecting high-school student would sooner have bitten off and swallowed the tip of his pencil than have committed that error. Prepositions in English take the accusative, also known as the objective, case. The trouble is that not very many college students could even tell you nowadays what a preposition is, what the accusative is, or, for that matter, what English is. A preposition, in grammar, is "a word that indicates the relation of a substantive to a verb, an adjective, or another substantive," according to the worthy *American Heritage Dictionary*, which in this instance, I am afraid, is not very clear. The old *Webster's Second* did it better: "A word generally with some meaning of position, direction, time, or other abstract relation, used to connect a noun or a pronoun, in an adjectival or adverbial sense, with some other word."

But the *Heritage* helpfully provides examples of prepositions: *at, by, in, to, from, with*. The *Oxford English Dictionary* is perhaps even more helpful; under *preposition*, it says: "One of the parts of speech; an indeclinable word or particle serving to mark the relation between two notional words, the latter of which is usually a substantive or pronoun; as sow *in* hope, good *for* food. . . . The following sb. [substantive] or pron. is said to be 'governed' by the preposition. . . ." Which one of these three definitions you find most useful does not matter; by any of them, *between* is a preposition. And what about the accusative, or objective? That, according to the *Heritage*, is "the case of a noun, pronoun, adjective, or participle that is the direct object of a verb or the object of certain prepositions." Note that this definition is not based on the English language, in which, strictly speaking, only pronouns have case endings—luckily or unluckily, as the case (not the case ending) may be. For ours is a language so uninflected (that is, without case endings) that it is, in this respect, much easier than almost any other. But the very ease lulls the mind to the few exceptions. The difficulties some people have with *who* and *whom* are well known; now comes the new problem with *between you and me*.

For, as you must know, *whom, me, him, her, us*, and *them* are the accusatives for what in the nominative is *who, I, he, she, we*, and *they*. And this is practically all there is to declension (case endings) in English. But for many people, even this seems to be too much. Had they studied any classical or foreign tongues, they would consider it a breeze—no, a windfall; they have not, however, and so, to make up for it, English has become Greek to them.

To continue. Prepositions like the aforementioned *at, by, in, to, from, with*—to which we might add such popular favorites as *be-*

*tween, for, over, under, beside, before, without, about, above, below, be-hind*—require the accusative in the pronouns they govern. So we say "for him," "without us," "beside them," "under whom," and so on. And in the old days, most people managed to say correctly "between you and me." Yet this, as you can doubtless see, is somewhat trickier—if anything so simple can be said to be tricky at all.

The problem here is that *you* is the only personal pronoun that does not have an accusative separate and different from the nominative, the case in which the subject of a sentence appears. Thus *she* becomes *her* in "I love her," but *you* remains *you* in "I love you." And that is how the confusion began: if something was between you and someone else and the *you* remained pristine, as if it were still in the nominative, why, asked our growing army of functional illiterates, shouldn't the other pronoun (or, more likely, "word" or "thing") remain equally unfiddled with: *between you and I?*

Of course, if it were the other way around, more people would get it right: *between I and you* would bother even some untrained ears. But out of politeness (or, more probably, habituation—for if we still had politeness, we would also have grammar, which is one of its forms), we mention the other person first, and so the un-changing first term precipitates inertia in the second—if inertia can be precipitated; perhaps *induces, continues, perpetuates* would be better.

There is, however, another, rather more odious cause for this error, which is known as a genteelism. People vaguely recollect that *It is me* is a vulgar, inferior form of *It is I*; that the correct, refined answer to *Who is it?* is *I*, not *me*. So, by a kind of dreadful linguistic social climbing, they decide that *I* is always a finer, clas-sier, more educated word than *me* and attests invariably to refine-ment, learnedness, breeding; whereupon *between you and me, for you and me*, and all the rest get *I*'s sprinkled all over them like cheap perfume. What ignorance began, snobbery finished off, and *be-tween you and I* is sweeping the country. As for poor Tennessee Williams, with his *between he and I* for *between him and me*, he is so far gone that he cannot even claim the inertia of the first pronoun as an extenuating circumstance.

But what is really wrong with *between you and I?* you may ask if you are an innocent, an ignoramus, or a false prophet like Wayne

O'Neil, a professor of linguistics at MIT and an associate professor at the Harvard Graduate School of Education; people, after all, will still understand what you mean.

Well, yes, in that particular instance they will still understand you. However, the trouble with grammatical errors—and in this respect they *are* like living organisms—is that they beget others, that they multiply and proliferate until all is error and confusion. Suppose, for example, that your *between you and I* practitioner graduates to something like "He is not crazy about you and she—about anybody." This might easily be heard as "He is not crazy about you, and she about anybody"—a very different kettle of fish and capable of eliciting a dangerous misconception.

You should see, then, that to avoid adding to the already raging chaos in English usage and communication, we must urgently stop *between you and I.* Otherwise, it will lead us to every kind of deleterious misunderstanding.

Let me give you a further example. When someone asks "Would you rather that I take you or she?" no one will know whether the choice is between who is to take him, say, to the movies or who is to be taken to them; it could mean that the invitation is either from a man or from his wife; it could also mean that the person invited is either you or your sister. Multiply this kind of obscurity, as committed by future millions, by an infinity, and you have a fairly accurate vision of hell: sentences and paragraphs will have to be resaid and personal and business letters rewritten and resent through the mail at who knows what cost in time, money, energy, and serious blunders.

What, then, are we to do about it? Simple: we fight. Whenever, wherever we hear someone say "between you and I" or one of the related horrors, and whoever the offender may be, we go into action. To strangers in the street, we may have to be polite; to superiors (in position, evidently, not in knowledge), we may even have to be somewhat humble. But correct them we must. To all others we may be as sharp, forceful, tonitruous as the circumstances permit or demand: let family, friends, and neighbors hear us correct them loudly and clearly—let *between you and me* resound across the land. Otherwise there will soon be no more communication between you and me.

GAY                    GAY

DESTROYING GOOD WORDS

# THE CHANGING LANGUAGE

# Destroying Good Words

**W**ith the possible exception of a baseball umpire or movie critic, there is no more popular object of abuse than the English language. The other day, at a lunch for the 1978 Polk Awards (journalistic awards more respectable but less prestigious than the Pulitzers), I heard Robert C. Toth of the *Los Angeles Times*, the winner in the Foreign Reporting category, repeatedly refer to "a media." Once, in fact, he said: "The media has a special responsibility. . . ." If there is a special responsibility the media have, it is to write good English and to know, for example, that *media* is the plural of medium, and so requires a plural verb.

A few days later, I was reading an article by Mel Gussow, a *New York Times* drama critic and reporter—and I stress that this was a piece of reportage, not a hastily written and edited review—where, disbelieving, I found: "Each of Mr. Fugard's plays . . . are themselves acts of contrition and ennoblement." The subject, *each*, is clearly singular, yet Gussow and the copy editor were content to let it multiply miraculously—an excellent thing in loaves and fishes, but sinful in syntax. What are we coming to when our big newspapers and their writers see no difference between singular and plural?

But let us give the press a rest for the nonce while we examine a different but equally sinister source of linguistic corruption: special-interest groups. Language, I think, belongs to two groups only: gifted individuals everywhere, who use it imaginatively; and the fellowship of men and women, wherever they are, who, without being particularly inventive, nevertheless endeavor to speak and write correctly. Language, however, does not belong to the illiterate or to bodies of people forming tendentious and propagandistic interest groups, determined to use it for what they (usually mistakenly) believe to be their advantage.

Take, for example, the aged. When I referred not long ago to *senior citizens* as an unsavory euphemism, George J. Friedman, of New York, was moved to compose a piece of ghastly doggerel accusing me of incompetence for not knowing that "that's what the aged like to hear,/Per Gallup, who, three years ago,/In survey was by them told so." Now, what these good folks prefer to hear, not in the least care I. They are the old, the aged or the retired;

they are not *senior citizens*, with grandiose implications of political importance well beyond the reduced bus fares and cheaper movie tickets they do in fact receive. Thus the fancy term is a mere trope—metaphor or circumlocution—that sounds, at first, hollow or jeering; later, stale and ludicrous. "An old man lay drunk in the gutter" is sad but unexceptionable. "A senior citizen lay drunk in the gutter" is risible.

There is nothing morally wrong with being old; it is precisely such supposedly status-raising phrases that begin to suggest that there is. I guess it all began when undertakers became morticians, and, when that wasn't fine enough, funeral directors. By tomorrow, they may be masters of obsequies. I can sympathize with people who dislike being called garbage collectors, though that is a perfectly useful and honorable calling—certainly better than that of structural linguist, semiologist, or punk-rock superstar. It is, in any case, not by changing their title to sanitation workers that they will upgrade their social position. Rather, it is by making the public comprehend their usefulness and dedication; otherwise people will disparage them just as stupidly and unjustly with "You sanitation workers, you!" By the way, have dogcatchers become canine euthanasianists yet?

Well, the tireless Mr. Friedman sent in still another missive, this time in prose, informing us that *policeman* is not a word destined to survive, as I had claimed. No, sir: "A few years ago, in a move to eradicate sexism in law enforcement, the New York City Police Department decreed the use of the neutered *police officer*." Look, I don't tell the police department how to catch *perpetrators*, and I don't want them to tell me how to speak English. Would people even understand a neutered, or castrated, headline that read "Acute Shortage of Police Officers," or would they shrug it off with a "So long as there are enough police sergeants"?

What I am leading up to is the wanton and shocking destruction of the good and necessary English word *gay*. One fine, or not so fine, day, some homosexual pressure group in America decided that the preferred term for *homosexual* was henceforth to be *gay*. And forthwith there was *gay liberation, gay pride, gay whatnot,* and, worse yet, the substantive *a gay*. Although there is considerable disagreement about how it all came to pass, the presumable source of the term is *gay boy*, the Australian slang for *homosexual*. Where, however, did the Aussies get it?

As Eric Partridge's *A Dictionary of Slang and Unconventional En-*

*glish* makes clear, the word comes from early-nineteenth-century British slang, where the adjective *gay* referred to "women leading . . . a harlot's life." Accordingly, *gay bit* was a whore; *gay house*, a brothel. What kind of honorific, then, is *gay*? *Homosexual* is a precise and dignified word, against which only two, equally unwarranted, objections are possible. First, that it is long. But, though brevity is a virtue, we have many four- or five-syllable words happily ensconced in everyday speech. No one has objected to and shortened *pediatrician* or *womanliness, paratrooper* or *dictionary;* then why shorten *homosexual?* Second, the once prevalent, now blessedly defunct, *homo* may rankle in some memories. But *homo* is merely Greek for *the same* and, although misleading and probably mischievous in this sense, is not intrinsically base, as, say, *kike* is. And if our society does not come to accept homosexuality, you may be sure that *gay* will, sooner or later, give rise to some similar pejorative distortion.

Meanwhile, there is every reason to object to a supposedly official word that carries clear implications of whoring. Apparently, some homosexuals who advocated it must have been of the "screaming queen" type, which ostentatiously acts out a parody of homosexual behavior. This is just as offensive as any crudely aggressive heterosexual behavior, e.g., pinching women's posteriors, whistling at passing females, et cetera. Such homosexual shenanigans might seem gay in the established sense of the word but are merely desperate, undignified, and pathetic. Other homosexuals may have felt that prevalent patterns of promiscuity in homosexual behavior (probably socially conditioned rather than inherent) justify the use of such a whorish word. That, however, is self-hate and should not be legitimized. And some self-deceivers and hypocrites may have actually believed that homosexual lives are merrier than heterosexual ones and so merit the appellation *gay.* Yet such manifest untruth cannot be endorsed.

To be sure, Partridge gives us two other slang meanings of *gay.* One is "slightly intoxicated," and though alcoholism seems to be a not uncommon phenomenon among homosexuals, it is hardly something that can or should be so memorialized. The other is "impudent, impertinent, presumptuous," and that at least applies to those who would enshrine *gay* as the correct term for *homosexual,* though this could hardly have been the intended meaning. But whatever the intention, be it noted that many, if not most, civilized homosexuals refuse to call themselves or others gay. On the "Dick Cavett" show, Gore Vidal rejected the word.

The problem is that this special-interest use of *gay* undermines the correct use of a legitimate and needed English word. It now becomes ambiguous to call a cheerful person or thing gay; to wish someone a gay journey or holiday, for example, may have totally uncalled-for over- and undertones and, in conservative circles, may even be considered insulting. The insulting aspect we can eventually get rid of; the ambiguous, never. What do we do about it? If we energetically reject *gay* as a legitimate synonym for *homosexual*, it may not be too late to bury this linguistic abomination.

There are, of course, many more examples of this nonsense emanating from minority groups or professions trying to upgrade themselves by bastardizing the language rather than by establishing their dignity through precept and example. Take the host of linguistic absurdities being perpetrated by the feminists, who have queered—if not expunged—such useful terms as, for instance, *young girl*, the feminine suffix *-ess*, and nouns ending in *-man* where this is clearly a generic term meaning a human being of either sex engaged in a certain activity.

Take the term *young girl*, or *girl*. Instead of enjoying girlhood, the feminists want to be *women* the moment they leave high school, if not before. How wrongheaded! There is something ineffably lovely about being a *girl*—very different from being a *woman*, which is wonderful in quite another way. So Humbert Wolfe's poem "Ilion" ends with the line "Girl, there were girls like you in Ilion!" Pity today's brainwashed poet who would write, "Woman, there were women like you in Ilion!" The lyric is about Trojan girls who "hoarded their loveliness, while Helen spent it," as any beautiful *woman* might have. The result was tragic, but imbued with romantic grandeur. These loveless *girls* merely tug at your heart wistfully, a distinction the poet wanted to make.

A reader, David Craig, from Baton Rouge, wrote in, objecting to my objections to *chair* as a replacement for *chairman*, which he finds preferable to *chairperson*. And he concluded by informing me that a magistrate in court is referred to as *the bench*.

*Chairperson* is certainly disgusting; but *chair* sounds, at best, like a fossilized metaphor or metonymy not worth preserving; at worst, like a stick of furniture. There is, moreover, inconsistency here, since women senators certainly want to be called senators, even though the *-or* ending is technically just as masculine as the enclitic *-man*. If neologisms are necessary, why not espouse *chair-woman*, though it may suggest an aged female in the Tuileries gardens who demands two francs from you for the use of a chair. Absurdity lies in wait everywhere. Now that women are entering the armed services, will the command have to be "Man and woman the guns [or lifeboats]"?

This is different from Negroes opting for *black* over *Negro*. *Black* means the same thing and was used all along, although formerly considered less polite than *Negro*. By shifting the preference, no harm is done to the language. As for magistrates acquiescing in or relishing the term *the bench*—surely language is too important a matter to be left in the hands of magistrates.

# U, Non-U, and You

**V**irtually nothing is so feared and hated in this allegedly egalitarian country of ours as snobbishness. There is no more detested creature anywhere—unless it be the elitist or the intellectual—than the snob, who cannot even enjoy the semifavorable publicity accorded bank robbers, necrophiliacs, and starters of forest fires. And yet H. B. Brooks-Baker, the publisher of *Debrett's Peerage* and, with the Viking Press, of *U and Non-U Revisited*, claims that England, the reputed cradle of snobbism, "is among the least snobbish and class-conscious countries. Far less so," he continues in the Foreword to *U and Non-U Revisited*, "than America, for example, which basks in the reputation of being the most democratic of nations."

As the jacket copy explains, the present tome is a kind of sequel to *Noblesse Oblige*, a book edited in 1956 by the late Nancy Mitford that "hit the world like a bombshell. Profiting from the researches of the philologist Professor Alan C. Ross, who had coined the expressions 'U' and 'non-U'—that is 'Upper-class' and 'non-Upper-class'—[Nancy Mitford] set about telling the man in the street just how common he was." I remember the immense sensation the book caused twenty-three years ago even in "classless" America, and the only reason I myself did not read it when everybody else did was snobbishness.

Just to show you how promiscuously and hostilely the word *snob* is bandied about, let me quote from an article on drag queens in the June 25, 1979, *Village Voice* by Edmund White, a respected novelist and a coauthor of *The Joy of Gay Sex:* "Disdain for drag is, I would contend, often concealed snobbism. Most gay transvestites, especially street drags, are either black or Puerto Rican. Discrimination against them may be both elitist and racist." First, I am surprised that a homosexual writer of White's talent and literacy espouses the dreadful abuse of the word *gay;* second, I am appalled at his subscribing to that bugbear of gutter radicals, the three-headed monster Snob-Elitist-Racist. Obviously the distaste of heterosexuals for drag queens—leaving aside the question of whether it is justifiable or not—stems from sexual sources: sexuality is so ingrained, so elemental a thing with us that the person whose sexual practices are antithetical to ours and who flaunts this antithesis becomes more resented than a mere religious, political, or social adversary. But whenever heavy demagogic weaponry is needed, *snob, elitist,* and *racist* get hauled out.

The origins of the word *snob* remain uncertain.* The late, sorely missed Eric Partridge, in his splendid etymological dictionary *Origins,* writes: "*Snob,* cobbler, hence (slang) a townee, a plebeian, hence a toady and a superior person: o.o.o." ("O.o.o." means of obscure origin.) Ernest Weekley, whose *Concise Etymological Dictionary* Partridge goes on to cite, argues that *snob* is related to *snip,* a tailor, suggesting kinship with *snub,* to cut short. Notice the implication that a snob is an inferior person trying to climb the social ladder, hence he is both "a toady" to those above and "a superior person" to those beside and below him.

What concerns me here, however, is whether there is such a thing as linguistic snobbery: the use of language to achieve or assert social superiority. Such language, though correct from the linguistic point of view, might be reprehensible in a larger, humanistic context and thus a good thing to avoid. As *Noblesse Oblige* made crystal clear, there existed an Upper-class English and a non-Upper-class one. The differences still exist, though *U and*

* I can find no evidence for the frequent assertion that *snob* derives from *s. nob.,* for *sine nobilitate,* as a designation for commoners on certain British rosters.

*Non-U Revisited* makes them only plastic, not crystal, clear. What the little book makes manifest, though, is that snobbery goes on and on, even if Thackeray, as long ago as 1846, wrote an entire book castigating the snob as one who "meanly admires mean things." As the new book demonstrates, however, distinctions between U and non-U in language are getting fuzzier, what with the non-U people trying to sound U, and the U ones, out of reverse snobbery, espousing non-U terminology.

Which brings me back to the question of snobbishness in the U.S.A., which does indeed flourish in various forms. For example, in Los Angeles you are mercilessly classed according to what make of car you drive. This kind of snobbery is the accepted thing there and has even spawned an appropriate reverse snobbery, whereby a beat-up old Chevy is considered in some circles more prestigious than the latest Jaguar, Mercedes, Porsche, or Rolls. Similarly, there is a plutocratic snobbery rampant from coast to coast; for instance, when country clubs can no longer discriminate along racial and religious lines, they resort to admitting members according to their income tax bracket.

Such things are, by and large, accepted as matters of course. Not so, however, linguistic snobbery, which is considered totally heinous and to be expunged by hook, crook, or napalm. There are, clearly, two possible places for linguistic snobbishness: in pronunciation and in vocabulary. Your linguistic snob (or U speaker) still tends to say de-*cay*-dence rather than *dek*-a-dence, even though current dictionaries usually list the former as a secondary and less desirable pronunciation. De-*cay*-dence makes more sense in terms of the word's Latin provenance and pronunciation; but who nowadays knows anything about Latin?

Likewise, the correct American pronunciation of *squalor* used to rhyme with *tailor* and was so given in *Funk & Wagnalls Standard Dictionary*, which in matters of pronunciation was ranked above even the good second edition of *Webster's*. Some thirty-five years ago, I heard of someone's not getting a job teaching in the New York public-school system because he made *squalor* rhyme with *holler*—though in England this was always the accepted pronunciation. Nowadays, I suppose, you don't need to know even the meaning of *squalor* to teach English anywhere; the assumption may be that you'll learn the meaning from experiencing it on the job.

Pronunciations change, and we change with them. There is an interesting discussion of language in *U and Non-U Revisited* among Professor Ross, Richard Buckle (author, ballet critic, and the book's editor), and Philip Howard (the language columnist of the London *Times.)* As an example of non-U speech, Ross adduces the tendency for the accent to shift from the first to the middle (actually the second) syllable in words of three or four syllables; he and Buckle cite and deplore, among others, *laméntable, preférable, exquísite,* and *marítal.* But Howard, who is more permissive, points out that there is something called the progressive accent, which evolves in the course of time "because we dislike a rapid succession of light syllables and find them hard to pronounce." He notes that *commendable* was once accented on the first syllable—thus in Shakespeare: " 'Tis sweet and cómmendable in thy nature, Hamlet"—but has since become *comméndable.* And he makes the usual defense for change: language is a living thing, we foolishly want the pronunciations of our childhood frozen for all time, and more of the like.

Buckle responds to this with an admirable *non serviam* hurled at the collective ignorance of the unwashed:

> You may be right that I am "frozen" in the customs of my childhood but I do think—or rather, feel—that to pronounce "exquisite" or "lamentable," and particularly "marital," with the accent on the middle syllable is vile. It is aesthetically offensive. I know the laws of beauty change, like everything else, but I should fight against that to the end of my days. Incidentally, can you imagine the French or Italians changing the pronunciation of a word like "formidable" or "amabile"?

Here, bless him, is the linguistic snob—or, as I prefer to call him, purist—speaking. When I hear, as I often do these days, *influence* pronounced by ignoramuses with the accent on the second syllable, it makes my blood freeze—and not in the customs of my childhood. What makes *inflúence* so ghastly is not necessarily its sound (though I think it is ugly) but its demonstration of the existence of people so uneducated, so deaf to what others are saying, so unable to learn the obvious that they are bound to be a major source of verbal pollution, linguistic corruption, cultural erosion. Their bad offices clearly won't stop at this single egregious error. When Howard cheerfully accepts this sort of thing, only to go on to bemoan the "vexing" loss of discrimination between *disinterested* and *uninterested*, does he not realize that it is the same persons who are guilty of both?

The point, as any snob can tell you, is that the melody of the English language is being ruined. Make the accent ( ´ denotes stressed syllable, ˘ unstressed) fall regularly on the second syllable in trisyllabic words, and you get what is called in scansion an amphibrach ( ˘ ´ ˘ ) where before there might have been a dactyl ( ´ ˘ ˘ ). This and similar changes would reduce English to a much more boring melodic pattern, such as that of, say, Finnish and Hungarian, with their monotonous stress on initial syllables.

Of course, it is British English that truly lends itself to snobbery. When, as Buckle claims, the U pronounce *garage* in the French manner, whereas "the middle-class pronounce it to rhyme with 'barrage' [that is, *bear*-azh]" while the "lower-class is 'garridge,'" you have a perfect spectrum: language as a total class indicator. Except that Ross disagrees and finds the alleged U pronunciation merely old-fashioned. Which is precisely what linguistic snobbery or purism is: old-fashionedness. Or take Ross's statement that the non-U pronunciation of *fiancé* rhymes with "pie fancy," whereupon Buckle contends that he thought the "usual non-U . . . was 'feonn-say.' U people wouldn't use the word anyway." Better yet: lower class, fie-*an*-cy; middle class, fee-*on*-say; upper class—no such word. One has just a one-night stand, an affair, or a marriage.

Well, we are a bit closer to classlessness in America, but there *are* differences, especially in vocabulary. As the "American Section" of the book indicates, there exist, for example, the non-U *chaise lounge, drapes, folks, hose, home,* for which the U words are *chaise longue, curtains, parents* or *relations, stockings, house.* (Though the list is not always accurate: thus *trousers* is not the non-U for *pants* but vice versa.) If you are the sort of person who thinks that to sound well brought up, educated, fastidious, and perhaps even old-fashioned is not shameful but distinguished, go ahead and be a linguistic snob. You may not want to be the last by whom the old is laid aside, but you certainly don't want to be the first to try the illiterate new.

# Should We Genderspeak?

**W**ords and Women: New Language in New Times, a book by two women journalists, Casey Miller and Kate Swift, proposes certain radical changes in the English language in order to make it more just and acceptable to women (Doubleday, 1976). This seems to be the first book-length treatment of the subject to have emerged from one of the major houses, though some of them have brought out guidelines in pamphlet form. The body of the book, containing some sensible suggestions as well as much unpersuasive special-pleading—along with a number of inconsistencies and grammatical and other errors (Michael Korda, for instance, appears as Alexander)—is summarized by the authors in the Epilogue, to which, for the sake of brevity, I primarily address myself.

The authors state their basic criterion admirably: "Does the term or usage contribute to clarity and accuracy, or does it fudge them?" Fine. Under their first rubric, "Animals," they ask that an animal become an *it* rather than a *he*, with which one cannot quarrel. Next, they suggest that babies, as well as other general categories, say, Americans or politicians, should not be regularly referred to by masculine pronouns. Here, again, one cannot but concur, though the authors go through an elaborate rigmarole instead of simply proposing that a baby, too, be an *it*. What to do with politicians and all other general categories is more problematic, though the authors' proposal that they be pluralized into a sexless *they* gets around most difficulties.

Now comes my first disagreement: female endings in -ess are, it seems, taboo. "Since authors, poets, Negroes, sculptors, Jews, actors, etc. may be either female or male, the significance of a word like authoress is not that it identifies a female but that it indicates deviation from the [alleged] standard. . . . An -ess ending . . . is reasonably resented by most people so identified. [What about those not covered by this "most": do they not resent it, or do they resent it unreasonably?] When it is relevant to make a special point of someone's sex, pronouns are useful and so are the adjectives male and female." Well, then, if *stewardess* is out, should we write, "The stewards wore blue skirts," implying that they were

DO WE GENDERSPEAK?

Scottish or transvestites? Or perhaps, "The female stewards wore blue skirts," leaving the reader to wonder what the male stewards were wearing?

In a review, must I write, "The female actors, on the whole, were superior to the male actors," and sound ridiculous, probably illiterate, and certainly prolix? Clarity and accuracy, which Miller and Swift demand, are importantly served by succinctness, and *actress* will always be shorter and clearer than *female actor*, which might easily mean a male impersonating a woman on stage, or an effeminate performer, or heaven knows what else.

If I write that Marisol is a fine sculptress, or Stevie Smith a distinguished poetess, I help those less informed readers who might not know that the artists in question are women. Unless we assume that male and female sensibilities are identical (thank heaven they tend not to be), it is helpful to identify Marisol's sex concisely and unaffectedly. How absurdly inconsistent to say that "when it is relevant" one may use pronouns or adjectives denoting sex, but not a suffix; is a suffix a dirtier thing than a pronoun or adjective? If I say to the restaurant hostess (she doesn't look like a host to me) to send over the waiter, though the person who waited on me was a waitress, I invite confusion and trouble.

Earlier (p. 126), the authors write: "Few women are asking to be called men, but more women than anyone has bothered to count are asking that they *not* be called men." What, I ask, is calling a waitress waiter, or an actress actor, if not calling her a man? It is perfectly true that in early English usage the same agent-noun referred indiscriminately to males or females, but that was then, before the language evolved and became codified. If one can complain about this codification, it is mostly because it did not go far enough—because, for instance, it did not posit a standard feminine ending, as there is in German, to designate females in all possible situations. How lucky the Germans are to have the *-in* ending, as in *Freundin,* a female friend, *Herrscherin,* a female ruler, *Lehrerin,* a female teacher, and so on up and down the line. Never has this ending been considered patronizing in German-speaking countries, only helpful for the terseness with which it dispenses useful information. It is good to know without having to ask nosy questions whether the guest you have invited is bringing a male or female friend to dinner—it helps balance the company. It is convenient for a woman to be able to say in a concise, unfussy manner that she wants a female gynecologist. And are we now to give up the relatively few cases in English where such instant clarification is painlessly available? Are we going to have to refer even to the Dresden china shepherdess on the mantel as a female shepherd?

Still, I understand and even sympathize with a woman's desire not to be called a poetess or an authoress, because there was once a kind of female-ghetto poetry and prose that gave *poetess* and *authoress* a bad odor. But *actress* was never pejorative, nor, certainly, were *empress, priestess, duchess,* and the rest. *Negress* and *Jewess* are not pejoratives, either—unless you take *Negro* and *Jew* to be insults. *Sculptress* is also blameless, for there was no female-ghetto sculpture, even if the reasons for this, I grant, were also discriminatory.

Now let me skip ahead in the Epilogue. Under "Job Titles," we find that *congresswoman, newspaperwoman,* and *forewoman* are correct

designations for women in those offices, and I couldn't argue with
that. But under "-*Person* Compounds," we are told that "*salesperson*
. . . doesn't seem to throw anyone into a tizzy" and is preferable to
*salesman* or *saleswoman* because "the need was felt for a common
gender term that could refer to either." This is strangely inconsistent. When there is *salespeople* (not to mention *staff*, *personnel*, or
*force* attachable to *sales*), why drag in the colorless and uneducated-
sounding *person*? Remember the ludicrous Miss Adelaide who la-
ments in *Guys and Dolls*: "Just from waiting around/ For that plain
little band of gold,/ A person . . . can develop a cold." And if
-*person* is so good, then why not *congressperson* or *newspaperperson*?
The authors imply that they prefer *chairperson* to *chairwoman*, perhaps because (though they don't say it) the latter reminds them of
charwoman. In any case, they like the metonymic *chair* best of all,
and (p. 76) refer to Calvert Watkins as "the distinguished chair"
of the Harvard Linguistics Department, which that distinguished
chairman may well abhor. Are we also expected to say, in a meeting, "Will the chair please yield the floor?"

Certainly Miller and Swift are right when in "*Man* as Typical,"
they reject things like "the man who pays taxes" in favor of *tax-
payer*, and substitute *workers* or *working people* for *working men*. They
may be right, too, when in "*Man* as the Species," they plunk for
*human beings* or *people* in preference to the generic *man* or *mankind*,
though they have a formidable lot of linguistic and literary history
going against them. Still, "Human beings are tool-using animals"
may be less ambiguous as well as fairer than "Man is a tool-using
animal." However, *humans*, which they also seriously advocate,
strikes me as facetious, like *equines* for horses.

Skipping again, I bristle at Miller and Swift's advocacy of *they*,
*their*, etc., as singular pronouns because "reputable writers and
speakers" have used them with indefinite antecedents. They cite
(pp. 135–36) a number of examples, e.g., Bernard Shaw's "It's
enough to drive one out of their senses" and Scott Fitzgerald's
"Nobody likes a mind quicker than their own." But the lapses of
great ones do not make a wrong right: a "one" is not a "many";
some*one* cannot be they.

Should women feel slighted by the correctness of, say, "Everyone must look out for himself"? Some obviously do, but are we to
believe that masses of girl children grow up miserable and psychi-
cally stunted by such constructions—as the authors maintain on

the basis of a few anecdotes about schoolgirls? Surely teachers and parents can explain this to most kids' satisfaction, and those girls who don't accept it are as likely to be "saved" by becoming fighting feminists as to be "doomed" by becoming domestic drudges.

The giveaway is the final rubric, under which the authors argue that the word *womanly* means that a woman is not courageous, strong, and resolute. It means no such thing. It means rather that she has certain physical and psychic traits, such as comeliness, elegance, gracefulness, unneurotic enjoyment of the opposite sex, maturity, and a sense of security and relaxation in being a woman. It means *not* feeling compelled to compete with men in every way, and not becoming (in Geoffrey Gorer's phrase) an imitation of man, as Miller and Swift, their protestations notwithstanding, would have her be. I am deeply worried when the authors define *androgyny* (p. 27) as "that rare and happy human wholeness," a state that, judging from their jacket photographs, they may indeed have achieved. In no sense, figurative or literal, do I take her-maphroditism to be a happy state of affairs.

But Miller and Swift, like many feminists, have set up straw men as adversaries in fields extending far beyond linguistics. Thus they keep referring to Otto Weininger's misogynistic *Sex and Character* as if it contained representative views, instead of being the brilliant but pathological work of a disturbed genius who killed himself very young, and whose theories are as exploded as those of Cesare Lombroso and Max Nordau. Doubtless, women are entitled to the process of getting the rights and freedoms granted to men; once these goals are achieved, however, and even before that, they can leave language alone. When women have full social, political, and economic parity with men, no schoolgirl will burst into tears over *himself* being used in the sense of *herself* too, or about "men and women" being a more common phrase than "women and men"—any more than French school-girls, I imagine, weep over their sexual organs being, in both high and low parlance, of the masculine gender.

"Far from implying sameness, however, the language of equal-ity emphasizes sexual differentiation by making women visible," our authors state. I doubt whether women's visibility will be achieved by calling usherettes ushers, or replacing *mankind* with the Miller-Swift coinage *genkind*. Equal job opportunities, salaries, and recognition are what will make women fully visible, something to be achieved not by meddling with language but by political action.

Yet woe betide if this is accomplished at the cost of sacrificing womanliness in women and manliness in men. Men and women must continue to attract each other through characteristics peculiar to their respective sexualities and sexes; a world in which we cease to be sexually fascinating to one another through certain differences will be a world well lost. And this may be a very real danger to—not mankind, not womankind, and certainly not genkind. To humankind.

# English Sans Footnote

The Hollywood screenwriter Philip Dunne has written a curiously symptomatic piece for *Newsweek* (February 13, 1978) about what is happening to our language. While quite correctly objecting to a number of abuses—most of them chronicled in this column over the past year—Dunne nevertheless has to have it both ways. In a manner doubtless learned in that grand school of compromise that is the movie business, Dunne apologizes for the very things he deplores: language, after all, is change, and the changes "are the result of inventive illiteracy over the ages. . . . So to complain about change, any change, is both pedantic and fruitless. In spite of all the efforts of purists . . . it will happen; more often than not, the result will be a graceful improvement."

Dunne feebly attempts to justify hating the errors that particularly annoy him by calling them "destructive changes" and blaming them on "bureaucracies both public and private," rather than on the sacred and unassailable American people. But after a fairly spirited philippic comes Philip's dispiriting cop-out: "I'm afraid that, in spite of the efforts of the [Edwin] Newmans and [E. B.] Whites, all these little horrors are embedded in the language, along with 'like' for 'as,' and 'you know.' " This statement is a perfect example of that weak-kneed liberalism which, while knowing better, abets, indeed invites, deterioration.

First of all, we'll get nowhere by blaming "bureaucracies," guilty though they may be. Nearly every change in language does, in fact, begin with some form of illiteracy, but an illiteracy that is seldom, if ever, inventive; it is also, without exception, the act of an individual. It was not a bureaucracy, public or private, that first said (to quote one of Mr. Dunne's examples) "Hopefully, it won't rain tomorrow" or (to quote one of mine) "Behave yourself, like you should." Bad usage is not the invention of an Aristophanic chorus of frogs croaking "like you should" in unison. It is the dirty work of private, individual batrachians—possibly scattered across the map, and committing the same breach independently but simultaneously. Still, they are all individuals, and the thing could be nipped in the bud, or in the tadpole. This would, however, presuppose a group of speakers who (a) knew better and (b) were not afraid of correcting an ignoramus—unlikely presupposition, alas, in this benighted, permissive, and demotically oriented democracy of ours.

Nevertheless, ignorant, obfuscatory, unnecessary change, producing linguistic leveling and flatness, could be stopped in its tracks by concerted effort. The fact that this has not often happened in the past is no excuse for the present. We have acquired a set of fine, useful, previously unavailable tools, culminating in the *Oxford English Dictionary* and a number of excellent treatises and handbooks on grammar. We now have the means to slow down changes in language considerably, if not to stop them altogether.

Well, not altogether, for some change is both wholesome and necessary. As new inventions, discoveries, concepts come into the world, new words are needed to designate them. "Cybernetics," "Oedipus complex," "filibuster" are cases in point. Slang, too, is welcome in its place, even though it is not, generally speaking, a graceful improvement, as Dunne would have it, merely an amusing or graphic alternative to standard usage. Thus "badmouthing" and "tossing your cookies" are jolly substitutes for "decrying" and "vomiting." But notice what happens to slang: it wears thin, becomes boring, and is superseded by new slang. There is already an antiquated sound to "tossing your cookies," though "badmouthing" still has its vitality. The point about slang is that it is, *grosso modo*, a metaphor, simile, or circumlocution invented by an anonymous poet in prose; it catches on for a while, eventually ceases to be unusual, clever, or amusing, and gradually fades out of the picture. It fades even faster if it is too long; the popular mouth prefers brevity. So monosyllables such as "cop" or "fuzz" will probably outlive such already obsolescent disyllables as "copper" and "flatfoot" and the by now archaic "peeler." Slang is like a joke: funny and viable only while it is new. But one does not get tired of "policeman," which is as basic as your basic black dress and never goes out of fashion.

To stay with our example: if uneducated ghetto speakers pronounce "police" as "pollis," and proceed to spell it in that way, there is absolutely no reason that the rest of us should stand by smiling sheepishly and let it become first accepted and then the norm, everyone allegedly being entitled to his ignorance. Rather than change the pronunciation and spelling, change (i.e., abolish) the ghetto. A decent school can teach "police" as easily as "pollis." There are, however, standard excuses adduced by well-meaning but misguided liberals or ill-meaning and unguidable ignoramuses (some of whom consult and misinterpret the *Oxford English Dictionary* to bolster their benightedness). Foremost among them is, "But look at Shakespeare [or Dickens, or Hemingway, or any other famous writer] who wrote X instead of the supposedly correct Y. If it's good enough for Shakespeare [or whomever], why not for you and me?"

Well, Shakespeare wrote in an age when what we call modern English was still in its formative phase. His grammar was good enough for his era; it is not good enough for ours—any more than his geography, medicine, or Latin is. As for more recent writers of distinction, their forte was not necessarily grammar; at any rate, they could occasionally slip up. Such lapses were duly noted and set down; sometimes with glee, sometimes dispassionately for the record. Yet merely because we cannot match the excellence of the great writers, we need not duplicate their errors.

My point is that things have at last been sufficiently established—classified and codified—and there is neither need nor excuse for changes based on mere ignorance. The fact that some people are too thickheaded to grasp, for example, that "anyone" is singular, as the "one" in it plainly denotes, does not oblige those who know better to tolerate "anyone can do as they please." The correct form is, of course, "anyone may do as he pleases," but in America, in informal usage, "can" has pretty much replaced "may" in this sense, and there is nothing more to be done about it; but we cannot and must not let "one" become plural. That way madness lies.

And don't let fanatical feminists convince you that it must be "as he or she pleases," which is clumsy and usually serves no other purpose than that of placating the kind of extremist who does not deserve to be placated. The impersonal "he" covers both sexes; however, in a girls' school, for instance, "as she pleases" obviously makes more sense and should be used. What we must get across is that, in language, at any rate, anyone may *not* do as he pleases.

My question to Philip Dunne is: How do you tell a "destructive change" from an "inventive illiteracy" or "graceful improvement"? Let down the barrier in one place, and all language is promptly trodden into the dust by a stampede of uninventive illiterates and graceless disimprovers. This always begins in slight, seemingly harmless ways. An advertisement for a Sony Dictating/ Transcribing Machine (why, incidentally, must the hyphen be superseded by that ugly slash?) begins, in bold print: "He thinks he's got it all. He doesn't." Clearly, that "doesn't" has no antecedent. The antecedent is " 's," which is "has" abridged; the slogan must, therefore, conclude: "He hasn't." Otherwise it means, if anything, "He doesn't think." Or consider something we hear in stentorian tones every Saturday from December to April on Texaco's opera broadcasts: "Texaco, who is proud to present . . ." Texaco, a company acting in unison, is an *it*; so it must be "Texaco, which is . . ."

Small matters, you say? Then consider these statements from a *New York Times* Op-Ed piece by Joseph A. Califano (January 25, 1978) sent to me by Rabbi Lyle Kamlet: "When I was appointed Secretary of Health, Education and Welfare, the relationship of smoking and health were not very much on my mind." A few paragraphs on, Secretary Califano writes, "In an urban area in California, one in twenty 11-year-olds smoke and one in five 12-year-olds smoke." In the first sentence, the singular noun "relationship" requires the singular verb "was." In the second, the subject is, repeatedly, "one," and so requires "smokes," the singular predicate. Let's hope that Secretary Califano is better at health and welfare than he is at education. But, as Rabbi Kamlet observed in his accompanying letter, such sloppiness "bodes ill more for the copy editor of the *Times* than for the careless Mr. Califano."

It is those who should know better who are truly guilty. It is through them that ignorance is allowed to maintain itself and spread. The end can only be chaos. Thus a good many readers—bless them!—sent me in response to my column on punctuation horrible examples of what one of them (Robert E. Friend) calls the Great Apostrophe Plague: the newfangled insertion of apostrophes in ordinary plurals. That this can lead to total insanity is confirmed by a brief but charming note from C. William Bradley, Jr., which reads in toto: "I doubt that popular confusion of plurals and possessives is endemic to New Orleans, where the presence of boiled crabs in a restaurant's repertoire is often indicated by a 'Boil Crab's' sign. But, certainly, no other city can boast a service station graced with the sign 'Larr'y 66 Service'!" The unfortunate man must think that, like a possessive, a diminutive demands an apostrophe before the last letter.

But Philip Dunne is willing to let it go at "all these little horrors are embedded in the language." And who, pray, allowed them to become embedded? As you embed, so you shall lie. Instead of embedding, let's start uprooting. Wouldn't it be nice if half a millennium from now people could read today's writers without elaborate footnotes and glossaries such as we require to read Shakespeare?

# THE ARBITERS

# Guarding the Guardians

**W**herever you look these days—including places where you least expect it—you find bad English. Casually skimming Frederick R. Karl's voluminous *Joseph Conrad: The Three Lives*, my eye caught "Napoleon, the man whom Poles hoped would help restore their country," and, later, "its less than 50,000 words stretched out to seven installments." Obviously, the first passage should have read "the man who"; the second, "fewer than 50,000." If some cursory glances into a huge book by a professor of English at the City College of New York, author of various learned tomes and winner of numerous awards, could yield two such whopping errors (which, moreover, got by the editors of Farrar, Straus & Giroux, one of our best publishing houses), how many more mistakes must lurk in those thousand pages? And in how bad a state must the English language be?

Just now, in the very first essay of *Celebrations and Attacks*, by Irving Howe, one of our leading men of letters, I came across the following: "as if to take a New York subway comes, as indeed it does, to taking on the weight of the world." Now, this may be a deliberate rejection of the subjunctive, which is required with a statement contrary to fact: "as if to take a New York subway came . . . to taking on." It is just barely possible, though, that Howe was thrown off by that "as indeed it does," making it look as if the statement were (not *was*) simple fact. But it isn't: the "as indeed it does" is an afterthought, a hyperbole, a parenthetic remark, and does not affect the grammatical status of the basic hypothetical statement. Yet deliberate rejection of the subjunctive by a fastidious writer strikes me as worse than an error.

All of this brings me to the two books I wish to discuss here: *What's Happening to American English?* (henceforth abbreviated as *AE*), by Arn and Charlene Tibbetts (Scribners, 1979), and *Word Abuse* (henceforth referred to as *WA*), by Donna Woolfolk Cross (Coward, McCann & Geoghegan, 1979). Of the two, *AE* is much the more important; it is a careful discussion, based on extensive research, of how English has been handled and mishandled, taught and *not* taught, in a representative cross section of American high schools. From this base, however, the authors go on to examine various other threats to English, a language whose condition they rightly perceive as critical. They also make sensible suggestions about what we can do, or try to do, about it.

I found particularly useful the authors' critique of the National Council of Teachers of English, a body so shot through with irresponsible radicalism, guilt-ridden liberalism, and asinine trendiness as to be, in my opinion, one of the major culprits—right up there with television—in the sabotaging of linguistic standards. Mrs. Cross's book is more of a general introduction to the manifold ways in which words are being abused and concerns itself largely with problems of jargon, propaganda, public gullibility, and ignorance. It, too, however, contains harrowing examples of failures of instruction and fiascoes of learning.

"In the 1970's," write the Tibbettses, "the corruption of the uneducated by a dozen forces in our culture requires us to be skeptical of their ability as word makers, and the decay of standards of speech and writing among the educated in this country may cause us to be a trifle more authoritarian in matters of usage." Very true, and so, without wishing to undermine the arguments of either of these most welcome books, I must nevertheless point out how even *their* authors have, to some extent, fallen prey to the linguistic anomie they seek to combat.

Thus we find in *AE* "The evidence presented bears few . . . connections to either the author's thesis or conclusion"; yet, in the best English, whatever follows *either* must be balanced by what follows *or*. Hence we need "to either the author's thesis or his conclusions," although "either to the author's thesis or to his conclusions" would be even stronger and better. Next we read, "Everybody involved . . . disclosed their illiteracy," where true literacy demands "his illiteracy." Furthermore, for "ladies' hairdresser," one should write "women's hairdresser," not because of trendy support for the more fanatical shock troops of feminism but because a hairdresser who restricted his clientele to women who are ladies would soon go out of business. The Tibbettses quote without demur the phrase "incredibly ponderous restatements of the obvious," but used in that way, *incredibly* is a nasty bit of jargon to be scrupulously avoided.

In "requirements as to type and quality," the *as to* falls into the category described by Fowler as "a slovenly substitute for some simple preposition." *As to* has its legitimate uses, but replacing a simple *of* or *for* is not one of them; in such cases, it is likely to generate needless ambiguity. In "good schools are much like each other," "one another" would have been correct, there still being (I hope) more than two good schools. Yet even "like one another" is illogical: one thing is like another; two things cannot be like their relationship. Why not just say "are much alike"? "A *Warriner*-type book" is offensive; good usage requires, at the very least, "a *Warriner* type of book," though there are more elegant ways of saying this. "Not as good as" is not so good as "not so good as"; after a negative, *so* is preferred to *as*. Again, "including, most importantly, a good principal," though widespread, is a fallacy; "most important," the elliptical form of "what is most important," is called for.

There follow two more serious errors. "She had been filled full of bad ideas" is obviously redundant: someone filled is ipso facto full. "Crammed full" or "stuffed full" is conceivable, though still, logically speaking, tautological. Particularly odious to me is "One uses them when he needs to," even though, I realize, this used to be taught (and probably still passes for) the correct form. This was, I fear, very bad linguistic policy. If the sentence in which it occurs is longer and more complex, the reader becomes confused: the *one* introduces a generalization, whereas the *he* suggests a specific person and sends the reader back on a wild goose chase for a missed antecedent. There is nothing wrong with "One uses them when one needs to."

Whereas *AE* is only intermittently marred by bad usage, *Word Abuse* is pockmarked with it. Although many of Mrs. Cross's errors were caught in the copy editing, many more survive in the finished book. I have space only for the most reprehensible ones. "We never see the world as the Shona or the Bassa—nor even the Chinese . . . do." In this statement, the initial *never* covers all the subsequent examples, although the author may have been thrown off by the dash into believing otherwise. Her error, however, is no different from the endemic "No eating nor drinking permitted"; indeed, elsewhere in *WA* we find "Nary a bloody knife nor a mutilated body." *Nor* either follows a *neither* or introduces an entirely new sentence or idea. *Anymore* in one word is offensive to good taste even though the worthy *American Heritage Dictionary* condones it. The *Oxford*, bless its heart, will have none of it, though the 1971 *Supplement* adds "freq. anymore." In addition, you do not "aggravate untold thousands," you *annoy* or *irritate* them (if, for example, you criticize them); *aggravate* means "exacerbate" or "worsen." We also encounter the ironic statement "You also don't say if something is going right, you say it is 'nominal.' " To begin with, "also don't" is less clear than "nor do you say"; more important, where *if* could mean either "whether" or "in case that," you had better avoid it. Then, rather than "anxious to prove" something, one is *eager* to prove it. News is not written "intriguingly" but *interestingly, provocatively,* or something of that sort; it may, however, concern somebody's intriguing *against* someone else. "Connotations are what evaporate in translations" is wrong, *what,* being synonymous with "that which," is singular— hence "what evaporates." Consider now "A popular magazine had a contest in which they invited its readers. . . ." A magazine is an *it,* not a *they;* should you, however, subscribe to that demotic plural, you cannot schizophrenically switch to the singular forth-with. "Not too many people . . . stop to think" is a popular and irresponsible use of *too* for *very;* there can never be too many thinking people in the world.

"Overly specific" is inferior to "overspecific," as "inside of her" is to "inside her"; deadwood is always undesirable. All reporters are "investigative," or should be; the epithet is redundant. "Stick-toitiveness" is a ludicrous coinage, made ghastly when spelled "stick-to-itiveness," as in *WA.* There follows an error committed even by some good writers: "When he was a kid, 'breaking your neck' was one of the only injuries there was." *Few* would be better than *only* here, but "injuries there *were*" is mandatory. The *were* goes not with *one* but with *injuries:* there *were* several (or a few) injuries, of which "breaking your neck" was one. "English critic Max Beerbohm" should read "the English critic," lest the meaning be taken as "the critic of English"; this is why we should avoid the construction "critic X" or "author Y," rampant though it may be. "Whole range of action" should, of course, be "whole range of actions"; *range* requires the existence of more than one action. "Competent language producer" is jargon for competent *speaker* or *writer.*

Such sloppinesses (and there are others as well) betoken an imprecise thinker, as is borne out by the following. On page 131 of *WA,* Mrs. Cross writes, "Sticks and stones can only break your bones; words can really hurt you," meaning that words can be worse than weapons. Fair enough, but on page 141, we read about guardsmen so "bethumped with words" that they fought back with "weapons much deadlier than words," that is, things like sticks and stones.

So although I urge you to read both these books, I also beg you to reflect on their caducity. *"Quis custodiet ipsos custodes?"* asked Juvenal: "Who is to guard the guards themselves?" By which he meant not those guardsmen bethumped by words but those persons in responsible positions who nevertheless act irresponsibly.

# The Best Policy

For some time now I have been reiterating that correct use of the language has much to do with logic; I should add that it entails also honesty. I use the word *honesty* in its broadest sense and propose to give some examples of what I mean.

A few months ago, an anonymous reader sent me several clippings from the Antioch College student newspaper that concerned the spellings *wimmin* and *womyn*, which a group of radical feminist students had managed to impose on restroom doors and a weekly student publication. (I may have these absurd spellings slightly wrong but distinctly recall that there were two separate but equally preposterous ones.) The object, obviously, was to get the hated syllable *men* out of the word *women*. Now, this travesty is, first of all, stupid. By the same illogic, we might have to change the spelling of *menstruation, menopause, mentality*, and heaven knows how many other words as they pertain to women (or *wimmin*). Moreover, such antimale fanaticism serves no intelligent cause and merely betrays a pathological streak in those who espouse it.

There is, however, simple dishonesty in this as well—in the attempt to palm off illicit coinage as coin of the realm. There is something deeply fraudulent about pretending that centuries of consolidated spelling and established usage are as nothing to the will of a few extremists, that certain urgent social problems in need of thoughtful political solutions can be settled by despotic invitations to illiteracy and chaos. And these lunatic-fringe feminists, endorsed by the craven college authorities, have instituted a reign of terror: surely the reason my correspondent chose to remain anonymous was that if I printed his name in my column, he would be torn to shreds, like Pentheus by the bacchantes.

From the same menagerie (or mynagerie) as the preceding comes an opinion by Judge Robert S. Thompson of the California Court of Appeals, forwarded to me by Katherine L. Walker, of San Francisco. The injudicious judge writes, "As I analyze the ovular case of *Coast Bank v. Minderhout . . .*" and appends a footnote, "The feminists among us are entitled to a word other than 'seminal.' " I was tempted to call this baloney but, not to offend the feminists with that offensive first syllable, will call it twaddle instead. The metaphorical *seminal* comes from the seed of plants, not men; to pretend otherwise is plainly dishonest.

There are many ways of cheating with language short of actually lying. The most obvious method is tendentious selectivity. In *Decadence: The Strange Life of an Epithet* (Farrar, Straus & Giroux, 1979), Richard Gilman makes fun in rapid succession of "a critic . . . in the *New York Review of Books,*" of "an eminent novelist-reviewer . . . in *The New Yorker,*" of "a writer on pop subjects who has himself a pop sensibility" in *New York* magazine, and of "a theater review by Julius Novick" in the *Village Voice.* One wonders why Novick is mentioned by name, whereas the others are allowed the palliative of anonymity: are some of them figures too powerful for Gilman to fall afoul of, while others are nonentities unworthy of mention? Whatever the case, language is used in a discriminatory and thus dishonest way here.

However, my main concern at present is honesty of style rather than of content, and for this purpose a very useful book has been published: *The Reader Over Your Shoulder,* by Robert Graves and Alan Hodge (Random House, 1979). Subtitled "A Handbook for Writers of English Prose," its *raison d'être* is to teach people to write precisely, clearly, and honestly. There is a slight dishonesty of salesmanship, though, in the very way the American publisher bills the book on the jacket: "Second Edition, revised and abridged by the authors." This is true enough as far as it goes, but it suggests a fresh, up-to-date revision. In fact, the original version came out in England in 1943 and was abridged and revised by the authors in 1947; this is the text that Random House has brought out thirty-two years later without any further updating but with, alas, additional typos.

The deterioration of copy editing and proofreading, incidentally, is a token of the cultural entropy that has overtaken us in the postwar years. Aside from routine misprints, of which there are quite a number, the "new" American edition foists on us such particularly confusing ones as "bought" for *brought* (page 29), "lecture of book" for *lecture or book* (page 31), "ration" for *ratio* (page 102), and "feet" for *fleet* (page 123) in Part I alone. More shocking yet is the statement (page 37) "We are confident that few of our readers noticed a trick played on them on line 12 of page 36." The reference is taken over verbatim from the British edition, where the trick indeed begins at line 12; in the American edition, however, it begins at line 6. Such sloppiness in book publishing would not have occurred a few decades ago on either side of the Atlantic.

It would have been a great blessing to bring out a newly and fully revised edition of the work. As it is, we find in it a quotation from a schoolteacher complaining of the deleterious effect of radio on the state of the language; just think what Graves and Hodge could have done with the ravages of television, assuming they had the stomach for watching it longer than five minutes. But whatever the shortcomings of this book—among which must be included the fact that it addresses itself to British usage rather than to American—it is better to have it reach us late than not at all.

Although the term *honesty* is never invoked by the authors, it seems to me to describe perfectly what they are after. Graves and Hodge are well aware of the difficulties of English, which, as a literary language, "has never crystallized the way that Italian, French and Spanish have done." But they find this "immense, formless aggregate" wonderfully susceptible to being adapted "to one's own temperament, environment and purposes" and "admit[ting] of such poetic exquisiteness" as more regimented languages do not allow. " 'Fixed' English," say our authors, "is an easy language to learn . . . but of free English . . . no wise person will ever claim final mastery—there is no discovered end." They "suggest that whenever anyone sits down to write he should imagine a crowd of his prospective readers (rather than a grammarian in cap and gown) looking over his shoulder." They go even further in their seemingly permissive approach: "As a rule, the best English is written by people without literary pretensions, who have responsible executive jobs in which the use of official language is not compulsory; and, as a rule, the better at their jobs they are, the better they write."

In 1979, this would be overoptimistic: few executives nowadays can write any better than the secretaries who do their actual writing, such as that is. But though the foregoing quotations may make *The Reader Over Your Shoulder* sound demotic or even demagogic in its approach to language, the authors' practice is much better than their preachment, and there is sterner stuff to come. True, "to write English perfectly is impossible in practice [and] there has never been a writer who did not have some blind spot in his reading eye"; nevertheless, "the writing of good English . . . is a moral matter," and also requires logic with a capital *L*. Needed, too, is a kind of honesty that Graves and Hodge describe as follows:

> No writer of English can be sure of using exactly the right words even in a simple context, and even after twenty or thirty years of self-education. But he should at least act on the assumption that there is always an exactly right word, or combination of words, for his purpose—which he will gratefully recognize as such if it happens to occur to him; and that, though he may not always find the right word, he can at least learn . . . to avoid the quite wrong ones, and even the not quite wrong.

Toward this end, Graves and Hodge posit twenty-five principles of clear statement and sixteen principles of graceful prose—the former to satisfy the requirements of sense, the latter those of sensibility—and proceed to give numerous examples of failures in each category, as well as corrected versions. In fact, Part II of the book is a series of substantial passages from well-known writers (the examples include every kind of expository prose); Graves and Hodge analyze in minute detail large and small deficiencies in them and then provide fair copies—the passages rewritten as they should have been composed at first, in the interest of clarity, elegance, and craftsmanly integrity.

Although I don't agree with every detail, I can warmly recommend the book as a whole to all readers, even those with no

serious writerly aspirations—perhaps especially to those. Yet what
I find of almost as great, though coincidental, interest is that writers as astute as our authors (Graves is very probably the finest
living poet in the English language, as well as one of its most
distinguished prose practitioners) make obvious mistakes. They
write (or quote without demur from other sources) "too final,"
although a thing is either final or not—never "too final"; "whether
we like it or no," which is obsolete—we now say "whether or not";
"human beings are changing continuously," where the correct
word would be *continually—continuous* means something unbroken,
uninterrupted, and applies, at best, to the changes of a chameleon;
"both grammatically and from the point of view of sense," which,
for the sake of balance and concision, should be "both grammatically and logically" or "for the sake of both grammar and
sense."

Such mistakes—and there are quite a few more—illustrate the
authors' point that nobody writes perfect English. But the book
goes a long way toward giving us precept and example for the
achievement of simple, good, honest expression of even very
complex ideas. It will protect you from writing, as Benjamin De-
Mott does in the *New York Times Book Review* of May 13, 1979,
"*The Star-Apple Kingdom* marks . . . the return, after an absence, of
a moving public speech to poetry in English." DeMott is too
bright not to know that a return predicates an absence. But he
wanted to make a grand statement without bothering to figure out
whether the absence in question was short, long, very long, or
merely imaginary. "Return, after an absence" resounds more por-
tentously than a naked "return" and seems, even if tautological,
more suited to cover up the vagueness and questionable honesty
of the assertion. Concision is honesty, honesty concision—that's
one thing you need to know.


# Jacques Barzun: Purism Without Petrifaction

There do indeed exist two cultures in our society, but they do
not face each other, as C. P. Snow argued, across a demarcation

line called the Second Law of Thermodynamics. The issue is not, I think, whether a person's knowledge pertains to the sciences or to the humanities, but whether a person has language or not. Wherever people foregather, one hears two kinds of talk: that which, by and large, can be called English; and that which is essentially gibberish.

English can be recognized as the tongue of Shakespeare and Milton, of Dickens and Faulkner; gibberish is the language surrogate made up of "oh, wow!" and "like, I mean," of "mind-blowing" and "hopefully." It is not, as you might assume, a matter of one culture or the lack of it, the way it used to be; it is truly a matter of *two* cultures, of which the lower is made up of a loose coalition of culturelessness and counterculture, of *arrivistes* and (we need the word) *départistes*. Social classes hardly exist any more, and the division between high and low, or popular, culture has been pretty much erased thanks to pop, camp, dropping out, turning on, various kinds of inverse snobbery and *nostalgie de la boue*, and the ubiquitous braying, screeching, howling of rock. Just about the only way left of telling the players apart—in the absence of programs and even uniforms—is by the language they use.

What creates this confusion bordering on chaos is the loss of boundaries. Intellectuals, or at least potential intellectuals, haunt rock concerts and body-building exhibitions, stock-car races and porn movie houses, while *hoi polloi* hang out at museums and art galleries, classy restaurants and ballet and opera houses. The biggest slob thinks nothing of wearing a Beethoven T-shirt, whereas the brightest college student cares mostly about David Bowie or Patti Smith. The one area in which distinctions still exist is diction: there are those who say "like I said," and those who would sooner bite off their tongues than say it; there are those to whom "whom" is sacred, and those who have forgotten that they ever heard it, if indeed they did.

There is, and can be, no compulsion: those who are awash in soap operas and situation comedies need not be channeled into chamber-music concerts, any more than fanciers of Pontormo should be compelled to immerse themselves in the iconography of *Peanuts*. But there is a major problem: those who care to acquire genuine culture, and who might want to start, quite properly, with learning their language, no longer know where to turn for help. I have had university students thrust under my nose A or even A +

papers whose grammar, syntax, and style would make the prose of anonymous hate letters and kidnappers' ransom notes appear positively Johnsonian.

It is no longer from our institutions of learning, grown permissive, that you can learn how to speak and write, as the published works of most of the new academics make abundantly clear. And this is no small matter: even with the best will, literate and illiterate people are finding it harder and harder to communicate. There is a language barrier behind which rises an even higher thought barrier, and no traffic, in either direction, can vault them.

In a recent movie column, I happened to dismiss (deservedly, it seemed to me) a certain northeastern university. In no time at all, I had a letter of protest from a special assistant to its president; it began: "Hopefully, all intelligent Americans" are against extending the freedom of the press to include such derogation, and wondered, "What viable evaluative criteria exists [sic]" for the conclusion that said university "is anything but the fine, distinguished institution that it indeed is?" Any institution that tolerates in such a high position a devotee of the impersonal "hopefully" (a.k.a. the floating hopefully or a misused modal auxiliary) and the singular "criteria," a fellow who wallows in such jargon as "viable evaluative criteria"—to say nothing of his bizarre concept of the freedom of the press—might indeed give rise to doubts about its distinction and fineness.

Another letter came from a young woman describing herself as a Liberal Arts "alumnus [sic]" of said institution; she considered my daring to "cast dispersions" on her alma mater "one of the worst failings a reviewer . . . may have." Clearly, this alumna had jumbled "aspersions" and "disparagement" and had never learned the difference between "can" and "may."

In a third letter, two Harvard students (one male, one female) accused me of contemptible "snobbism"; they went on to declare that "Harvard, where [I] had earned [my] Ph.D. thesis, is loathe [sic] to take credit" for me. They also instructed me that my use of "graduated" was incorrect, the proper form being "was graduated." Not only did they confuse the adjective "loath" with the verb "loathe," they were also benighted enough to write "earn a Ph.D. thesis," though one writes a thesis and earns a Ph.D. They were also mistaken about "was graduated," the common usage having shifted to "graduated" (see the *American Heritage Dictionary*), and, to top it all, in one place they put a period outside the quotation marks—a lapse one would not have expected from high-school students in palmier days.

In our time of linguistic—and thus cultural—misery, how welcome was the publication of Jacques Barzun's *Simple & Direct: A Rhetoric for Writers* (Harper & Row, 1975), a book that, taken to heart and mind, might actually teach people how to write correct English, and, after that, how to speak it. For I am convinced that correct writing comes first: there is no way of teaching the mouth except through the eye and the hand. We all know that things go in one ear and out the other, but not in one eye and out the other; and even if the left hand doesn't know what the right hand is doing, that is all right as long as the right is not doing it wrong.

It would be impossible to tell you in this little space all about Jacques Barzun and his work. He is an eminent historian and writer on almost every aspect of the arts, the sciences, and the social sciences. In a recent *Festschrift* in his honor, Barzun's bibliography covers more than twenty-two pages. It includes books on, among other subjects, the heritage of Darwin, Marx, and Wagner; the concepts of classicism, romanticism, and modernism; Berlioz; race; science; the art of teaching; the energies of art; and the nature of intellect. It further contains articles of the most varied sorts, as well as translations of French belles lettres, chiefly plays. Barzun is the historian as polyhistor, one of those rare scholars who give polygraphy a good name. For many years he taught at Columbia, where he was at various times dean, provost, and university professor, the highest academic rank; retired from teaching, but ageless and active as ever, he is an editorial consultant at the publishing house of Charles Scribner's Sons.

Some seventeen or eighteen years ago, I was the associate editor of The Mid-Century Book Society, whose editors were W. H. Auden, Jacques Barzun, and Lionel Trilling. My principal duty was to put out *The Mid-Century*, the book club's monthly magazine, to which Auden, Barzun, Trilling, and, a little later on, I were regular contributors. In those days, Barzun gave me a number of invaluable pointers about writing, the most astonishing of which was the suggestion that I refrain from using in the same passage the words "regiment" and "calvary," because, in that context, readers were sure to misread the latter as "cavalry." This struck me as a bit farfetched at the time; still, I dutifully changed "calvary" to "golgotha."

I remember well the excitement of working with those three distinguished men. I was amused by their widely divergent attitudes toward corrections in their copy. Auden, who took his fugitive essays much less seriously than his poetry, dashing them off somewhat carelessly, left the straightening out of his prose entirely to his editors, whom he treated with a charming mixture of gratitude and indifference. Trilling I would call up and have interesting telephone conversations with: sometimes he agreed to a proposed change, sometimes not. Barzun was a problem: he required very little editing, and accepted less. If I called him up to make a gingerly suggestion in the most respectful tone, I got a crisp, curt, audibly smiling reply; he would make quite clear why he was sticking to his guns, and that was that. After a while, I gave up trying; most of the time he was right, anyway, which entitled him to an occasional idiosyncrasy, or even lapse.

But to get back to *Simple & Direct*. It is a book that may irritate a few people because of a certain doubleness of tone: at times, it seems to address itself to sophisticated, consenting adults; at others, it becomes rather more schoolmasterly, with the swish of the ferule heard between the lines. Yet how sensible and useful Barzun's precepts are, how encompassing and enlightened his views! And how pregnant his formulations, as in "Ideas will best slide into a reader's mind when the word noise is least." And "Readers vary in their awareness of bumps, but smoothness is so glasslike a property that the smallest flaw spoils it." And further: "Communication is most complete [*sic*] when it proceeds from the smallest number of words—and indeed of syllables." Again: "Writing is a social act; whoever claims his neighbor's attention by writing is duty-bound to take trouble—and in any case, what is life for, unless to do at least some things right?"

Barzun, you might say, stands for purism without petrifaction; though conservative, he is by no means inflexibly opposed to change, provided the change makes sense. He has wonderfully cogent opinions on such matters as "like" and "as," "who" and "whom"; on jingles, genteelisms, the uses of the apostrophe and hyphen, and hundreds of other such matters, as he takes his readers (always with appropriate exercises and occasional examples of good writing from rather unusual sources) through the mysteries of diction, linking, tone and tune, meaning, composition, and revision. To give you a sense of Barzun's mind and style, and a demonstration of how fully he practices what he preaches, here is a sample passage:

[It is not] enough to pay attention to words only when you face the task of writing—that is like playing the violin only on the night of the concert. You must attend to the words when you read, when you speak, when others speak. Words must become ever present in your waking life, an incessant concern, like color and design if the graphic arts matter to you, or pitch and rhythm if it is music, or speed and form if it is athletics. Words, in short, must be *there*, not unseen and unheard, as they probably are and have been up to now. It is proper for the ordinary reader to absorb the meaning of a story or description as if the words were a transparent sheet of glass. But he can do so only because the writer has taken pains to choose and adjust them with care. They were not glass to him, but mere lumps of potential meaning. He had to weigh them and fuse them before his purposed meaning could shine through.

This is beautiful writing from every point of view: a perfect blend of the sweet and the useful. But, as Barzun admits, no one is perfect, and so we find a few, very rare slipups even in this excellent book. We read, for example, about possibilities canceling "each other" out where more than two are involved; here, "one another" would be preferable. It seems captious to me to carp at the U.S. Postal Service's use of the "stamps . . . have been gummed" on the ground that " 'gummed' . . . means licked and affixed to the envelope." The *Oxford English Dictionary* gives the definition "to coat or smear with . . . gum" along with "to fasten . . . with gum." Again, we read: "Telegraphese is by no means down-to-earth; it is but another affectation, particularly when it is not really stripped bare, but mixed and mannered. . . ." Here one sentence contains two different "but"s, the first an adverb, the second a conjunction. This sort of thing creates confusion.

Yet these are footling matters. If you read this short book, two things will stay with you if nothing else does: the sense of someone happily, inspiredly, and above all requitedly in love with language, and the pleasure that such love communicates even to the

casual reader. You may, at the very least, develop respect for
language, out of which further good things may gradually evolve.
I, for one, am very glad, in retrospect, that Barzun made me
change that "calvary" to "golgotha." It was, to use a lovely phrase
of Barzun's about the effect of his good friend and colleague
Lionel Trilling on his students, "a reshaping of the mind, not an
indoctrination." That one could use such foresight and courtesy to
forestall misreading—to make some hypothetical reader's sailing a
little smoother—is something that would never have occurred to
me. Now it is something I can never forget.

## Edwin Newman Bares His Civil Tongue

Edwin Newman's *A Civil Tongue*, published by Bobbs-Merrill,
in 1976, is a sort of sequel to *Strictly Speaking*, which I regrettably
missed. True, the new book's jacket quotes Bob Woodward:
"Even funnier, even better than *Strictly Speaking.*" But what about
Bernstein? I can no more believe Woodward without Bernstein
than Abercrombie without Fitch. The jacket has an endorsement
from one Richard H. Revere as well. Is that Richard H. Rovere
reverentially rechristened?

In any case, *A Civil Tongue* is an annotated compilation of just
about every type of error that makes language in America, if not
quite yet a lost cause, less than a going concern. With demonic
acumen, Newman adduces 196 pages' worth of grammatical errors. Clichés, jargon, malapropisms, mixed metaphors, monstrous
neologisms, unholy ambiguities, and parasitic redundancies, in-
terspersed with his own mocking comments, puns, anecdotes,
pastiches, bits of autobiography, and exhortations to do better.
The examples are mostly true horrors, very funny and even more
distressing. That some of our leading politicians, educators, artists, scholars, clergymen, journalists, military men, and other assorted leaders and luminaries—as well as plainer folk—could write
or utter the godawful gobbledygook here assembled is more than
tragicomic. It is very nearly tragic. Worse than a nation of shop-

keepers, we have become a nation of wordmongers or word-butchers, and abuse of language, whether from ignorance or obfuscation, leads, as Newman persuasively argues, to a deterioration of moral values and standards of living.

"We are safe when language is specific," Newman writes. "It improves our chances of knowing what is going on." Among hundreds of examples, Newman cites, "The purpose of this letter is to historize the philosophical infrastructure Craig Computer Center abides, regarding applicant referrals." Well, that is only an employment agency speaking, or partly speaking. But here is the Nashville School Board stating its intentions: "Programmatic assumptions will be specified, competencies identified, a rationale developed and instructional objectives stated. Pre-assessment, post-assessment, learning alternatives and remediation will be an integral part of instructional modules within the framework of program development."

Birch Bayh is quoted as saying, "Energywise, economywise and environmentalwise, we have become obsessed with the problems"; Allison Cheek, the first Episcopal woman minister, declares, "I will not let the church inferiorize me again." A Lincoln Center program note reads, "Dvořák was a late bloomer, compositionwise"; a sign at the University of Pittsburgh announces "an elevator outage." The CIA has a "nondiscernible microbionoculator," which turns out to be a dart gun with a silencer. Muzak justifies its repellent product by calling it "sonorous design to humanize man-made environments" and says it "promotes the sharing of meaning because it massifies symbolism." Charles G. Walcutt, a graduate professor of English at CUNY, writes, "The colleges, trying to remediate increasing numbers of . . . illiterates up to college levels, are being highschoolized." A coordinator of research of the department of education of an eastern state refers to "summarizative descriptions."

Newman quotes copiously from an article, "Formative Hermeneutics in the Arting Process of an Other: The Philetics of Art Education," by Professor Kenneth R. Beittel of Penn State, published in *Art Education*. It is all inscrutable jargon, and not in the least hermeneutic. The Navy Finance Center in Cleveland offers "lecturettes"; Kissinger refers to "a hypothetical situation that does not now exist"; and the U.S. commander in South Korea declares that if the North Koreans attack, "Our firepower will have a tremendous impact on their ground troops, breaking their will in addition to killing them." Professor Herbert Stein of the University of Virginia writes that FDR "holds the record for most times elected President in one lifetime." Something is sold in stores that calls itself an "aerated nondairy creamer." Newman rightly observes, "One blanches to think what [it] would be called on the basis of what it is rather than what—dairy cream—it is not."

After many, many more such varied abuses held up to our scorn, Newman concludes: "The use of language that is at bottom nonsense leads . . . to the advocacy of nonsensical ideas and, by the law of averages alone, to the adoption of nonsensical ideas. At the least, the language and the ideas go hand in hand." And further: "The appeal of [bastardized] language lies in its slipperiness. It sounds as though it means [sic] something especially to those who do not look at it closely. It serves as a fence that keeps others outside and respectful, or leads them to ignore what is going on because it is too much trouble to find out. For those inside, either effect is useful." What Newman wants is that "clarity and genuineness come together" and that with "some knowledge . . . some imagination, and a sense of delight in what language can do," we repossess the fun that good, natural English offers us.

The book stands for all the right things, and is peccant only in two minor but irritating ways. That there are occasional errors— "deprecatingly" for "depreciatingly," "a bookstore which" for "a bookstore that," a couple of faulty agreements and a captious attack on the useful word "demythify"—is not so much Newman as human. More objectionable is the tendency to hit us over the head with an excess of examples of the same mistake, and still more injurious is a certain self-indulgence—Newman's permitting himself too many lengthy and often unfunny puns, labored imaginary dialogues, and other smart-alecky ways of making fun of verbal crimes that speak, or shriek, for themselves.

At times, the book feels like a surfeit of those squibs at the bottom of *New Yorker* pages, with the patronizing comments getting out of hand—as when the absurd jargon of "instructional modules" makes Newman become more absurd and write about silent students to whom all this talk has given "throat modules. The teacher, a son of the Ould Sodule and mindful of the maxim, Spare the rodule and spoil the child, says he will codule them no longer, and all go back to work, including a set of twins who are as alike as two peas in a podule."

This sort of thing is self-destructive. It weakens the striking power of Newman's important arguments, which are, at other times, reinforced by pertinent, pithy witticisms like the reference to General Washington's "revolutionary-type war," or the joke about news conferences being "part of the interface [a vogue word Newman correctly loathes] process, which reaches its ultimate expression when all parties turn the other cheek." But intermittent slickness and incidental smugness aside, *A Civil Tongue* is a valuable compendium of *pseudodoxia epidemica*, as Sir Thomas Browne called his collection of vulgar misconceptions, and I wish only that there were more watchdogs like Newman in positions so visible and prestigious, and barking, like him, up the right tree. Most other newsmen, alas, are very ordinary dogs, and what they do to the tree of language relieves only them.

# THE GENIUS OF LANGUAGE

# The Sacred Trust

Language, my lovely concern (if I may adapt from Malherbe), leads me to mistrust habitual offenders against good usage. Their offenses take many shapes. They may betray something like tone-deafness in music, as when Vincent Canby, the *New York Times* film critic, consistently writes "disinterested" to denote lack of interest, for which the correct word is "uninterested" ("disinterested" means unbiased, impartial). Or they may betray a mind insensitive to logic, as when Joan Mellen, a professor of English at Temple University—where, to be sure, she teaches film courses, thank God, not English ones—refers in her book *Voices From the Japanese Cinema* to a "three-part trilogy about the Second World War." Though a three-part trilogy is undoubtedly preferable to a two-part one, common sense, I think, is better yet.

However, let me not dwell on appraising the diction of individuals or professional strata; let me try, rather, to speculate a bit about what has been called the spirit or genius of a language (as in "genius loci," the genius or spirit of a place), which varies so greatly from language to language and tells us almost embarrassingly much about the people who speak the tongue in question.

I just returned from a short journey through France and Italy—a *truly* sentimental one, I'm afraid, I being made of less stern stuff than my illustrious predecessor—where I had ample opportunity to reflect on the differences among languages and the cultural differences they predicate. It all began with a little item in the movie column of *France-Soir*, in which a film was described as *"une comédie à la française sur fond de cocuages"*: "a comedy in the French manner against a background of cuckoldings." Now, this would be unheard of in an American newspaper: "Cuckoldings," or "cuckoldry," simply would not do. The word has become, for all practical purposes, an archaism. Manifestly, the phenomenon it describes is anything but obsolete, yet no new synonym for "cuckoldry" has evolved. What has happened is that we have lost our sense of humor about marital infidelity (at least as practiced by wives, in contradistinction to husbands), assuming that we ever had it, and think of it only in earnest, moralizing terms. "Adultery" is our word for it. And it is a grave business, in theory, at any rate—the stuff not of comedy but of marital drama.

When you look at our theater and cinema, you find virtually no such thing as comic cuckoldry in it. Currently on Broadway, for instance, there is *Agamemnon*, which is partly about cuckoldry, but is ancient, tragic (thus really about adultery), and Greek (even if a Rumanian charlatan named Serban has made a hash of it); *Chicago* has something in it about unfaithful wives, but it is all buried under other plot and production elements and lost sight of; *Otherwise Engaged* has a bit of wifely infidelity in it, but it is British, and in sophisticated Britain cuckoldry still exists—besides, the husband gives even more than he takes, so that what is sauce for the goose is actually a swimming pool for the gander. In *I Love My Wife*, something is afoot that might be called the son of cuckoldry—wife swapping—but it is never consummated. Which is characteristic of American comedy in general: infidelity is contemplated, hovered over, and finally avoided, the coitus interruptus or clean dirty joke being the staple of American screen and stage fare.

Granted there is the long-running show, *Same Time, Next Year*, about a man and a woman, married but not to each other, who once a year spend a special night together, not so much making love (though that, too) as lovingly discussing their respective families. It is all so sweet and innocent that you can hardly call it cuckoldry or adultery—or even sex. In other words, in our theater as in life, a concept that is very much *à la française* cannot be served up *à l'américaine*. I cannot help wondering whether if cuckoldry could be seen more facetiously in art, and therefore in life, our disastrous divorce rate might not go down a bit.

In Rome, I was having lunch with Lina Wertmüller, the marvelous director, and her husband, Enrico Job, the artist and the art director of Lina's films. Candice Bergen and Giancarlo Giannini, the stars of Lina's first English-language film, *A Night Full of Rain*, were also with us. Lina was saying how much she loved Art Nouveau, called Liberty in Italian, and wondered, along with Enrico and Giancarlo, why the word "liberty" seemed to be on the decline in English, superseded by "freedom." Miss Bergen explained that "liberty" was a longer word, syllabically, and rather old-fashioned now. True, but somewhat circular as an argument: "Liberty" is obsolescent because it has become obsolete. But Miss

Bergen had a good point there about length: we are becoming mortally afraid of—or simply unacquainted with—long words.

Consider, though: could Patrick Henry have made it with "Give me freedom or give me death"? It had to be "liberty." Partly for reasons of scansion: a great prose epigram functions as a line of verse, and in this tetrameter line the first half would have been perfectly trochaic, "Gíve mĕ fréedŏm," and the second, after the caesura, perfectly iambic, "ŏr gíve/mĕ déath." That is too symmetrically *un*balanced to be rhythmically viable. The touch of irregularity caused by the extra syllable in "liberty" saves the cadence.

But there is more to this. "Liberty" ends on a so-called open syllable, i.e., on a vowel. The "y" becomes in the mouth of an orator an extended "ee" that resonates on and on: "liberteeee"; it stands in contrast to "death," a closed syllable, i.e., one that ends on a consonant that cuts the vowel off. Try as you may to draw out the "ea," the "th" is right there to put a stop, or quietus, to it. "Freedom" ends similarly on a closed syllable—an unaccented one at that—so there is no way in which the "dom" can be prolonged; the famous but feeble verse notwithstanding, "freedom" does not ring—"liberty" does. But "liberty" strikes today's Americans as a big word; the democratic thing is to speak small.

After lunch, I watched Miss Wertmüller direct Candice Bergen in the dubbing of the new film. Parts of the dialogue, for various technical reasons, were not recorded in direct sound during the shooting; they had to be "looped" in afterward at a sound studio. In this particular scene, Miss Bergen, who plays an American photographer traveling in Italy, leaps to the defense of an Italian woman whom a man has been ostensibly beating up; since it is a medium-long shot and the lip movement is not very apparent, there is some freedom (if not liberty) in improvising the English dialogue. In Italian, says Lina, the American woman would shout to her Italian "sister" something like "I couldn't just stand there and let him beat you like a dog." Candice Bergen wonders whether an American would say "beat you like a dog." All right, Lina replies, how about "like a horse" or "like a donkey"? But we don't say those things, either.

Why not? Is it that we have become too urbanized for such country phrases? Or that the ASPCA has taught us better manners toward our animals? Or that we are hypocrites who do in fact beat dogs, horses, or donkeys, but do not admit it in our parlance? Or are we Anglo-Saxons simply more humane than those nasty Latins?

There were by now several Americans in the studio making suggestions; one heard "beat her like dirt," "like a slave," "like a nigger," and sundry other things, but they all sounded wrong. Either we don't beat any creature habitually or we don't own up to it linguistically. Conceivably, it is an honest language, after all, that makes a clean breast of animal abuse; and the nation that speaks it an honest people. Well, brutal but honest. Certainly there is a great deal that can be deduced about national traits from the genius of a language. French, for example, has a perfectly civilized locution for a severe beating: in French, you beat someone "like plaster." Plaster, you see, cannot take offense; indeed, it wants to be beaten, i.e., slapped on.

In an interesting popular book on the French language, *Parler croquant* (which could be translated as "to speak like a peasant," or "clodhopper talk"), by Claude Duneton, the author advocates the liberalization and democratization of the French language and plunks for the simpler, livelier, more colloquial way in which English allegedly expresses itself, as against the more formal, abstract, aristocratic turns of French. These Duneton perceives as imposed by nobles and academicians—and later by the bourgeoisie—on peasants and proletarians, the real people. He admires English for being made up by the people themselves for plainer and more practical purposes, often in juicier forms. Claims Duneton: "The fear of being ridiculous in English is the fear of being a pedant. It must be admitted that the opposite is frequently the case in French: one is afraid of being ridiculous by using a language that is too clear, comprehensible to everybody."

It is undoubtedly true that many Americans have a horror of consulting a dictionary and consider any reading matter that periodically obliges them to look up words a sort of disgrace. The hate letters I receive at *New York* magazine just for my alleged sesquipedality are legion. Less hatefully, a law student at a Midwestern university actually wrote me a letter asking for the meaning of one of my words because the nearest unabridged dictionary was at the library, clear across the street from him. But there are also letters from happy readers thanking me for expanding their vocabularies, though these frequently come from foreign-born

Americans. Now, I can easily see being bored, annoyed, even put off by having to do dictionary work; but hate—sheer burning, raging, uncontrolled hate—in return for a bit of linguistic education (dare I call it maieutics, inasmuch as the writer is the midwife between the reader and the dictionary?) seems a mite excessive. Yet there it is: the American wants it short and simple, unlike, say, the Latin.

Take the willingness with which Italian adds extra syllables to a word—any word—whereas in English we tend to begrudge Vladimir Nabokov a single letter: when, with admirable precision, he writes "a leathern coat," we call it fussy, antiquarian, pedantic. Some years ago, there was a film by the late Pier Paolo Pasolini entitled *Uccellacci e Uccellini*, which means "the big birds and the little birds"—or, still more literally, "big, ugly [or mean] birds." It is all done with suffixes appended to the basic word *uccello*, bird. Besides the diminutive *-ino*, Italian boasts the augmentative *-one*, as well as the pejorative augmentative *-accio*. The title was officially translated into English as *The Hawks and the Sparrows*, which was inadequate: it did not emphasize the fact that these birds (a metaphor for people, of course) were all the same kind of beings, *uccelli*; some were small and helpless, while others were large and predatory, but, as members of the same family, they were all supposed to love one another. Bringing in different species, you lose the implied moral imperative. The Anglo-Saxon, or American, need for brevity, however, was well served with words of one or two syllables only.

The way imagery is used in a given language is, of course, extremely revealing, too. Serbian folk poetry, for instance, which is our closest modern-day link to Homer both in its structure and in its mode of performance, uses a formulaic metaphor to describe the mouth of a pretty girl: "Her mouth is a box of sugar." Why, you might ask, would the Serbian folk bard have differed so strikingly from folk poets of other nations, to whom female mouths suggested roses or rosebuds and such, not a prosaic box, however sweet its contents? Because, I submit, for the Serbs—oppressed and plundered for centuries by the Turks—a box of sugar represented something more than just sweetness: incalculable riches. Anyone could grow a lousy rose on his patch of land, but to own a lasting supply of sugar! . . .

To go from one extreme to the other, people have often wondered why the basic imprecation of Hungary—so unlike the curses of other peoples—should be (I am putting it somewhat more politely) "a horse's member up your anus." Why isn't it something about the promiscuity of your mother, the looseness of your saints, or the unmentionable things you should do to certain parts of yourself, as in other, more civilized languages? The answer is that the Hungarians were, from way back, an equestrian people who, whether or not descended from Attila the Hun, rode roughshod over lands and peoples, devastating them by cavalry attacks and sheer hoof power. A Hungarian of those days lived on his horse; his saddle, under which his slices of beef were stored, even acted as his meat tenderizer. For such a centaur, the fitting thing to threaten with was his horse's penis up the enemy's soft human behind.

And what about that conceivably greatest of English losses vis-à-vis the other European languages: the loss of the personal pronoun's second person singular form—the absence of "thou," except, perhaps, in talking to God? In how many European works of art—and, better yet, lives—does the great moment occur when two beings who were until then "you" to each other suddenly, perhaps in the middle of lovemaking, become "thou"? And, conversely, what stunning effects of solemn distancing are achieved when "thou" suddenly reverts to "you"! In English, none of this. The only intimacy left us is with God, and even that is rapidly growing obsolete.

So let us think about what languages—or just *the* language—can do for a culture, or for us. Grasping this, let us avoid such boorishnesses as using "disinterested" when we mean "uninterested" and such monumental idiocies as "three-part trilogies." Language is a sacred trust: we should nurture it, polish it, encourage it to grow new branches; instead, we kick it around, blunt it, and smash it at the peril of our very souls.

# Do You Speak Humor?

International understanding is a delightful thing. How nice it was at the 1978 Pula Film Festival, in Yugoslavia, between viewings of films, to find a group of critics and scholars from various

DO YOU SPEAK HUMOR?

countries in agreement about the vast overratedness of that self-inflated, dismally repetitious, barely second-rate fictionist Isaac Bashevis Singer. The discussion profited from the fact that everyone spoke English well enough to be able to convey his dislike, which, regardless of his country of origin, was very nearly identical with the other fellow's. But at the magnificent Roman amphitheater, where the Yugoslav films of the past year were being shown to some twelve thousand people night after night, things were a bit less cozy for some of my fellow critics who did not speak Serbo-Croatian and had to use earphones, and who afterward complained bitterly of the inadequacies of the simultaneous translations into their respective languages.

How marvelous it would be to have a universal language, one was induced to think, whatever its name and provenience; it would mean having to translate into only one other language, and that one so well known everywhere as to make a truly satisfactory rendering relatively easy. Which, in turn, made me wonder whether we did not already possess, unbeknown (preferable to *unbeknownst*) to us, a universal tongue. Could not that lingua franca be, not Esperanto, Volapük, or even English, but humor? At times, when twelve thousand people endowed with the cultural, religious, and other differences prominent among Yugoslavia's constituent republics, all represented here, laughed in thunderous unison so that Emperor Vespasian's mighty arena had to withstand assaults stronger than those of time, I wondered whether it was too much to assume that a touch of humor makes the whole world kin.

But is humor really a language? And, if so, what kind? And is it truly universal? The effect of humor, laughter, is certainly universal; but is its cause equally ecumenical? Would the majority of people the world over really find the same things funny? Some aspects of humor obviously depend on our familiarity with a given language—puns, for example, whose hero and martyr, James Joyce, taught English in Pula between 1904 and 1905, as a plaque testifies. But consider also this: the Women's Campaign Fund, one of the most influential feminist organizations, has sent out a brochure soliciting contributions, and the subheading, writ large, reads: BREAK THE VISCIOUS CIRCLE. The text itself begins (in only slightly smaller print): "That viscious psychological circle has kept many women out of office." Should not these eminent postulants, some in very high office, who seek election or reelection funds, know how to spell *vicious?* Such illiteracy—obviously not shared by all the illustrious signatories—not only does not make me reach into my pocket, it also prevents me from keeping a straight face. But how many feminists—even aside from those whose fanaticism excludes a sense of humor—in the Women's Campaign Fund would actually find this contretemps funny?

Funniness, as we all know, comes in two forms, wit and humor, and some of our best minds have toiled over defining the distinction between them. Rushing in where cooler heads might abstain, I would say that *humor* is basically good-natured and often directed toward oneself, if only by subsumption under the heading "general human foolishness"; *wit*, on the other hand, is aggressive, often destructive (though, one hopes, in a good cause), and almost always directed at others. It would perhaps not be an excessive oversimplification to say that humor appeals to general masochism, whereas wit caters to general sadism. Humor also tends to be spread out, leisurely, more diffuse than wit, which is usually pinpointing and epigrammatic.

Let's try a few examples of humor. Everyone knows the famous Abbott and Costello routine "Who's on first?" This is a good specimen of vulgar but infectious humor—a little lower than the angels, but higher than a banana peel. Note that much of the comedy depends on obtuseness, or at least misunderstanding, allowing the hearer to feel superior or, at worst, not inferior to the purveyors of such foolery. For something higher, consider Falstaff's remark "I am not only witty in myself, but the cause that wit is in other men." That is a supremely humorous, rather than witty, line: first, because Falstaff, though funny, is not particularly witty—hence lack of self-knowledge on the part of the speaker that permits us to feel pleasurably superior to him; second, because Falstaff is jovially aware of his fatness and perhaps even folly as butts for jests—hence an admission of fallibility and further encouragement to us to condescend to it mirthfully.

Take, however, a maxim such as this one, attributed to (among others) William James: "There are two kinds of people in the world: those who divide people into two kinds, and those who don't." Is this humor or wit? On the surface, it is a benevolent and droll way of saying that all people posit such division, even the ones who, like the speaker, seem to be above such strategies. But this is also rather cleverly put, and the listener cannot help feeling (rightly) that the speaker knows what he is saying, namely that even the listener is locked into a schema of two-way partitioning from which no one can escape—a threatening ideological confinement.

We get unquestionable wit, however, with the following remark, which I am inclined to consider the cleverest piece of capsule dramatic criticism I know of: W. S. Gilbert's comment on Beerbohm Tree's performance as Hamlet—"Funny without being vulgar." This is the epitome of wit, irony, subtle devastation; it sounds as if it were exquisite praise until, a second or two later, it explodes into perfect disparagement: what could be worse than a funny tragic hero? I attempted something similar years ago in a Harvard publication while reviewing a Cambridge production of Cocteau's *Orpheus*: "When, in the second act, Paul Schmidt esuriently kisses the front half of a horse, a production that has generally been living beyond its means finally manages to make ends meet." Less genteelly and succinctly devastating than Gilbert's sally, it is nevertheless an example of irony; that is, seeming to say one thing while conveying its opposite. But irony, on which a great deal of wit is based, is a device remarkably little understood by the typical American, who is far too bluff and foursquare for such Old World deviousness.

Wit, then, is seldom harmless: at the very least, it is likely to offend its target; but those who miss ironic implications, and those who out of soft-heartedness or mere insecurity are apt to put themselves into the victim's shoes, are equally likely to be offended and resent the ironist.

Speaking of shoes, a Hungarian critic at Pula told me a joke now very popular in Budapest. At a scientific congress in the heart of Siberia, Brezhnev encounters a distinguished Soviet atomic physicist, winner of every conceivable Russian award, walking through snow and ice with only one shoe on. "Comrade professor," asks Brezhnev, "isn't it carrying academic absentmindedness a bit too far to walk around in this cold without your other shoe?" "On the contrary," replies the Lenin Prize laureate, "it was quite a piece of luck to find even this one." The joke—witty rather than humorous—expresses Hungarian hatred of Russia, which so underpays its great men (according to the joke) that they cannot even afford a pair of shoes, and which, in 1956, treated Hungary considerably worse. Wit, then, can be *revanchisme*, a way of getting even: a device that can deliberately irritate an entire nation. By now you must see the importance of differentiating between humor, which is basically innocent merriment, and wit, whose claws pierce dangerously through the glove of irony.

To put it another way, whereas humor is for both those who identify themselves with (avoid the psychiatric jargon "identify with") the teller and those who sympathize with the subject of the joke, wit is only for those secure enough to identify themselves with its perpetrator. What deuniversalizes wit as a language even more, however, is the frequency with which it eludes less sophisticated audiences. Thus I have recently come under fire for having given the play *Tribute* what many readers consider a too favorable notice; I have also received some fan mail for my presumed enthusiasm for this "heartwarming" work. The truth of the matter is that though I found the play superficially amusing and amiable, I also thought it inconsequential and given to rather too calculated wooing of sentimental spectators. My very title, "Assent for *Tribute*" (a pun on "Millions for defense, but not a cent for tribute"), should have been a warning; describing the play as "the most comforting news this side of a cure for cancer" should have alerted even flightier readers to "Slow down: irony at work."

The sad truth of the matter is that people, as a rule, do not laugh at the same things or at the same time. Dejan Karaklajić, the young Yugoslav filmmaker, is only the most recent film or theater person to tell me that successive audiences consisting of seemingly similar people will laugh at different parts of a movie or show, some guffawing blissfully where no joke was intended. Many years ago, Danny Kaye, giving a talk at Harvard, was asked by a member of the audience which nation had struck him, on his extensive travels for UNICEF, as having the most outstanding sense of humor. Claiming first that they were all alike, Kaye suddenly corrected himself, and answered, "Yugoslavia." But when I later questioned him about the nature of this humoristic superiority, he was unable to define or even describe it.

Still, I believe that there exists a grammar of humor that could be universal but for two things: much of humor is wit, and wit rubs many more people than its direct object the wrong way; and even humor, let alone wit, has, like any other language, illiterates unwilling or unable to learn its grammar and syntax. So there goes another universal language down the drain.

# The Wit and Wisdom of Catch Phrases

Let us forget about grammar and syntax for the nonce—everybody else is doing it. The front-page obituary for Alfred Lunt in the *New York Times* (August 4, 1977) begins: "Alfred Lunt, who with his wife, Lynn Fontanne, reigned for nearly 40 years as the leading couple of the American stage. . . ." If Alfred was, as this sentence would have it, a leading couple and had a wife to boot, the Lunts must have been the number one ménage à trois of the American theater. Or look at the front page of the *New York Times Book Review* of July 17, and you read this in a review by James Atlas: "Rolfe was . . . a 'homosexual paranoid' for whom writing was incidental to the dominant purpose of his life: to punish . . . those whom he fancied had 'provoked . . . [him].' " If that second "whom" were the object of "punished," it would indeed have to be an accusative "whom." It is, however, the subject of "had provoked," i.e., those who, he fancied, had provoked him, and so takes the nominative case. (But, then, there is not much copy editing at the *Book Review*; otherwise, on page 3 of the same issue, Francine du Plessix Gray could not have gotten away with a reference to the woman mystic "Joan of Norwich." That fifteenth-century recluse was called Julian, or Juliana, of Norwich.)

So let us escape from all this for a while and advert to a fascinating subject raised by the American publication of Eric Partridge's *A Dictionary of Catch Phrases* (Stein and Day, 1979). Eric Partridge, as many readers will surely know, is not only one of the great lexicographers of all time, whose important dictionaries and linguistic studies are legion, but is also a literary scholar, editor, and autobiographer. A New Zealander by birth, he has lived and worked for many fruitful years in England and is still going great guns at age eighty-three.* The three books of his I have found particularly useful—indeed indispensable—are *A Dictionary of Slang and Unconventional English; Origins: A Short Etymological Dictionary of Modern English;* and *Usage and Abusage: Guidelines to Proper Usage of the English Language. Shakespeare's Bawdy: A Literary and Psychological Essay and a Comprehensive Gloss* is not far behind in

---

* He died on June 1, 1979, after this article was written. He was working on his language books indefatigably until the end.

handiness. But any one of Partridge's dozens of books is bursting with the most helpful and most lightly worn erudition, set forth with a humor and humanity that wonderfully feed on each other.

The new lexicon deals with catch phrases British and American of the last five centuries and has that admirable virtue common to all of Partridge's publications of being a good deal more than the title implies and thus of interest to people who may not care a rap about catch phrases but who will find themselves unable to tear their attention from the pages of this capacious and captivating book.

What is a catch phrase? one may ask at this point. Partridge is humble enough to claim not to know exactly how it differs from a proverbial saying, famous quotation, or even cliché, although he accepts the definition of a friend: "A phrase that has caught on and pleases the populace." Accepts it, that is, with two emendations: he prefers "saying" to "phrase" and "public" to the tendentious "populace."

A saying that has caught on with the public, then. Partridge begins his all too brief introduction with a quotation from Part II of Robert Louis Stevenson's *Virginibus Puerisque:* "Man is a creature who lives not by bread alone, but principally by catchwords." And here, in Partridge's dictionary, they all are—well, perhaps not quite all, but oodles of them from five centuries and four continents (Australia, South Africa, and Canada are represented almost as copiously as Britain and the United States), gleaned from the listening of Partridge himself and his many friends and correspondents and from countless books (books on the present subject and on related matters, but also books of fiction and nonfiction of every kind), as well as plays and movies.

Take a typical entry: *"I wouldn't trust him* (or, the occasion demanding, *her) as far as I could throw him* (or *her).* This c.p. [catch phrase], applied to a spectacularly unreliable person, dates from c. 1870. In April 1967, Dr. Douglas Leechman told me, 'I recently encountered "I wouldn't trust him as far as I could throw an anvil in a swamp" '—a Canadian variant. Then there's the South African *I trust him as far as I could throw a piano,* 'which I heard from a Springbok in the Western Desert in 1942' (Yehudi Mindel, 5 May 1975).

"Cf. two further variants: *I wouldn't trust him with a kid's money box* (specifically, utterly dishonest), C 20 [twentieth century]; and I *wouldn't trust him with our cat* (of a man with an unsavoury sexual record)."

That is a better known catch phrase; here now is the entry for a less familiar one: "*I didn't ask what keeps your ears apart.* This low, very witty c.p., dating since c. 1949, is the devastating counter to the low comment, or rejoinder, *balls!* or *ballocks!, nonsense!* Probably suggested by *to have more brawn* (or *balls) than brains.*" Or take this: "*Don't look down—you'd soon find the hole if there was hair round it!* is an army drill sergeant's admonition to recruits as they fumble to fix bayonets—when practised, they don't need to look: late C19-20. Ribald and pertinent."

Many catch phrases are sexual or scatological (including some that sound harmless enough, like, say, "Pop goes the weasel!"), and most of them are witty, or at least clever, even if their allusiveness is no longer readily understood. Some are splendidly graphic, e.g., "like a one-armed paperhanger with crabs" or "If he fell in the shit he'd come up smelling of violets."

Frequently catch phrases are ethnic in origin, for example, "I need that like I need a hole in the head" or "I should live so long!" These Partridge correctly identifies as being primarily of Jewish descent. Catch phrases may also have a class origin and can be interesting because of their social implications, as, for instance, "Some of my best friends are Jews," an obviously anti-Semitic locution ("current since the early 1930's, with equivalents in other European languages"), though one that, as Partridge reminds us, can be, and has been, turned as easily against other groups. It is typical of this dictionary that Partridge, in the best (albeit lost) tradition of lexicographers like Dr. Johnson, will permit himself speculations or asides; thus he muses upon this last one: "Sometimes one wonders why, there being so much racial prejudice and even hatred about, there haven't been even more wars. The true miracle, the enduring miracle, the greatest miracle of all, is that, so far, the human race has succeeded in surviving the human race; clearly the age of miracles is *not* past."

This refers, of course, to another catch phrase, "The age of miracles is past," which, Partridge informs us, "was contentiously used by freethinkers during C18, challengingly by agnostics during C19 and by all cynics and most skeptics in C20." That is a good specimen of the evolution of catch phrases and of the societal implications underlying them, implications that are sometimes not quite obvious. Take the entry *"Something nasty in the woodshed—he* (or *she) has seen.* Applied—in ironic derision of too many psychiatrists' too glib explanations—to 'a crazy, mixed-up kid': British and Australian: since the mid-1930's. Esp. in reference to one's mother (or, less violently, a dearly loved sister) making love, usually with 'the hired help,' in a woodshed or other outhouse." It had never occurred to me that this was a dig at psychiatry—and I am still not entirely convinced that it is—but it surely presupposes the existence of psychiatric awareness within a society.*

Occasionally catch phrases involve more than a little learning. Consider this one—and I give it also as an example of a longer entry in the dictionary, although some of the most informative and stimulating ones are three or four times as long (and, for that reason, not reproducible here): *"Illegitimis non carborundum!* Literally, 'Let there not be a *carborundum*ing by the illegitimate!'—Don't let the bastards grind—hence, wear—finally, get—you down or break your spirit!: carborundum (silicon carbide), being extremely hard, is used in grinding and polishing: owing to its apparently having the form (*-undum*) of a Latin gerund, the word has prompted a piece of delightful mock-L. From being an army Intelligence c.p. of 1939–45, it became, as early as 1940, a more general army c.p., chiefly among officers. I have often wondered which classical scholar, irritated and exacerbated almost to desperation, coined this trenchancy; and I like to think it was my friend Stanley Casson, who, born in 1889, became Reader in Classical Archaeology at Oxford and who, after directing the army Intelligence School early in WW2, went to Greece to lead the resistance there and was killed mid-April 1944, a learned, witty, gallant scholar and man of action.

"The phrase had by the late 1940's gained a fairly wide currency among the literate. In 1965, Mr. Barry Prentice assured me that, in Australia, its use was by no means confined to those who had a little L.

"In Martin Woodhouse's novel, *Rock Baby,* 1968, it occurs allusively thus: *'Nil carborundum,* all right, I thought. Don't let the bastards grind you down, like it says in the book, but how was I to set about it?' "

<hr>

* I have been informed by Robert Loomis, of Random House, that the phrase comes from *Cold Comfort Farm,* a novel by Stella Gibbons.

It is curious that Partridge, who usually does not miss a trick, seems unaware of *Nil Carborundum*, the play by Henry Livings that the Royal Shakespeare Company put on in 1962; otherwise, what a delightful entry, including the touching tribute to a dead friend, whether or not he actually coined the phrase.

But it is time to ask ourselves what the values of the *Dictionary of Catch Phrases* are. It does not give us a full definition of a catch phrase, after all, because it does not define what the differences between it and a cliché or a proverbial saying are. Yet in various entries Partridge will say that such and such is not really a catch phrase but a cliché, implying that he is working from unstated criteria. In an earlier book, *A Dictionary of Clichés*, he gave us a rather explicit introduction; the introduction to the present tome—out of modesty, I presume—is rather too skimpy.

Nevertheless, this dictionary has obvious values, both positive and negative. One can surely enjoy or learn from a catch phrase without having a foolproof definition of it. Partridge's work elucidates numerous catch phrases that might baffle us in our reading, especially of texts from the British Commonwealth. It also offers pertinent insights into the byways of language, which is to say of cultural history, and there are a good many entries that will elicit hearty laughter or heady speculations about personal and social psychology. And there are some catch phrases left that are still less than well known—at least in this country—and so can be re-used to redound to the user's glory in much the same way that a good but little-known joke well retold can make its purveyor appear to be a witty fellow.

The book's negative value may, however, be greater yet. For these catch phrases are, initially, some (usually anonymous) persons' clevernesses and are not for you if you would rather an inventor than a borrower be. Let your own creations become, if they are worthy of it, the catch phrases of tomorrow. Meanwhile, if you are any sort of author writing about yesteryear, you may profitably use these catch phrases to season the dialogue of some of your more outer-directed characters.

For a literarily engaged reader, Partridge's dictionary has a strange, wistful, indeed melancholy, value. Who knows—might I not have said something like "Formerly I could eat all—but now I leave nothing"? I would then, however, merely have restated a catch phrase already immortalized in Dean Swift's *Polite Conversa-*

*tion.* And, going from gourmandising to its aftereffects, could I not, in a rare moment of inspiration, and punning on "bird" and "turd," describe a fart as "the cry of an imprisoned turd"? Yet any congratulations from others or from myself on this *boutade* would be premature—or, rather, the opposite—for Partridge tells me this is a catch phrase from circa 1930 or a little earlier. The lexicon, then, is a sadly useful catalog of verbal inventions already invented.

Still, there remains the pleasure of reflection to which the book gives rise, as when one comes to realize how very many of these phrases originated in the armed services or among Jews, blacks, and other minorities. This can lead us to insights into the very nature of wit. For these felicitous verbal turns or sallies are our answer to constraints, whether of army or ghetto life or, worse yet, of war. Wit becomes, then, an expression of human resilience, of compensation through word power, which the close proximity of fellow sufferers in army installations or ghettos provides with an immediate and enthusiastic audience and a sort of oral Xerox process.

Or you might be led to speculate, for instance, about why so many catch phrases are taunts or put-downs. Clearly, this is so because the liberating power of wit is greatest when it offers a socially or otherwise encumbered person a chance to get even, at least verbally, with his oppressors. Not for nothing is the German word for "quickwitted" *schlagfertig,* which is to say ready for blows, and, indeed, ready for battle. Similarly, the frequent obscenity and scatology of these sayings is explicable, I think, as either a mild rebellion against social inhibitions or a safety valve: pent-up drives can be released most innocuously in sayings legitimized, as it were, by being catch phrases.

Yet many catch phrases are good-natured and humanistic, e.g., "There's life in the old dog [or "old girl"] yet," which has been with us since the mid-nineteenth century. To reiterate: a catch phrase is something to be both admired for its initial ingenuity and avoided for its present staleness. *A Dictionary of Catch Phrases* both elicits the admiration and facilitates the avoidance.

# Sesquipedality, Anyone?

**W**e have always been told to refrain from belching in public, to yield our seats on the subway to old people, and to avoid using big words where simple ones will do. The implication was unmistakable: there was no time when a short, sensible term could not, virtuously and profitably, replace a big bad word. The use of idle and ostentatious polysyllables even had a suitably gruesome name: sesquipedality, or sesquipedalianism.

*Sesquipedalian* comes from the Latin word *sesquipedalis*, "of a foot and a half in length," referring to long and ponderous words, the *sesquipedalia verba* Horace brought to our attention in his *Ars Poetica*. In English, the word is almost always used in a facetious or derogatory context, as when Robert Southey referred to Stephen Hawes's verses as being "as full of barbarous sesquipedalian Latinisms as the prose of the *Rambler*." Now, Hawes's poetry I would not wish on anyone, but Dr. Johnson's periodical, the *Rambler*, whatever the ultraconservative poet laureate Southey thought of it, is something all of us can learn a thing or two from. Though the simple word is often the best, there are also times when the less obvious, less current, and, usually, longer word is preferable.

I've taken, almost at random, this sentence from issue number 122 of Johnson's *Rambler*. It is a description of the Earl of Clarendon's style: "But there is always Dignity in his Negligence, a rude inartificial Majesty, which without the Niceties of laboured Elegance, swells the Mind by its Plenitude and Diffusion." Suppose Johnson had wanted to delatinize that sentence and make it less sesquipedalian—the sort of thing that, happily, never occurred to him. He might have concluded as follows: "swells the mind by its fullness and reach," the best Anglo-Saxon approximation I can come up with. But here *fullness* would have been less good than *plenitude;* the latter, besides sounding more majestic, suggests ripeness and abundance as well. And *diffusion* conveys the ability not only to reach but also to penetrate, infiltrate, permeate.

Now, of course, neither *plenitude* nor *diffusion* is truly sesquipedalian in the way that a word like *misocapnic* is (I take sesquipedalian, like big, to mean either long or rare or both). Suppose you read that the country is becoming more and more misocapnic or

WHERE WERE YOU IN THE ANTELUCAN HOURS?

that there is an increasing number of misocapnic regulations in public places. You would have to know more than a little Greek to figure out that this grandiloquent coinage means antismoke, or antismoking. Such sesquipedality is grandiose and obscurantist unless it is put to comic use; even then, however, it works only if you can sneak in an explanation and so keep your readers or listeners.

Conversely, a word like *ipseity*, meaning personal identity, or selfhood, does not sound especially grandiose. Still, it is of virtually no use—partly because its sound is not impressive or melodious and partly because words like *identity*, *individuality*, and *selfhood*, besides being more familiar, communicate shades of meaning more precisely.

There are, to be sure, tricky borderline cases. Take the adjective *antelucan*, meaning predawn; the shorter *Oxford English Dictionary* defines it as "of or pertaining to the hours before dawn," whereas the *American Heritage Dictionary* does not contain it. It has the advantage of being a manifest, bona fide adjective, as opposed to *predawn*, which is obviously makeshift, a substantive pressed into service as an adjective—just like *makeshift*, for that matter. But it is a *recherché* word ("elucubrated," as your sesquipedalians would say) and a trifle vague. Does it refer to the time immediately preceding dawn, which *predawn* suggests more strongly, or does it cover several hours, in which case *nocturnal* might do just as well?

In this connection it is interesting to recall T. S. Eliot's long grappling with a passage from "Little Gidding," the last of his *Four Quartets*. A verse that originally read "We turn upon the first-met stranger at dawn" became, after numerous recensions, "The first-met stranger in the waning dusk." From amid his prolonged birth pangs, Eliot wrote John Hayward, his friend and mentor:

> I am still, however, wrestling with the demon of that precise degree of light at that precise time of day. I want something more *universal* than blackout . . . something as universal as Dante's old tailor threading his needle. . . . I have been fiddling with something like this: The stranger in the antelucan dusk/The stranger at the antelucan hour. Perhaps it is too self-conscious, and belongs rather to a Miltonic than to a Dantesque passage? . . . The image should be both sudden and homely, with the precision of country terminology for these phenomena. . . .

In an earlier letter, he had observed: "There is probably some dialect word for this degree of dawn; but even if I could find it, it probably wouldn't do."

There is much more agonizing over this word reproduced in Helen Gardner's excellent monograph, *The Composition of "Four Quartets."* For our purposes, it is enough to note that Eliot, for all his elitism, rejected *antelucan* and finally settled on the periphrastic "in the waning dusk." The latest example of the word recorded in the *OED* comes from De Quincey: "this practice of crepuscular ante-lucan worship, possibly having reference to the ineffable mystery of the resurrection." In that context, flanked by *crepuscular* and *ineffable*, *antelucan* does not sound half bad, though still a trifle abstruse. There may be cases where, if only a recondite word is available, circumlocution is the proper solution.

If you would enjoy a repository of *sesquipedalia verba*, I can recommend Russell Rocke's the *Grandiloquent Dictionary* (Prentice-

Hall, 1972), though it is, of course, not all-inclusive and though I often disagree with Rocke's notions of what is grandiloquent and of what is euphonious and what cacophonous. Thus Rocke lists consecutively *"purulent,* Of, containing, or discharging pus; suppurating,"* and *"quadrumanous,* Having all four feet adapted for use as hands . . . ,"* and considers the former euphonious and the latter cacophonous. I, on the contrary, feel that *quadrumanous* rolls sumptuously off the tongue, whereas *purulent,* with its reiterated *u,* suggests either echolalia or baby talk.

In any case, I must congratulate Rocke on his diverting and by no means useless compendium even while wishing it were—not complete, for that would be impossible—merely more informative. We are never given sources for the words or samples of actual use except for those Rocke himself concocts occasionally. So the resonant *ioblepharous* is given, as usual, without an etymology (it comes from the Greek: *io-,* a combining form meaning violet, and *blepharon,* an eyelid), and the definition simply reads: "Violet-lidded; describing the presence of coloring on the eyelids of a female person or statue." But where did Rocke find the word? It is neither in the *OED* nor in *Webster's Second.* Is it a hapax legomenon (a term found only once anywhere), or does it occur frequently in literature, or did Rocke himself coin it? We should be told.

It is curious to find *incrassate* in the book but not the related *inspissate;* it is nice to get *floccillation,* but why is it misspelled "floccilation"? And why don't we get its more austere synonym, *carphology*? But at least we do find reproduced here the longest word in the *OED*—and thus, presumably, in official English—*floccinaucinihilipilification.* Here, instead of giving the pronunciation, Rocke merely remarks, "Good luck"; his definition is "the action or process of estimating a thing, idea, etc., as worthless." The "as" is superfluous.

Looking at sesquipedality from a practical point of view, we can posit certain guidelines. What makes English such a rich language is that it represents the confluence of Greek, Latin, and Old French words brought in largely by the Norman conquest and the staunch Anglo-Saxon words that refused to bite the dust with poor Harold. Consequently, we very often have a choice—say, between *heavenly* and *celestial* or *clumsy* and *maladroit.* To stick with just those two pairs, let me show you that there is a time for the simpler and a time for the fancier. It is safer to confine *celestial* to astronomy and *heavenly* to sacred or profane enthusiasm: Venus *is* a celestial body but *has* a heavenly one. In the latter manifestation, she is often represented as *callipygian*, or *callipygous*, which, for my money, beats the hell out of "having beautiful buttocks." The shades of difference between *clumsy*, or *awkward*, and *maladroit* are not so patent; by and large, the elegant sound of *maladroit* (its Gallic provenance in itself assures a certain chic) takes some curse off clumsiness yet remains more physical than *awkward*, which is more abstract.

While reading the recently published and absorbing *Nabokov-Wilson Letters: 1940–1971* (Harper & Row, 1979) I found that in the first years of the correspondence, when the Russian-born novelist very much wanted to impress the American critic who became his protector, business adviser, and friend, he three times used the word *gnoseological* (from *gnoseology*, which *Webster's Second* defines as "the theory of the origin, nature, and validity of knowledge"). The word fades from the later correspondence, when Nabokov no longer needed to impress Wilson, though he continued to indulge his sesquipedalian tastes in his other writings. It is out of exasperation with Nabokov's verbal excesses that Wilson, in attacking his former friend's translation of *Eugene Onegin* in his notorious polemic against that work in the *New York Review of Books* (July 15, 1965), wrote about "my departures from the 'literal,' which have been obelized by Mr. Nabokov (I hope he has to look up that word). . . ." I doubt, though, whether Nabokov had to, but *you* might want to do so.

Incidentally, some misunderstandings between these two extraordinary polymaths stemmed from the fact that Nabokov's bible was *Webster's Second*, whereas Wilson's oracle was the *OED*; *gnoseological*, for instance, appears in the former (though spelled *gnosiological*)* but is curiously absent from the latter. Consequently, in *Strong Opinions*, Nabokov was to write: "The second unabridged edition (1960) of *Webster's* [is something] I really must urge Mr. Wilson to acquire."

To summarize. Used judiciously—in particular, facetiously—big words can be very apt. By and large, no word, whether short or long, humble or proud, is meant to rot in the dictionary; but some

---

* Gnoseological is apparently Nabokov's misspelling.

words grow old and die. A great many big ones can be used forcefully for special effect: Shakespeare's "No, this my hand will rather/The multitudinous seas incarnadine" would not be nearly so cosmic with smaller words. Fustian, of course, is foolish, but fastidiousness is fine. One last caveat: sonorous associations matter. The word *discommode* is impaired by its suggestion of *commode*.

# THE MEDIA

# Gloom at the Top

This time I resolved to examine what was happening to English in the pages of the *New York Review of Books*, the literary-political review with the highest prestige in America, rivaled only by one or two quarterlies. The only reasonably fair way of conducting a quick investigation was to pick an issue at random and peruse it from cover to cover; the issue I alighted on was that of November 23, 1978. Herewith some of my findings.

The lead is a review of Philip Rahv's *Essays on Literature and Politics 1932–1972*, by Frederick Crews, a professor of English at Berkeley and author of several books of criticism, among them *The Pooh Perplex*. Professor Crews's review is thorough, informative, and lively, but not without lapses in diction. We read: "This rule applies nowhere more strikingly than to *Partisan Review*, the longest-lived . . . of all our magazines." A minor error to note is that although *long-lived* is hyphenated, the comparative *longer lived* and the superlative *longest lived* are not when they follow a verb—implied or stated. More disturbing is the faulty construction "nowhere more . . . than to." *Nowhere* is static, *to* is dynamic; it would have been preferable to write "applies to nothing more strikingly than to. . . ."

Again, "Twenty-four respondents concurred with Phillips's and Rahv's proposal" is incorrect. When a genitive involves two persons in a joint undertaking, creation, business, or possession and those persons' names are linked by an *and*, only the second name takes the *'s*; thus "Kaufman and Hart's plays" (for those they wrote together, "Kaufman's and Hart's" for those they wrote separately), "Ferdinand and Isabella's reign," "daddy and mummy's bedroom" (but "daddy's and mummy's rooms" if they sleep apart), and "Phillips and Rahv's [joint] proposal." Further on, we read about "one time champions of proletarianism"; the adjective meaning "former" is spelled *one-time* or *onetime*.

The next review, of three books about the pros and cons of ETI (extraterrestrial intelligence), is by Martin Gardner, who, like many writers about science, commands an English superior to that of his colleagues in the humanities. Only one sentence bothers me: "A cube has the same structure for a blind man's touch that it has to one who sees it." *Blind man's,* a genitive, demands a parallel genitive, such as *one's* (which, however, would not work here); otherwise *one* seems to refer back to *touch.* Correctly, then, "A cube has the same structure to the touch of a blind man as to the eye of a sighted one"; or "A cube's structure is the same to a blind man's touch as to a sighted man's eye."

Next comes a review of Anthony Burgess's *1985,* by Clive James, a London literary journalist. Here purists would object to the so-called fused participle in "A good case can be made for Zamyatin, Huxley, and Orwell having struck deeper than the science fiction writers." They would insist with Fowler that the sentence should read, ". . . for Zamyatin's, Huxley's, and Orwell's having struck deeper. . . . " *Having,* they would say, is a gerund (a.k.a. verbal noun) modified by an adjectivally functioning genitive, *Zamyatin's.* But this is one of those disputed areas of English grammar, and there are many civilized persons, not to mention eminent grammarians, who would cheerfully go along with Clive James. The fact that there are three nouns involved makes the case of the Jamesians even stronger; all those apostrophes and extra sibilants add up to heavy going. But if there were only one noun, I would probably vote with Fowler: "A good case can be made for Zamyatin's [or "Huxley's" or "Orwell's"]. . . ." And if the three writers had been named in the previous sentence, I would insist on "A good case can be made for their [not *them*] having struck deeper. . . . "

We come, next, to James's flippant evaluation of *A Clockwork Orange:* "A handy transitional primer for anyone learning Russian, in other respects it is a bit thin." No need for fancy discussions of syntax to convey the immediate need for a noun or pronoun to which the phrase "a handy primer," et cetera, can attach itself; the sentence would be very much sturdier and clearer written as follows: "A handy primer for anyone learning Russian, it [the book] is a bit thin in other respects." James is a bit sloppy about word order, as also in "the arts are really rather a dangerous occupation," which would read less fuzzily as "a rather dangerous occupation."

Again, James writes, "He is an individualist by instinct—a valuable trait in a personality, but a limited viewpoint from which to criticize a whole society." This doesn't work. The "valuable trait" is, presumably, instinct; but instinct is not a "viewpoint" (quite aside from the fact that centuries of sound tradition have hallowed *point of view* as preferable to the Teutonism *viewpoint*). What James seems to mean is that the point of view of the "individualist by instinct" is not a good one from which to criticize a whole society; in other words, he has changed antecedents in midstream, from "instinct", to "individualist by instinct," which is impermissible. Finally, after describing a certain conviction of the British managerial class, James writes: "Burgess shares the same irritable conviction." This is redundant: you cannot share a *different* conviction. It has to be either Burgess "shares the conviction" or something like "voices the same conviction."

The next piece is an excerpt from a soon-to-be-published diary by Lincoln Kirstein, which contains a number of mistakes; before we criticize them, however, let us wait and see whether the copy editors at Knopf let them pass in the final version. There follows a snide review of Günter Grass's novel *The Flounder* from the envious pen of Nigel Dennis, the British novelist, playwright, and critic. After ridiculing Marilyn Moorcroft for confusing, in an article about Grass, *content* and *contents* (another case of sibling rivalry), Dennis goes on to make an error at least as offensive. He speaks of the novel's division "into nine hunks, each hunk celebrating one month of parturition." Now, *parturition* is the act of giving birth; if it took nine months, or even one, both mother and child would be dead ducks. What Dennis meant is *gestation* or *pregnancy*. (Oddly enough, the same error was committed by the reviewer of this book in the *New York Times.)* Dennis is as careless a reader as he is a writer: he speaks of the Flounder's trial taking place in Bonn, when Berlin is named over and over again as the locale; he writes of the prehistoric mistress-mother's "six tits," although Grass makes a great deal of her *three* breasts.

In a review of Nelson Goodman's *Ways of Worldmaking,* the Harvard logician W. V. Quine displays expectable precision where grammar and syntax are concerned but indulges in rather frivolous wordplay. The piece begins: "This book is a congeries. Not indeed an incongruous congeries, as of congers and costermongers, but withal a congeries to conjure with." Somewhat preposterous, too, is the peroration in which Quine expresses horror at the fastidious author's use of the word *acquacentric:* "Why the Italian, or indeed anything to do with Latin, when [Goodman] could have played 'hydrocentric' straight?" I suppose the argument is that *centric* derives from the Greek *kentrikos* and so demands a compound that is entirely Greek derived, not Greco-Latin; the Italianate "c" in *acqua* is probably just a typo. But English compounds don't follow such a rule—witness *hypersensitive* (Greco-Latin), and a host of others.

Robert Mazzocco's review of Robin Maugham's *Conversations with Willie: Recollections of W. Somerset Maugham* is rife with lapses. Thus "*Cakes and Ale* is a sparkling work, with *Don Fernando* [W. S. Maugham's] best single achievement. . . . " How can two separate books constitute a "best single achievement?" "Animadversion *to* art" should read "animadversion *on* [or *upon*] art." "Gentry class" is manifestly redundant for *gentry*. In "He took the animal side of Maupassant, stripped it of its passion, placed there instead obsession and compulsion . . . " there is no actual error, but the construction is needlessly confusing; one is apt to misread it as "placed there instead *of* obsession and compulsion" and be thrown for a loop.

"So many of his tales deal almost exclusively in the world of gossip" is a careless conflation. One can deal either *with* the world of gossip or, simply, *in* gossip; with "in the world of gossip," one needs a different predicate, say, *move.* For "The mutual basis of the above quotations," the correct English would be "*common* basis." Again, "but if [Maugham] assiduously read Spinoza, Kant, and Schopenhauer, he never absorbed them as Proust, say, absorbed Bergson" is ambiguous. Did Maugham read those philosophers assiduously and still fail to understand them completely, or did he, perhaps, not even read them all that carefully? A simple *though* instead of the *if* would have made what I take to be Mazzocco's meaning perspicuous. Finally, what kind of syntax is this: "About homosexuality, obviously he harbored an unappeasable guilt over it throughout his life"? Why not simply, "About homosexuality he obviously harbored an unappeasable guilt throughout his life"?

Well, I am running out of space, even though I have covered only about half the articles in the magazine's November 23 issue. Robert O. Paxton, a professor of history at Columbia, and Thomas R. Edwards, a professor of English at Rutgers, commit only one or two errors each. But Daniel Aaron, a Harvard professor of English and American literature, is guilty of eight solecisms; Henri Zerner, a Harvard professor of art history, is guilty of four. Marshall Sahlins, who professes anthropology at the University of Chicago, errs some fifteen times in an admittedly long piece.

Herewith my tentative conclusions: men of science and philosophy come off better than those of literature and the social sciences, though there are exceptions. But the real culprits are the editors of this high-toned journal.

# Verbal Barbarisms

**B**arbara Walters is the face, personality, and mind (in descending order of conspicuousness) that launched the famous $5 million contract making her the cynosure (in ascending order of importance) of career women, TV viewers, and media people everywhere. Whether before, on NBC's morning news show, or later on ABC's evening one, or whether on her celebrated hour-long specials, Barbara has been the biggest woman on television for so long that it seemed incumbent on me to check out what kind of literacy she spreads among five million dollars' worth of television viewers. So I caught two of her specials in 1976 and 1977: the one that was split between the Streisands (Barbra and Jon) and the Carters, and the one dedicated entirely to a fond farewell to the Fords. I also read most of her book, *How to Talk With Practically Anybody About Practically Anything*, which comes with an endorsement on its cover from the late Jacqueline Susann: "She's warm, she's exciting, she's Barbara!" The third of these contentions seems indisputable.

The Walters book is of that time-dishonored sort we owe to the aptly named Samuel Smiles, father of self-help, and it purports to teach "how to get beyond the superficial smalltalk that most people substitute for communication; how to take the terror out of meeting someone from another league." Barbara, you see, used to be terrified, she tells us, by the proximity of an Aristotle Onassis or a Truman Capote, but she cured herself, and now, with her help, so can you. Her medicine is homeopathic: become a celebrity yourself. Apparently, it doesn't take much; of a woman friend of hers she says, "She has . . . no actual claim to fame except for her interest in people," which is to say eagerness to meet the famous—just about all you need for your own celebrity. She, at any rate, has made it, and informs you from the eminence of her celebrity that "the same techniques that result in fifteen minutes of smooth informative chat with the husband of the Queen of England [how much more prestigious-by-association that sounds than a mere Prince Philip!] are just as helpful when I meet a new neighbor." Dear democratic Barbara, as willing to talk with a simple neighbor as with a crowned, or near-crowned, head—well, perhaps not actually talk with both of them, but certainly use her techniques on both.

How artlessly it all hangs out: "The saving quality in any question you ask a celebrity is empathy," she begins, and continues, "I'm always won [for "won over"] by people who want to know my schedule." So, you see, the celebrity used for illustrative purposes is none other than Barbara Walters. With even more palpable ingenuousness, she tells us that when she thinks of all the rich and famous and infamous folk her job has permitted her to meet, she would gratefully do it for nothing. Even if she didn't make the statement a second time, in italics, I would believe her, *I would believe her.*

Of course, the advice disbursed, like everything else about the book, is semiliterate trash (I may be too kind: quarter-literate may be more precise), as when she states that "deep breaths are very helpful at shallow parties," or when she instructs depressed women readers to "wear your most smashing outfit; maybe something a bit kooky that you'll have to live up to." Such "techniques" may work for Barbara Walters, the robot of social technology, but they are fairly worthless when handed down to mousy secretaries or repressed housewives who turn to her book for succor. Walters butters up these wallflowers: "You're bathed, deodorized and sweet breathed [*sic*] . . . you're all set for hours of superb conversation." Even the makers of Ban, Badedas, and Binaca would not have the audacity to tout their products as miracle drugs that turn Dumb Doras into Dorothy Parkers. Yet Barbara informs her trusting clientele: "People are going to gravitate toward you even before you open your mouth." Well, certainly not after it. For, the suckers are told, "when you say to the statesman, 'Do you believe in immortality?'—you'll have it made." The statesman will have to be a diplomat indeed not to take to his heels after such a gambit. And dear Barbara offers no helpful suggestion about how Joan Blow is to get near a statesman in the first place.

Might it not be better to advise these insecure people to cultivate their minds—to acquire a little literacy and so avoid being crashing bores? But what can we expect from Miss Walters, who uses *overly* for over, *wracked* for racked, *intriguing* for fascinating, *wrong-taste remark* for remark in bad taste; who writes "Don't expect that his real personality *is* like his professional one," "employment-wise," "none *are* snobs," "those kind of *agog* questions" (agog is an adverb, not an adjective), "now we neither wear them on camera or off" for "now we wear them neither on camera nor off," and who spells acerbic *ascerbic.* And so on and on.

But there is greater illiteracy at work here—an illiteracy of the soul. It is illiterate and vulgar the way the understatedly overdressed Walters sidles up, physically and verbally, to a celebrity, fixes her distended eyes on him or her and, after telling us in her book not "to probe the sensitive areas right after the introduction," proceeds to probe the sensitive areas right after the introduction. She can hardly wait to ask Gerald Ford whether it is true that, *as people said,* he was crying when Betty had to concede the election for him. With Jon Peters, she cannot blurt out soon enough that *"some people* have been saying" that he might be Barbra's "ruination." With the Carters, she is a bit slower to urge them to tell about each other's irritating habits, and they, bless them, do not rise to the bait.

With this lascivious prodding goes, of course, hypocrisy. To Peters, Barbara says banteringly, "I hope you didn't hear what I just said about you," and then, with the same sweet jocularity, repeats it for him. The nasty queries and comments are always attributed to "people" or "some people"; they clearly have nothing to do with any unwholesome curiosity Barbara herself might harbor. When she is obliged (by whom: her conscience, history, God?) to ask the Carters in what kind of bed or beds they sleep, she rolls her eyes in indignation (mock indignation, needless to say) and prefaces the question with, "I don't know how to ask this, so I'll just ask it." After a good while on the subject, she interjects with a kind of shy, virginal salaciousness, "You're not embarrassed? I am," and continues with the topic. When at last she has squeezed the subject dry while having thus covered her front and flanks, she proceeds to cover her rear with, "I don't know whether you want to go on any more, but *I* don't." In her book, when giving advice to her publicly sweating or menstruating readers, she refers to "perspiration or other stains," so that you find out what she's talking about only when you get to the remedy, "one terrific red dress . . . to wear on the dangerous day." Butter would not melt in that capacious mouth, and menstruation would not even enter it.

What is the key to Walters's success? On your TV screen, you behold a large but sleek common-looking woman, with a brashness that has been cosmeticized into proto-polish, who might be the wife of a Seventh-Avenue clothing magnate or, as it happens, the daughter of a man who owned a large, vulgar night club. She wears her bought respectability with a certain bravura, although her overeagerness to be gracious collapses when, for instance, Streisand's phone rings in mid-interview and Walters shrills in mingled panic and outrage, "Don't answer the phone!," the Park Avenue gloss on her voice cracking to reveal the Bronx. The voice is basically one of those unresonant, gray ones, and when the conversation turns to something truly awesome—such as Jerry Ford's no longer getting helicopters and limousines to wait on him, or the bed habits of the Carters—it is lowered to a stage whisper.

The facial expression tends to be solemn verging on blank. One senses such intense concentration on the dialectical rigors of interviewing that the gaze perforce turns inward; the eyes, in a faint scowl, roll back into that head preoccupied with its Pythian profundities. But then Barbara remembers and opens her eyes wider before lowering her lashes demurely, thus bringing her most powerful feature into full play. I mean the muscle in her upper eyelid, which in her case is unusually prominent and produces the effect of dimples on both sides of the root of her nose. Such dimples attest to intense concentration and cerebration, and are what sets Barbara off from television's numerous Walters epigones.

Yet this muscle, I venture to guess, is worth only about half of that $5 million contract; the other half is owed to her mentality, which is the perfect mean: the absolute, unwobbling midpoint of averageness. Barbara's golden-mean mentality, you see, is what asks all those impeccably average questions that are burning in the inarticulate but inquisitive depths of every average to subaverage soul, aching to find a voice, however flat and lusterless, in Barbara Walters. When she asks Jon and Barbra why they haven't married after three years of living together, you just know that she is articulating the question that has been trembling on every impeccably average pair of lips from Brentwood to Brooklyn, from dentists' offices to imitation Louis XVI living rooms.

In fact, when Blair Sabol in the *Village Voice* defends Walters as the most effective "female" personality around (quotation marks Miss Sabol's, though, for slightly different reasons, I heartily concur with their use), she argues, "It could be that a lot of Americans are more interested in the Carter's [*sic*] sleeping arrangement than in hearing prefab answers to cabinet choices." I am mildly surprised at this special pleading from the usually sensible Miss Sabol, but I assume that being a guest on Barbara's old "Not for Women Only" show can do wonders in eliciting pro-Walters sentiments.

Anyhow, I do not dispute that the general state of literacy is so low that most people are interested only in questions about the Carter boudoir—although I doubt whether the alternative questions need be as grim as Miss Sabol proposes—but that is precisely my point: why commit so flagrantly the blackest sin a personality, "female" or otherwise, can commit—pandering to the public? If there is to be any kind of literacy in this society, it can come only from *not* pandering so wholeheartedly and effusively to ignorance, crassness, and sterile curiosity. But just watch Barbara's face in an agony of concentration, hovering on the brink of what may instantly turn into sobs or orgasm, as she leans toward Streisand to suck every drop of answer out of her, and asks in choked-up tones why she is attacked so much: "Is it because you are a prima donna and you're a tough, difficult lady? Is it because you are a woman? Is it what?" Oh, the urgency and exquisite illiteracy of that "Is it what?"

And don't think that Barbara Walters is unaware of her importance. In her book, she cites as an example of untoward gushiness the woman who greeted her after a lecture with, "All I can say is, *Thank God for Barbara Walters!*" Comments Barbara: "I'm as fond of approval as anyone but it's unnerving to be deïfied." Yet, surely, if someone thanks God for something, that thing is not thereby deified. Now, if the woman had said, "Thank Barbara Walters for God," *that* would have been deification. But that Walters should refer to what is merely rather fulsome praise as deification—what are we to make of that? Is it arrogance? Is it stupidity? Or is it what?

But don't expect me to feel sorry for Harry Reasoner, for all that. Not for someone who signs off with "Good night from Barbara and I." And speaking of sign-offs, there is that already notorious one with which Barbara concluded her Carter interview: "Be wise with us, Governor, be good with us." It is mildly revolting, but not, I think, because it constitutes, as Morley Safer perceived it, a papal precept to newly made cardinals. I found its derivation in the schlock fiction Barbara must have been reading in pre-Sarah Lawrence days and cutting her spiritual teeth on. I mean the sort of novel where the adorably virginal heroine, finally yielding to her defloration-bent lover, jumps into bed in her slip, pulls the covers up to her chin and whispers, "Be kind to me, darling. Be gentle with me." And that's why they love Barbara Walters from DeKalb Avenue all the way to Dubuque.

# Word Crimes at the *Times*

The English language is being treated nowadays exactly as slave traders once handled the merchandise in their slave ships, or as the inmates of concentration camps were dealt with by their Nazi jailers. The other day, the radio announced that, according to figures just released by the Census Bureau, "four out of a hundred Americans usually speak some language other than English." "True," I exclaimed, "only they call it English." I am by no means a professional grammarian; still, I try to do right. It is like making a citizen's arrest: whoever notices a crime being committed, regardless of his or her own imperfection, should endeavor to bring the culprit to justice.

The crime begins in the cultureless home and the shoddy schoolroom as much as in the streets. When the Democratic majority leader, Tip O'Neill, can declare that Wayne Hays should step down out of respect for his "fellow colleagues," the rock bottom of linguistic ineptitude has been reached. If a prominent public figure does not know that *colleague* means fellow something-or-other, what does he know? Yet the ultimate proving grounds of linguistic irresponsibility—or stupidity—are today's media. You need sink no lower than the culture sections of the *New York Times* in 1976 to get your linguistic hackles up.

To go on with the Hays motif, Robert B. Semple, Jr., reported from London in the *Times* of June 21 that Tom Stoppard's *Dirty Linen* "could not have appeared at a more fortuitous moment" because of its applicability to the Hays affair and its consequent timeliness. What Semple meant is a felicitous or opportune moment, whereas *fortuitous* means accidental. But because *fortuitous* and *fortunate* sound alike, they have become confused, and create an even greater confusion when, for example, a reader cannot tell whether "a fortuitous meeting" means a happy reunion or merely a chance encounter.

In the *Times* of Sunday, July 25, there was an article about the Venice Biennale by Paul Overy, the art critic of *The Times* of London. Here we read that "There seemed a general consensus that the best of the post-war environmental works was by . . . Maria Nordman." The statement should have begun: "There seemed to be a consensus," because things can seem *true* or *ridiculous* or *to be*, but they cannot just *seem*, and because consensus is, by definition, general.

The front-page article in the *New York Times Book Review* on June 6 was a critique by David Halberstam of *Lyndon Johnson and the American Dream.* The third sentence began: "Too, he is no longer around to serve as a custodian-censor of his own story. . . . " *Too* is not a word that can begin a sentence, as *also* and *moreover* can. There may be a rhyme in this, if not a reason: an initial *too* could be heard as *two*, making the hearer anxious about having missed point *one*. However that may be, it is firmly established usage that one does not lead with "too," and the sensitive ear bridles at the initial *too* just as it would at something like "As well, he is no longer around."

In the *Times* of July 4, Robert Brustein, the distinguished drama critic, dean of the Yale Drama School, and director of the Yale Repertory Theater, shows a little too much independence from grammar when he writes about "four days in June, [when] Yale . . . played host to the artistic directors, managing directors, board members, and other delegates of . . . non-profit . . . theaters in a

conference designed to air their mutual problems and concerns."
*Mutual* means that A is or does to B as B is or does to A; it does
not mean that A is or does to C as B is or does to C. If two types or
groups of theater people had problems with each other (as is often
the case, but is not meant here), those would indeed be mutual
problems. But survival was a problem for *all* the people at the
conference, so what they had were *shared* or *common* concerns.

In the next paragraph, Brustein writes: "What both conferences
shared in common . . . " This is disconcertingly sloppy: *both* already makes *shared* a distinct redundancy, but "shared in common" is arrant tautology, staggering from a writer of Brustein's
stature.

In the *Times* of July 31, Judith Weinraub reports from London
on Delphine Seyrig. The actress and militant feminist is appearing
there in an obscure production whose political message she en-
dorses. We read: "The power struggle Miss Seyrig has been bat-
tling is an essentially feminist one." But "to battle" does not mean
to wage a war; it means to combat, to fight against, and so Weinraub is saying the opposite of what she means. In any case, one
cannot even wage a war against a power struggle. On August 3,
Judy Klemesrud, reporting on the literary-social-gastronomic life
of Bridgehampton, writes: "Here are the rundowns on the two hot
spots, *neither* of which *have* ever been especially praised for *their*
food." (Italics mine.) And this from a culture reporter! On August
5, Lawrence Van Gelder, in a review of the film *Survive!,* mentions
"the wracking issue of survival that depended upon cannibalism."
The plane of these particular survivors may have been *wracked*
(though *wrecked* is now the usual form), but the painful business of
survival, which put them on the rack, was a *racking* issue. These
mistakes are from the daily edition of the paper; in the Sunday
edition, as noted, things are no better. On August 1, Joseph Mor-
genstern writes, "Selznick was intrigued," a flagrant Gallicism.
And in a paean to the wretched Robert Wilson, John Rockwell
offers "put in words" for "put into words," the pleonasm "com-
ponent parts" for "components," "mutual creativity" for "joint
creativity," and the incorrect agreement "The new ensemble . . . *is*
a tighter . . . group. . . . And *they* need to be." Such shabby writing
is, alas, the norm, not the exception, in most of what goes into
almost any issue.

One of the worst offenders is Clive Barnes, stylistically as well as grammatically. On July 31, he writes about a Dennis Nahat ballet, *Brahms Quintet*, that it is "graceful, even clever [earlier he said, "very bright, honest"], but so much less a commentary on the music it is commenting on that it becomes a minor bore." I am not even talking here about Barnes's notorious "jesuitical two-step," as I once dubbed it, consisting of criticism that goes one step forward and, immediately, one step back—how can something very bright, honest, graceful, and clever be a bore?—but about the absurdity of "less a commentary." Less than what? We don't have a clue. Barnes concludes the short piece with an announcement of the loss of his opera glasses: "If anyone picked up . . . a pair of Tasco Bantam Hunter opera glasses, could they please send them back to me." This should read, of course, "would he please send them back." Or, to oblige the feminists, "would he or she."

The day before, reviewing *As You Like It* at Stratford, Connecticut, Barnes was "grateful for the adaptizing scenery." Even if this was a misprint for *adapting*, it still wouldn't make sense. Mind you, I am not against coining words when the coinages are really helpful, but for what earthly purpose do we need *adaptizing*, except perhaps for a foundling's simultaneous adopting and baptizing? What Barnes means is *adaptable* or *versatile*.

Why, you may ask, is correct speech and writing important, as long as the meaning is clear? Well, to begin with, in incorrect usage the meaning is often unclear. For example, when Anthony Burgess (who is considered by many, not excluding Mr. B., a black-belt-champion wielder of words and usage) writes in his Foreword to *Moses:* "Narrative verse—as you can see from *Aurora Leigh* as well as the *Odyssey*—anticipates the cinema," the ambiguous, and thus objectionable, construction does not quite obscure the meaning: what we see from *Aurora Leigh* as well as *from* (the sentence should run) the *Odyssey* is the coming of cinema. But suppose the statement were: "What we can see from Manhattan as well as Brooklyn is the Statue of Liberty"; the meaning then could be either that the statue is equally visible from both boroughs, or that it is visible only from Manhattan, just as plainly as Brooklyn is visible from there.

Clarity and succinctness can both be victims of faulty English, but the greatest loser, I dare say, is elegance. I couldn't disagree more with the structural linguists and their disciples—and thus with most dictionaries in current use—when they contend that "language is what is spoken by the people" and, as if it followed like the night the day, that "language is a living thing, not something codified by pedantic scholars." Yes, a living thing in the sense that new conditions or discoveries require new words, sometimes even new meanings for old words. But not at any price—not if lucidity must be sacrificed. We cannot, because certain ignoramuses think that *fulsome* means the same thing as *full*, only more elegantly expressed, allow *fulsome* to become an acceptable secondary meaning of *full*. That way lies chaos. Abuse of this type, among others, proliferates.

Of course, we are not going to jail the abusers of language, any more than we would lock up people who pick their noses at the dinner table; but we will not condone, let alone imitate, their behavior. Yes, language is a living thing, insofar as it is what people use in daily intercourse—but *which* people? The sensitive, concerned, and discriminating ones, who have applied themselves to questions of language (not necessarily in schools—good English can, like other things, be self-taught); or the uncaring know-nothings who have no sense of the elegance, the grace, of good speech?

And, be it said, correctness does not mean dull conformity; there are many very different ways of expressing the same thing properly. The good speaker, like the good painter, tennis player, or lover, has a technique and a style that are distinctly personal. To be sure, not having certain educational benefits makes it harder to master language—though I should think that the people who write for the *Times*, or at least their editors, would have had those benefits.

Yet when Theodore Bernstein, the language expert of the *Times*, advocates the dropping of the accusative *whom* as an unnecessary source of confusion, he is merely pandering to those who cannot cope with inflection, which, in English, is rudimentary anyhow. Even if that accusative serves no other purpose than to separate the goats from the sheep, it has earned its place: let it be the sign by which the believers in good usage recognize one another.

# WRITERS OF ENGLISH

THE GOOD AND BAD OF GORE VIDAL

# The Good and Bad of Gore Vidal

**W**here, figuratively, does Gore Vidal live? Is he, as many claim, an essayist of distinction who has wasted his time writing undistinguished novels, plays, screenplays and, formerly, even teleplays? Or is he a novelist of distinction who can toss off a clever essay or write for the stage and movies merely to support himself in the style to which he has become accustomed? But, then, as John W. Aldridge reminds us in *The Devil in the Fire*, "Vidal . . . rather dramatically announced . . . that he had finally discovered the novel form to be unworthy of his talents." And where does Vidal live literally? One has heard glowing descriptions of his fabulous Roman apartment. But what, then, is American television to him, which he also seems to inhabit, not only appearing on every conceivable talk and interview show but also on "Mary Hartman, Mary Hartman"? A home away from Rome?

Is he perhaps more interested in politics than in belles lettres? Many of his novels, plays, and essays deal with politics. He is descended from Senator Gore of Oklahoma, has hung around the White House, and has even run for political office, without success. In an interview in *American Film*, in April 1978, the interviewer remarked, "It's been said on more than one occasion that you should be President." To which Vidal responded: "I think you're quite right." Was he serious, or was it a put-on meant to dazzle the public? Yet, for all his television exposure, he has not really made much of an impression. Philip Roth once asked a student of his, "Who is Gore Vidal?" and was told, "A society hairdresser who has written a book or two." This despite the fact that Vidal has debated most of the great minds of his day on television, including Norman Mailer (successfully) and William F. Buckley (unsuccessfully).

As Ned Rorem, the composer, diarist, and essayist, has noted in *Critical Affairs*: "Tennessee Williams and Edward Albee, for example, are certainly more famous than their works, while Myra Breckenridge [*sic*] is surely more famous than Gore Vidal. [Not famous enough to resist misspelling.] But where Albee and Williams have *peaked*, as the saying goes, Vidal remains stable, he being also a mind, an *idea* mind." (If you are going to be a mind, that, I would say, is the best kind to be.) Accordingly, Vidal's new collection of essays, *Matters of Fact and of Fiction* (Random House, 1977), has received many glowing reviews, even though Vidal condemns the purveyors of "book-chat," as he calls them—the very people who have made him famous. So, too, have a few lawsuits and his self-confessed bisexuality, which some still consider scandalous. Indeed, when I glanced at the entertainment page of the *Times* the other day and saw the headline WARHOL'S DESCENT INTO GORE, I thought for one uneasy moment that our most venerable middlebrow publication had sunk to a gossip sheet— but it turned out to be merely a review of *Andy Warhol's Bad*, a rather gory movie. At this point, you may ask yourself what all this has to do with The Language. I was just coming to that.

I think that Gore Vidal's greatest service to this society could be the proper packaging of his style and language. I do not see fiction as his true medium. As I wrote in a review of his *Burr: A Novel* in the *New Leader*, Vidal's characters "are all intelligently conceived and observed, but they lack that racy, idiosyncratic, autonomous selfhood that severs the umbilical cord between a character and the mind that gave birth to him." Of course, if Vidal were an experimenter or innovator—or what he calls, somewhat scornfully, "an R. and D. (research and development) writer"—this would not matter. But Vidal is pleased to consider himself what he is, an old-fashioned R. and R. (rest and recuperation) writer, and that requires full, three-dimensional characters.

Vidal is not really a playwright, either. In fact, it is for some unfavorable reviews of his plays that I earned my place in his *sottisier* in an essay entitled "Literary Gangsters," which appeared in his penultimate collection. Apropos his play *Weekend*, I wrote in *Commonweal*: "Like his characters, [Vidal] seems to care only in a narrow way about achieving his aims—in this case, to write a successful Broadway play—and there is no sense of feelings, intellectual passion, human concern beyond the basic requirements." And I spoke of "a basic coldness in the author." So, in "Literary Gangsters," I became—along with Robert Brustein, Richard Gilman, and the aforementioned John W. Aldridge, all of whom had given some Vidal product a less than ecstatic review—an outlaw: "There is nothing he cannot find to hate. Yet in his way, Mr. Simon is pure; a compulsive rogue criminal, more sadistic Gilles de Rais than neighborhood thug. Robert Brustein . . . is not pure;

he has ambitions above his station. Mr. Simon knows that he is only an Illyrian gangster [a reference to my origin, or, as Vidal put it a few lines earlier, "a Yugoslav with a proud if somewhat incoherent Serbian style"] and is blessedly free of side; he simply wants to torture and kill in order to be as good an American as Mr. Charles Manson, say, or Lyndon Johnson."

I quote this at such length in order to show that, proud or not, Vidal's style is rather incoherent: if I am a Gilles de Rais, who among criminals had the kind of preeminence Vidal would arrogate to himself among writers, how can I also be, as Vidal remarked at the end of his essay, a common mugger "who still prowls the criminal night, switch knife at the ready"? Inconsistency is only part of it, however; disingenuousness is the rest. For Vidal writes that "though no [journal] holds [Simon] for long, the flow of venom has proved inexhaustible." Well, in 1970, when he wrote this, I had already put in ten years as the drama critic of the *Hudson Review* and eight years as the film critic of the *New Leader*. A reputable essayist ought to get his facts straight no matter how intense his antipathy to his subject.

Here let me quote the beginning of the biographical notice attached to the manuscript of a famous twelfth-century troubadour: "Peire Vidal was of Toulouse, the son of a furrier, and he sang better than any man in the world, and he was one of the most foolish men that ever lived, for he believed that all things that pleased him, or that he wished, were true. And song making came more easily to him than to any man in the world, and it was he who made the richest melodies and talked the greatest nonsense about war and love and slandering of others." Gore Vidal likes to play verbal games with his name and find significance in them; perhaps he can find . some parallels between himself and his Provençal namesake.

Still, Vidal is an essayist of talent. I am not sure that I would bestow on him the mantle of Matthew Arnold or Edmund Wilson, as Stephen Spender does in his notice of *Matters of Fact and of Fiction* in the *New York Times Book Review;* nor am I quite convinced that Vidal's "paradoxes at their best rival Oscar Wilde's best," as Edmund White asserts in his review of the book in *Harper's*. But the new collection contains some very good pieces, as weighty as anything in Oscar Wilde and easily as witty as the best of Matthew Arnold. The learning may not be as encyclopedic as Edmund Wilson's—certainly the approach is less lofty—but it is considerable all the same. Vidal, who prides himself on not having gone to college (which makes his hatred of academe rather excessive, considering that he was never its victim), is the best kind of autodidact: neither a stilted show-off like Edward Dahlberg or Kenneth Rexroth, nor a geyser of garrulity like Henry Miller. I guess Rome, now that the mephitic exhalations from the Colosseum have been checked, is no longer as perilous as it was in Daisy Miller's day; and it is certainly provincial and uneventful enough to allow Vidal plenty of time to read and cultivate his idea mind.

At least three essays in *Matters of Fact and of Fiction* are extremely diverting and useful. There is "The Top Ten Best Sellers," in which Vidal, who must be as much of a speed-reader as he is a speed-writer, analyzes the ten best-selling books of 1973, all of which he has actually read. Since very few people of Vidal's intelligence have the acumen and celerity required for this task, we get a rare, fascinating, and rewarding evaluation of America's favorite reading in a given year. Characteristically, however, though Vidal makes some very good observations along the way, he does not quite manage to come up with a conclusion that goes beyond the fact that most of these novels were spawned by the kinds of movies their authors grew up on.

"The Hacks of Academe" is a review of *The Theory of the Novel: New Essays*, edited by John Halperin, and provides Vidal with a fine platform from which to inveigh against academic writing and rail at the teaching of literature in the universities. There are several brilliant paragraphs here, too long to quote, but I can reproduce two pregnant and pertinent sallies: "The efforts of the teachers now under review add up to at least a half millennium of academic tenure." And this, about Donald Barthelme's latest novel, which "is written in a kind of numbing baby talk reminiscent of the 'see Jane run' primary-school textbooks. Of course Mr. Barthelme means to be ironic." And now the sentence that kills: "Of course he knows his book is not very interesting to read, but then life is not very interesting to live either." This is a kind of reductio ad absurdum in reverse: inflation ad absurdum, and it makes Barthelme (whether deservedly or not I don't know, not having read *The Dead Father*) sound like a pretentious ass.

In "American Plastic: The Matter of Fiction," the unhappy Barthelme gets it again. This time Vidal surveys not only Barthelme's own books but also those of the four colleagues Barthelme seems to admire above all others: Gass, Pynchon, Barth, and Grace Paley. Barthelme and Barth come off very badly; Pynchon less than well; Gass with only a flesh wound or two mixed with considerable praise; and Paley very well indeed. Yet Vidal is again inconsistent: in his summation, he writes, "The meager rattling prose of all these writers, excepting Gass, depresses me." He has by this point clearly forgotten all about Paley.

Whether or not one agrees with Vidal's judgments, there are some trenchant formulations in this essay. Speaking of Pynchon's prose, Vidal attributes its failings to the "rattle and buzz that were in the air when the author was growing up, an era in which only the television commercial was demonically acquiring energy, leaked to it by a declining Western civilization." Or, discussing the esoteric French critic Roland Barthes's book-length analysis of Balzac's story *Sarrasine*, in which, among other things, Barthes distinguishes between "writerly" and "readerly" texts, Vidal observes that his "style seems willfully complicated. I say willfully because the text of itself is a plain and readerly one in no need of this sort of assistance, not that Barthes wants to assist either text or reader." Note how that last bit, spoken, as it were, out of the corner of the mouth in a throwaway manner, casually punctures the hell out of Barthes. (It would seem, incidentally, that the pentagrammaton BARTH makes Vidal see red: Barth, Barthes, and Barthelme all get skewered.)

Better yet is the following: "Like *so* many of today's academic critics, Barthes resorts to formulas, diagrams; the result, no doubt, of teaching in classrooms equipped with blackboards and chalk. Envious of the half-erased theorems—the prestigious *signs*—of the physicists, English teachers now compete by chalking up theorems and theories of their own, words having failed them yet again." Note how an abstract concept—the English department's wishing to compete with science—is translated into an image, slightly absurd but very concrete and with some basis in reality, to make a sharply visualized hyperbole that sticks in the reader's memory.

The essay that is generally considered the best in the book is "Some Memories of the Glorious Bird and an Earlier Self," which starts out as a review of Tennessee Williams's *Memoirs* but turns into a double portrait: recollections of Williams and Vidal when they were much younger and saw a lot of each other in the heady atmosphere of Rome in the late forties. Italy was ecstatically bursting into liberation after Fascism; they, no less ecstatically, after the constricting puritanism of America. I find this essay less satisfying, chiefly because it is too discursive and falls finally between the stools of criticism and reminiscence while trying to encompass both. Here, too, certain devices of Vidal's are too heavily leaned on—the ironic anticlimax, for example: "[Williams] was thirty-seven; but claimed to be thirty-three on the sensible ground that the four years he had spent working for a shoe company did not count." Or, about Harold Acton's autobiography: "The ongoing story of a long and marvelously uninteresting life . . . a little volume called *More Memoirs of an Aesthete,* a work to be cherished for its quite remarkable number of unaesthetic misprints and misspellings." And, again, about a piece of nonsense in Acton's book: "Splendid stuff and I wish I had said it. Certainly whoever did was putting Acton on." In all of these cases, terms of seeming praise—*sensible, marvelously, remarkable, splendid*—are just setting up the victim for the kill. But this strategy, however overworked, does produce one gem; after quoting some of the young Truman Capote's sexual braggadocio, Vidal remarks: "I should note here that the young Capote was no less attractive in his person then than he is today."

Perhaps even more than as an essayist, we need Vidal as a television personality. I could not disagree more with James Wolcott (the *Village Voice,* May 9, 1977), who rejects Vidal's "lecturing his countrymen [on TV] on the folly of their ways." Vidal's intelligence, *pace* Wolcott, does not "curdle" on television and his quick mind—prejudiced in many ways but still quick and clear— buttressed by a delightfully ironic wit, is just what the American public needs, particularly when it is expressed in magisterially cutting, fastidiously cultivated language. Quite rightly, Vidal deplores what he calls the American lack of a sense of humor—really a lack of wit and, above all, irony. Frequent exposure to his manner, consisting in equal measure of a devastating irony, a lucidly applied and expressed culture, and a casual arrogance, might give those in TV land an idea of which way lies civilization, which is where Vidal lives.

# Authors Without Fear or Shame

In the beginning was the word. But by the time the second word was added to it, there was trouble. For with it came syntax, the thing that tripped up so many people. And they're tripping up more than ever today. It is amazing to find even some established American writers committing the kinds of grammatical errors that in the days when college was not yet junior high school, and high school not yet kindergarten, would have been unacceptable from a mere student.

Thus a friend called my attention to a recent book by Arthur Miller, *In the Country* (Viking Press, 1977). The very first sentence begins: "Born and raised in city apartments, it was always a marvel to me." What, we wonder, is that "it" that was born and raised in city apartments and a marvel to Arthur Miller? Turn the page, and there is an even more glaring syntactical lapse: "Later that afternoon, eating a sandwich in the sun, the first itching began on my belly." Visualize it, if you will: an itch in the late afternoon, eating its first crepuscular sandwich. And, impudent son of an itch that it is, presuming to eat it on the belly of one of our foremost playwrights.

Sure, you say, a misplaced antecedent, a dangling construction; but what of it? Everyone gets the point, anyway. That is not always the case, however; sloppy syntax can very easily obscure or distort the writer's or speaker's meaning. But even when the meaning is discernible, as here, the improper construction puts a banana peel under the sentence and reduces our Ibsen from Brooklyn to a grammatical vaudevillian. Bad grammar is rather like bad manners: someone picking his nose at a party will still be recognized as a minimal human being and not a literal four-footed pig; but there are cases where the minimal is not enough.

To make writing and speaking a little more complicated, there is also the problem of imagery. So much of what we commit to other people's hearing or reading is simile or metaphor, and bad similes and metaphors hurt the sensitive eye and ear. So it is astounding to see the usually fastidious Joyce Carol Oates, a poet as well as a fiction writer, perpetrate the following in the *New York*

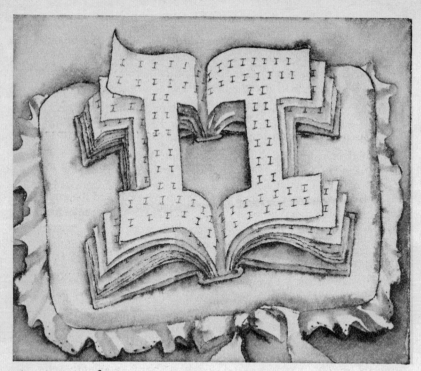

AUTHORS WITHOUT FEAR OR SHAME

*Times Book Review* of April 3, 1977: "Nor do the parallels between the two American women become too aggressively pointed." Parallels are lines that run side by side; in no sense can they be pointed.

And, alas, where there is careless imagery, there is usually inadequate grammar. In her very next sentence, Miss Oates refers to a conversation "between" three people. Now, I realize that in our sadly permissive dictionaries "between" is becoming acceptable as a synonym for "among." But do not buy this, good people; the "tween" comes from the Anglo-Saxon *"twā,"* meaning two, and if we start meddling with such palpable etymological sense (who cannot hear the "twain" in "tween"?), we become barbarous or trendy, even if we happen to be in the dictionary business.

My point is that people who are consistently untidy or ignorant about grammar and imagery are usually not to be trusted in other areas of taste and discrimination. Jean-Luc Godard, the revolutionary filmmaker, who is hardly an old-fashioned pedant, once observed that the choice of a type of shot in a movie is really a moral choice. A bad metaphor, too, is, among other things, a moral lapse. Consider this image from a current novel, Anne Roiphe's *Torch Song*, a veritable treasure trove of the most laughable fiascoes of diction this side of Rex Reed (who, being manifestly subliterate, remains *hors concours*): "I stood naked . . . my kinky pubic hair sprawling like urban blight over the tops of my thighs."

This is about as defective a simile as you can get (and the novel pullulates with them) because it does not make sense on any level. It is wrong visually, because urban blight is not kinky or comate. It does not work in terms of tone: urban blight is an environmental and social problem; excess genital hair is a private and highly subjective one. And even nowadays, when the pubic has pretty much gone public, the two do not mix well conceptually. Nor, most important, is this image in good moral taste—and I do not mean anything so trivial as sexual decorum. A petty personal preoccupation should not, even casually, be aggrandized by the writer's trying to give it tragic dimensions—exaggerating it, even metaphorically, into a universal calamity. That is repellently self-serving.

To test my theory that there is a nexus between bad writing and a failure of the ethical-aesthetic sensibility, I decided to examine Erica Jong's new novel, *How to Save Your Own Life*. From previously published excerpts and from various reviews, I deduced that the book was in less than exemplary taste, broadcasting the sort of private, intimate details about easily identifiable persons that only a cad would reveal to the world's prurience. Gossipy writers usually adduce two justifications. One: All novelists use data from their personal experience. True, but only vulgar and unimaginative ones spread it around in the manner of gossip columnists rather than imaginatively transforming it after the fashion of genuine artists. Two: Why can't you tell about others if you tell about yourself as well? To this there are three objections: (a) you have the right to make a pig of yourself, but not of someone else; (b) for being indiscreet about yourself, you get, in this absurdly confessional age, high marks for candor and honesty—when all you are doing is showing off what a hell of a guy or gal you are,

boasting about the number and variety of orifices you have penetrated or been penetrated through; and (c) bad writers always
have a way of incriminating other people's characters rancorously
and ruthlessly; self-incrimination, however, takes on the tone of
compassion, of waxing tender over one's own foibles. *How to Save
Your Own Reputation* [for good money] *While Smearing Everybody
Else's.*

In a certain metaphorical sense, Jong's book suffers from a failure of language that can be called pronoun erosion. There is no
real he, she, or you in *How to Save Your Own Life;* the author never
gets beyond the hypertrophic "I." Have you noticed that in the
overwhelming majority of modern novels the only real, three-
dimensional, fully developed—living, breathing, and fornicating—
person is the author, that is to say, some unmistakable alter ego
and mouthpiece of the novelist? There are many "others" in
Jong's book: some good, some bad. Foremost among the bad, and
most lovingly dissected, is Isadora-Erica's ex-husband. But he
never comes to life, never has an authentic personal existence.
Foremost among the good is Isadora-Erica's current (at least I assume still current) lover, Josh, a writer and a supposedly enormously decent, clever, wise, sensitive, and perceptive fellow. Yet
we learn very little about him beyond the fact that he has a furry,
warm, crooked smile (or is it face?), and that Isadora need only
think of his hot, thick, huge cock for her generous cunt to start
overflowing. (I am paraphrasing closely, needless to say, not in-
venting.) From now on, it will be hard for his friends not to view
the poor fellow as dehumanized into a mere piston of above-
average circumference and temperature.

My hypothesis was right. The novel is a self-serving, egomania-
cal, monstrously self-righteous tale, even while it pretends to be
scrupulously self-incriminating: Look at me—I am peccant in
small ways but also beautiful and brainy; a dazzling talker, brilliant writer, faithful friend; a basically fine person and fabulous
lay; deservedly famous yet an almost model modest, self-sacrific-
ing wife abused by a lousy husband, and a truly model mistress
for the perfect lover, whom I have found at last (gloat, gloat!),
though there are times, my God, when even he does not treat me
quite so well as I deserve. And with this insufferable tone goes, as
I suspected, every kind of bad writing, grammatical and stylistic.

The amusing thing is that Jong holds grammar in high esteem.

When she and her soul-mind-and-sex brother, Josh, make fun of a California how-to book entitled *If I Knew Who I Was, I Would Tell You*, our fellow writers exchange the following comments: "Isn't it, 'If I knew who I *were*'?" "Not in Big Sur, it ain't. . . . Grammar is bourgeois and repressive." So our two literary lights actually think that correct usage demands here the subjunctive "were," which would be the case only if the statement were contrary to fact, e.g., "If I were king." But it isn't. The author says that he *actually* doesn't know who he is. So the correction is wrong. (But the title is also wrong: it should be *If I Knew Who I Am*, because the problem is not who the author was in an anterior existence or childhood, but who he was all along and still is.) Yet the two illustrious ignoramuses feel vastly superior to Big Sur: *they* know that grammar is *not* bourgeois and repressive.

Still, there is virtually no grammatical error Miss Jong doesn't commit. Herewith a few samples. We get "deformed . . . to" for "deformed into"; "a mammoth pudenda" for "pudendum"; "I was obsessing" for "obsessed"; "I was conflicted" for "in conflict"; "post coitus" for "post coitum"; "anymore" for "any more"; "unbeknownst," a vulgarism, for "unbeknown"; "circular staircase" for "spiral staircase"; "intrigued" for "fascinated"; "lady writers" for "women writers"; "if it was him" for "if it was he"; "none of them are" for "none of them is"; "It might have smelled like garbage—but it was home" for "It may have"; "Everyone lies about their feelings" for "his feelings"; "telling each other" for "telling one another" (more than two people being involved); "I couldn't help but notice" for "I couldn't help noticing"; and so on.

Jong writes: "I felt incredibly guilty." At the very least, this is jargon—a meaningless "incredibly" thrown in for emphasis. But it is also ambiguous; at first, the reader may think that Jong is a responsible writer who meant something like a guilt feeling that lacks credibility. On closer perusal, such is not the case. Again, our author writes, "Her pelvis felt like someone had knotted the bones." It should, of course, be "as if someone had knotted the bones." If we make the mistake of trusting Jong's grammar, we tend to read "like someone [who] had knotted the bones" and assume that a "who" was accidentally dropped. Whereupon we are brought up short: knotted what bones? And, as a last example, take the incorrect use of "hopefully": "She felt the base of his penis throbbing as all the filaments flew flew flew into her womb and hopefully caught." Is Jong trying to tell us that the filaments were filled with hope? Not even she would go that far. She means that she hoped they would impregnate her. But the reader is thrown off his course, a discomfort to which no decent writer would subject him.

Now for a few samples of stylistic inadequacy. For a supposed poet, Jong has a staggering propensity for banal, shopworn imagery that often hurtles into outright cliché. "I was smiling so hard, I felt my face would crack"; "The air conditioning seemed to have given up the ghost"; "It all seemed like some sort of nightmare"; "her shelflike bosom"; "his voice a steel trap"; "to pull it out now, like a rabbit out of a hat"; "I rewind the film backward . . . and my life flashes past in reverse"; "I am already miles, light-years away"; "He came, groaning for me across forever"; and many, many more.

Her imagery errs in numerous other ways as well. Sometimes the image doesn't take us far enough from the original situation to make the trope striking: a beginner's anxiety on skis "feels like coming to the top of a staircase, looking down, and forgetting how to walk." Clearly the tenor (to use I. A. Richards's terminology), "skis," and the vehicle, "staircase," do not create the exciting resonance of very different things coming aptly and tellingly together. Sometimes the images are distasteful in their self-importance: "I was sinking into the grave . . . as surely as the Jews at Auschwitz"—how dare this little humdrum neurosis compare itself to the Holocaust? Often the images are imprecise: "Each of us only feels the torn lining of his own coat and sees the wholeness of the other person's"; this would make just as much sense the other way round—each of us noticing the other person's torn lining but not his own—and metaphors, unlike coats, should not be reversible. Or the image is cheap as well as vague: "California is a wet dream in the mind of New York"; "Someday every woman will have orgasms—like [sic] every family has color TV." (Can orgasms be bought like a television set?)

At other times her images cancel one another out through sheer excess—a kind of metaphorical redundancy. In an unhappy marriage, "the bed might as well be a raft in a shark-infested sea. You might as well have landed on a dead planet with no atmosphere." One or the other, please; the two together fight unto the death of both. Altogether, Jong tends to be redundant: "My cunt growls, howls, bays at the moon"; "so breakable, so fragile";

"I was also over the hill, too old"; "this prodigious miracle, this wonder," which manages to be a double redundancy. Even more unfortunate are the many stillborn jokes, some of them hoary gags like "deadlocked wedlock," some of them new but awful, such as this description of fellatio: "I put my best tongue forward" (how many has she got?); or the evocation of a WASP female lover's mouth eating her "Jewish pussy" as "the mouth that roared," by way of a feeble punning allusion; or this attempt at explaining a lesbian adventure with an epigram: "If men were the question, perhaps women were the answer," where far too great returns are expected from the cheap trick of turning an obvious "problem" into a supposedly clever "question." Often the cuteness takes a scatological or scabrous turn. Seeing a telephone in a producer's bathroom, Isadora-Erica wonders, "What producer, however crass, would negotiate on the phone while grunting out a large turd?"

Part of language—of any good language—is silence: knowing when to stop and let the unspoken speak for you. It is no service to Josh to quote him as saying in the midst of intercourse, "I love your pee, your farts, your shit, your tight snatch." A good writer can suggest such things without having to spell them out. But clearly Jong wants her bodily functions canonized, there being no bounds to her megalomania. In one passage she tells us that she knows things about love that neither Doris Lessing nor Tolstoy perceived correctly. And, in my very favorite passage, she rebukes "all of the greatest fiction of the modern age [for showing] women falling for vile seducers and dying as a result. . . . *Someone*," she continues, "had to break the curse, *someone* had to wake Sleeping Beauty without ultimately sending her to her destruction."

Can you divine who that wonderful, italicized someone is? Yes, you guessed it: it is our fearlessly and ungrammatically flying author, with her previous novel, and with this new piece of Jong.

# No Help for Teachers of English

**W**hen the man from the State Education Department tele-phoned to ask me to appear on a panel discussion for high-school

teachers of English about ways of teaching students how to write
our language, only a heart of stone could have resisted. The man
sounded so young, eager, stumbling, earnest, awed, well-inten-
tioned, that one had to accede to his request. I got the impression
that I was to appear on a panel with a few teachers, and that other
writers, individually, would appear on other panels, all in the
interest of helping to drum a little more literacy into the hardened
skulls of New York public-school pupils. Next to signing petitions
on behalf of writers in Siberian labor camps, a worthier cause
would have been hard to imagine.

Having accepted, I was soon deluged with letters and phone
calls in which this kindly supervisor of Urban School Services
kept checking up on whether I still intended to come, or making
sure that I had not forgotten. In his last call, the kindly supervisor
informed me that I was to be at the auditorium of the Graduate
Center of the City University of New York at three-thirty on the
appointed day, i.e., half an hour before starting time, possibly for
some setting-up exercises to limber me up for the event.

When I arrived at a quarter to four, the auditorium—which, I
guess, holds about three hundred fifty people—was nearly full. I
was directed backstage and, turning back, found myself closely
followed by Susan Sontag. My surprise grew as I took in the
people seated around a large backstage table: these were no hardworking but unsung heroes of secondary-school linguistics;
rather, they were, in alphabetic order, Caroline Bird, Hortense
Calisher, Ralph Ellison, Jules Feiffer, Francine du Plessix Gray,
Nat Hentoff, Martin Mayer, Edwin Newman, Arthur Schlesinger,
Budd Schulberg, and Gail Sheehy. After the symposium had begun, we were joined by the fourteenth panelist, Jimmy Breslin.

Never before had so many stars been assembled for one panel;
clearly, it was not so much a symposium as it was the Milky Way.
The kindly supervisor (who, to my added astonishment, turned
out to be a man of mature years) informed us that we were to talk
three minutes each, in alphabetical order; this was to be followed
by discussion among the panelists, and followed, in turn, by questions from the floor; after that, there would be informal conversation over refreshments—all this to take two hours, from four to
six. I marveled at the man's innocence. Was it not miracle enough
to amass fourteen such well-known speakers; did he actually expect the further miracle that fourteen such usually highly paid

and articulate mouths would open only to close again a measly three minutes later? No honorarium and only three minutes of limelight? Besides, how much light can even a star shed in one hundred eighty seconds on such complex problems?

All aflutter, the kindly supervisor's spouse now proceeded to serve coffee and cookies, while hubby invited us beamingly to plan our strategies backstage under his gratified regard. It became evident that having collected us like so many living autographs, he was not about to share us right away with *hoi polloi*, whatever the ostensible purpose of the convocation. By now, though, it was four-ten, and the packed hall was bursting with standees as well, justified impatience audibly seeping through the walls. Edwin Newman sensibly suggested that we go out and begin, to which the kindly supervisor assented with mild reluctance.

We were to be seated in alphabetical order except for Francine Gray, who, because she was on crutches, received the chair nearest the exit. Alphabetizing had evidently given the State Education Department a bit of trouble; for example, Schulberg, Sheehy, Sontag, Simon, and Schlesinger were seated in that order, which, you will grant, bears a rather remote resemblance to the alphabetic. Still, we were ready to start, but what was the subject? In a letter of December 6, 1976, signed by two representatives of educational agencies and two of City College, the topic was given as "The Writer, the Student, and the Creative Act." In a letter of January 12, 1977, the kindly supervisor referred to it as "The Author, the Student, and the Art of Writing." In a letter from the director of English of the Center for the Humanities and the Arts of the Board of Education of the City of New York, Division of Educational Planning and Support, dated February 15, 1977, it was "The Author, the Student, and the Art of Teaching." In a letter from the assistant to the director, dated February 28, 1977, it was "The Author, the Student, and the Art of Teaching Writing." Plainly, the Author and the Student were fairly constant, but the third ingredient had a protean tendency.

Having introduced the event and the participants, the kindly supervisor was faced with a problem: the discrepancy between his list of panelists, which was properly alphabetized, and the actual seating order, which wasn't. This resulted in some curious stumblings, greatly enlivening his introductions. However, in defiance of any order, Edwin Newman was called on to open the proceedings on the strength of his two books on English abusage. He proceeded to discourse well beyond his allotted three minutes in the breezily discursive manner of those books. Impishly, he cited grammatical and stylistic lapses ranging from an inscription on our very auditorium door, NO FOOD NOR DRINK ALLOWED IN THE AUDITORIUM, to an Aspen seminar on health care full of references to "interdisciplinary interfaces." He ended with an eloquent excoriation of "a boneless language full of gas—for concealment, or even to conceal that there is nothing to conceal."

The next speaker was Caroline Bird, whose main point was that since the kids were better at talking than at writing, they should be given a good dose of public speaking. Next, Jimmy Breslin, who had just lumbered in, declared that creative writing could not be taught any more than could piano playing, and that kids should be encouraged to write in their own juicy street language. Bedford-Stuyvesant is the Dublin of America; if you could post a nun with a ruler on each of its stoops, you'd have writing a hell of a lot better than what comes out of the suburbs.

Hortense Calisher was next and warned against labeling as elitist the striving for excellence. She advocated a middle path between functionalism and higher things. Ralph Ellison was for reading aloud in class to make the written word as exciting as the exchanged one, and for drawing on Afro-American traditions of music and dancing to help channel kids into literature. Jules Feiffer began with: "Writing is too serious a business to be left to the schools," which went over like a lead balloon, or perhaps a balloon in one of his cartoons. He told of the poor schooling he had received until television, the movies, and comic strips came to his educational rescue. Kids in the streets speak very colorfully and eloquently, and must be allowed to use their own tongue; eventually, as he knew from his own experience, grammar and syntax take care of themselves. We should stimulate the desire to communicate instead of assigning reading "as dense as mathematics."

Nat Hentoff went on for a good twelve or thirteen minutes and was for making kids write from their own experience and also not from it, but drawing on "fantasy and plain old logic." The idea is "to bring the world into the classroom—all the worlds, including [the students'] world." Differing with some previous speakers, such as Breslin, Martin Mayer asserted that writing was a skill that could be taught, just like piano playing. He was dubious about using the kids' conversation as a model for their writing, thus disagreeing with Feiffer, and agreed with Newman about the harmfulness of too much television. Reading one another's stuff out loud was fine, but it should be on "very specific and not very expressive subjects," such as the description of a photograph. But teachers must not put "correctness" above "precision" and lack the sensitivity to grasp a gifted student's special style.

Then came death in the afternoon in the form of Budd Schulberg's address, delivered haltingly and lasting seventeen and a half minutes. We were regaled with a lengthy anecdote about a poem the young Budd had written, which his mother had declared a work of genius, and his father a piece of drivel. We heard quite a bit about his father the producer, along with an anecdote about one of his father's screenwriters, who pronounced a story by the still young Schulberg vomitory. We then learned about the gifted blacks Schulberg taught in his workshop in Watts, and about the even more gifted blacks he is now teaching on West One Hundred Forty-ninth Street. He raised at considerable length the question of one black kid, Sammy Harris, who could write publishable poetry but was a high-school dropout. What are we to do about such kids? Could we perhaps institute special classes for students "who just like to do one thing, say, write poetry"? Schulberg asked, and was about to go on speculating on what makes such Sammies run when he was interrupted in mid-sentence, during one of his characteristic pauses, by a round of applause, which forced him to stop.

Gail Sheehy warned against too much reading aloud and plunked for more writing from the kids' own experiences. There must, however, also be reading, only not of the advanced kind that would make them cry out in despair, "How can I become that obscure?" She extolled the uses of reading nonfiction, which could teach such practical things as "how to make love" or "how to be a hooker," and which sounded rather like a curriculum based on the collected works of Gail Sheehy. Read a piece, say, about someone being assaulted in the street, then make the kids write about such an experience in their own way.

Susan Sontag took an adversary position: kids should not so much be taught how to write as how to think, how to get more information later on when they need it, and how to discriminate among various forms of information. The school should not be overambitious; teaching how to live or how to make love is up to the culture as a whole. Reading aloud is fine, but writing should not emphasize self-expression; better to imitate really good writers who can be assigned in small doses—a paragraph or a page—and then imitated by the students.

My own comments called for a kind of practical cynicism; in opposition to Feiffer, I urged teachers to appeal to such common and excusable human failings as pride and acquisitiveness as stimulants to learning. I also warned against the permissive posture and read a horrible example from a *New York Times* article in which one James Flightner, a professor of languages at the University of Montana, argued against his university's new writing requirements on the grounds that (a) there are no objective standards of good writing, (b) college students should not be required to have skills the high schools failed to give them, and (c) one should not introduce one more obstacle in the path of social mobility. My suggestion was to weed out the Flightners of this world while they were still in high school, before the waves of upward mobility have carried them to college, graduate school, and professorships—even in Montana.

Arthur Schlesinger made the practical suggestion that more funds be allocated for adjunct teachers—possibly middle-aged female college graduates—who would do nothing but correct papers and thus make possible increased writing practice; unfortunately, he neglected to say where these funds were to come from. Francine du Plessix Gray argued like Sontag that good writers should be the models for student papers and recommended close reading of Orwell, Agee, and Walt Whitman's prose. She was also for writing descriptions of "a narrow thing—a table, not even a room," and for the avoidance of "relevant stuff," in whose irrelevance she firmly believes. She called for a revival of letter writing, which had so well maintained culture in former centuries, and proposed exercises wherein kids wrote letters to a loved one, so that writing might become an act of love, friendship, even lust, and, ultimately, survival.

In short, the teachers were told that creative writing could be taught, and that it couldn't be. All writing should be based on personal experiences and be highly self-expressive; it should also imitate the classics and not be self-expressive at all. There should be much reading aloud, perhaps coupled with singing and dancing; there should be less talk and more writing. Kids should be taught writing by way of living, lusting, and loving; grand existential strategies should be strictly avoided, and kids should learn to think, explicate texts, and do research. Above all, kids should be allowed to use their own jargon, dialect, lingo; above all, kids should be taught through imitation of superb writers how to transcend their own lingo, dialect, jargon.

But all these fine contradictions seemed to me rendered perfectly academic and useless when the first questioner from the floor mentioned that the National Council of Teachers of English had firmly adopted a position fully entitling students to speak and write in their ethnic sublanguages, i.e., street language, dialects, admixtures of foreign tongues, etc. That puts a clean end not only to panels on how to teach English but also to English itself.

However, lest you think that the panel was so much wasted time and energy, let me hasten to tell you that I just received a form letter in which some official connected with the symposium asks for my signature on an enclosed label, to be used as part of a commemorative mural made of "newspaper clippings, name cards, programs and autographs of the authors who participated." Say not the struggle naught availeth, as long as it yields a collage, a piece of junk sculpture, or a wall suitable for wailing.

# LANGUAGE AND THE PERFORMING ARTS

# Why Reed Can't Write

**R**ex Reed is the most read, seen, and heard film and theater reviewer in this country. Millions read (or, at any rate, have access to) his column, which is distributed by the Chicago Tribune–N.Y. News Syndicate; further millions of nonreaders can catch him on the "Tonight Show," where he is one of the regulars, on "The Gong Show," or on his spots on CBS radio; and tens of thousands of select women and homosexuals can enjoy him also in the pages of *Vogue*. In many a culturally underprivileged American home he has become the archetype of the critic; in superficially bright circles he passes for a fearlessly outspoken wit; and one professor of cinema at a California university has dubbed him "the thinking man's John Simon." Having previously reviewed a collection of his interviews, I felt it was time to investigate his criticism as well.

In perusing some of Reed's pieces in *Vogue*, I came upon some truly remarkable formulations. For example: "The note of reigning terror is struck in the first scene (a dull woman's body is being examined by a Fascist doctor)." A dull corpse? How many witty ones has Reed known? But a corpse so dull as to strike a note of terror? That *is* dull, even for a corpse. As you watch *Bugsy Malone*, Reed informs you, "your heart is likely to hum with huggable good humor." Have you ever tried to hug a humor, good or bad? And how does a heart hum good-humoredly: like an efficient workshop or like a contented theatergoer emerging from a tuneful musical? Elsewhere we read, "The entire film shrieks with hypnotic tension," although hypnotic tension does not shriek and doesn't even exist—under hypnosis one is relaxed.

Brian De Palma, the director of *Obsession*, "has a strong sense of the importance of atmosphere and coats the screen with a veneer of decaying doom." Doom does not ordinarily come in veneers, still less is it decaying. But what I really want to know is this: when does De Palma shellac his screen—during the projection or before? And how many coats does he apply? Then there is John Wayne in *The Shootist*: "After two hundred movies, he still knows how to riddle the box office charts with bullets of victory." I have heard of leaden bullets, even silver ones (in *Der Freischütz*, though opera is beyond Reed, who once referred to the Anvil Chorus from *Aïda*), but bullets made of victory? And if Wayne shoots the box-office charts full of holes, who will be able to read his prominence on them? Again, *Network* "is a combination of apocalypse and ambrosia that is mystifying." Such a combination would indeed be mystifying, if only it were possible. Apocalypse is something revealed, ambrosia something eaten; the two have nothing in common beyond the alliterative initial.

Reed's brain is incapable of grasping how metaphors work. He can manage the kind of hyperbole that may pass for wit in the epicene milieu, as when he says of the all-star cast of *Voyage of the Damned* that "the list goes on for days," though gross and unclever exaggeration is of little value elsewhere. So, too, in a review of *The California Reich*, we are told that "there are scenes to turn your hair silver." The correct cliché is, of course, to turn it *white*, but Reed either can't even get his clichés right, or thinks by a slight modification to turn them into gold. He is even worse at recognizing fossilized metaphors that still have to be handled with care; of *Voyage of the Damned*, he writes: "The film has stretched itself to encompass a wide panorama of endurance and experience," where "stretched itself" evokes the small specific movement of, say, a cat, and therefore cannot encompass large abstractions like endurance and experience, which, to make matters worse, Reed lists in anticlimactic order.

But never mind metaphors. Reed doesn't even know how to use words. "Everything is massively researched," he writes, not realizing that *massive*, except when meaning bulky or imposing, is a vogue word, suitable perhaps for a *Vogue* column, but not for literate consumption. He refers to the Peter Finch character as part of the "subplot" of *Network*, even though Finch is what the main plot revolves around; Reed thinks he is clever to coin the term "morallegory," blissfully unaware that allegory is always a moral or moralizing genre. Elsewhere there is talk of Bette Davis's "masklike, map-lined face," without understanding that that would mean a face lined with maps. He speaks of special effects "executed on a considerable scale," a reference, however vague, to their size. But special effects have nothing to do with size, and can be measured only by their deftness or verisimilitude.

For total verbal and stylistic breakdown, however, consider this about *Network*, where the Faye Dunaway character is described as "a pathetic speech major." *Pathetic* is, again, a vogue word, singularly inappropriate for that hard character, unless perhaps she majored in making speeches full of pathos. "Dunaway," we read, "is the embodiment of how career robots are supposed to think, yet she's the one who has premature ejaculation." How do we get from career robots to the wholly unrelated premature ejaculation? The *yet* implies that career robots usually have punctual ejaculations, except in the unfortunate case of Miss Dunaway; but even Reed couldn't mean that. And what about female ejaculations in the first place? Not since Victorian times has anyone—even if he never had sex with a woman—assumed that women "spend" or "ejaculate." Of course, Reed may be trying for a metaphor here, but even metaphor must abide by some kind of logic.

Let us now turn to Reed's syndicated column in the *Daily News* and, instead of skipping around, examine a couple of specimens in greater detail. Here are some excerpts from the one on *Voyage of the Damned*, a shoddy film that Reed regards with "veneration and love." It will be "a sad and despondent loss for anyone who misses it," which might look like a kind of syllepsis—a rhetorical device of which Reed, we may assume, has never heard—but is actually a case of simple ignorance of the meaning of *despondent*, which can apply only to people. After inept syllepsis, incompetent synesthesia, as we read about "the fragrance of human spirit," an attempt to objectify a windy abstraction with an irrelevant olfactory reference.

To continue with *Voyage of the Damned*, agreement of subject and predicate is not for our Rex; consider "a purpose and a persona that adds weight." Neither is there any kind of consistency. The passengers of the S.S. *St. Louis* are "joined in a common bond of hope. Their joyless fates hang in the balance while the heartless structures of diplomatic red tape barter for them like cattle at a livestock show, yet they dance to Glenn Miller's 'Moonlight Serenade.'" A common bond of hope sounds rather inspiriting; but no, these are joyless fates that hang in the balance. If, however, they are already defined as joyless, what kind of balance can they still hang in? Perhaps that common bond of hope is actually wound around their necks. Meanwhile, heartless structures are bartering for them. Has a structure ever had a heart, to say nothing of its bartering? But this is a structure of red tape: something like a card castle, I presume, only made of tape instead of cards. These tape structures are bartering like cattle at a livestock show, while the traders, I suppose, stand by tethered and mooing.

The wonderful image continues; it seems that the dancers' "minds and dreams are in fragments, like splinters of broken glass." Luckily no one is dancing barefoot; even so, when there are glass splinters of *both* minds and dreams littering the floor, the going must be treacherous. It seems, further, that "every performer" responded with "collective sincerity and craftsmanship," which tells me what made most of those performances so rotten: lack of *individual* craftsmanship. There is a "massive job of cutting and editing," which must be massive indeed because "cutting" and "editing" are synonyms and typical of Reed's mindless word-mongering. Reed admires "Ben Gazzara's strength, sweating desperately and boiling with rage." A strength that sweats and boils simultaneously must be a truly remarkable sight for a gaze that could penetrate all that steam, especially as its "pleas fall on deafened ears." Again, cliché has been distorted into nonsense: ears deafened by what? Perhaps by Reed's prose.

Equally admirable, apparently, is "Julie Harris's encyclopedia of facial emotions," though Reed fails to specify the number of its volumes. A facial emotion, I dare say, is either something like an expression, only more histrionic, or else a feeling had while one receives a facial. Such an encyclopedia, in any case, deserves to be printed on facial tissues. But all the performances are "etched in blood, preserved in beauty," though blood cannot be etched in, even with beauty as a preservative. The people are "honest and sympathetic beyond offensiveness, and the tears they extract are profoundly honorable." How one is honest and sympathetic beyond offensiveness defies exegesis, but even the image of tears, however profoundly honorable, being extracted is more than a little troublesome. Perhaps Reed really meant teeth. The film certainly set mine on edge.

Reed returns to the charge when he writes of his having been moved "to tears without embarrassment or guilt"; could it then be that when he weeps over Judy Garland and other such camp favorites, he does recognize the guiltiness of his tears? Anything can happen, though, in these parlous times "when even the best work is usually aborted and compromised." How could work be both aborted and compromised, unless today's movies are, like young ladies of yesterday, compromised after having undergone what used to be termed an "illegal operation." But once a film has been aborted *or* compromised, how can it be—usually, yet!—part of "the best work"? *Voyage,* Reed continues, "is an amazing thing to applaud." Quite so—rather like applauding the new *King Kong* or *A Star Is Born*.

Our man is no less literate and eloquent when he turns to the theater, in this case to Joseph Hardy's feeble revival of *The Night of the Iguana*. Here, for instance, the flabby and unprepossessing Sylvia Miles is described as "a handsome predatory bird gnawed by the unpleasant prospect of oncoming menopause," a trope that beggars comment. The characters "pass through the transitory crossroads of life," even though crossroads can be neither passed through nor transitory. In the original Broadway production of *Iguana*, we learn, the actors "attacked its feast of poetry with hammers instead of chopsticks." Poetry, clearly, is an Oriental dish. *Iguana* is to be credited "for [it should be *with*] being a play of shadow and substance sweeping away the cobwebs that cloud the soul and reaching out bravely to touch the hearts of others." Dear Rex does not understand that in the phrase "shadow and substance" shadow represents nonexistence, a negative value. But what is most impressive here is the play's ambidexterity, which can sweep cobwebs off a soul with one arm while reaching for the hearts of others with the other.

Richard Chamberlain, "one of America's finest actors . . . glowers at the heads of his stricken public." This may account for his poor performance; it would have been better for him to look at his fellow actors. He "slices to the core of what ails the man [he portrays], exposes it, then sews it up again in self-defense." What's the point of all that slicing and exposing, only to sew it all up again? And sewing in self-defense? Well, if the needle is long enough, it just might parry an attack with chopsticks. As for Dorothy McGuire, she enacts an "old maid with hidden feelings of observation and understanding so full of pride and kindness." I never knew that observation and understanding were feelings; still less that they could be simultaneously filled with the sin of pride and the virtue of kindness. That, I suppose, is what they call mixed feelings.

While the rest of the audience is "stricken" and "hypnotized," Rex is first left "slack-jawed," and then begins "to tremble." Much of this is brought on by Miss McGuire, who "moves like a poem," though we are never told whether her poetry is lyrical moo goo gai pan or epic eggroll. Reed finds it a "heart-piercing experience," which shows how dangerous chopsticks can be in unskilled hands.

I could go on quoting forever, but must conclude with an excerpt from Reed's review of *Providence*, where this "often . . . confusing to comprehend [*sic*]" work is declared Resnais's "most
coherent and moving film. Pay attention to detail and allow it to
wash over you like a warm surf and you'll be rewarded." It takes
singular obtuseness not to recognize that paying attention to detail
is the exact opposite of letting something wash over you like
warm surf, but at least there can be little doubt about which of
those two approaches Reed takes in his criticism. And is there
anyone left—with the possible exception of Professor John Russell
Taylor of U.S.C.—who thinks that a mind so confounded by
words and images is capable of that clarity that is the minimum
requirement for any sort of cogent criticism?

# Masters of the Maladroit Metaphor

Today let us advert to matters of style, which are as much part
of the language as questions of grammar. More precisely, I wish
to examine metaphor and its role in our speaking and writing. A
simile, as you will recall, is a comparison including *like* or *as*—e.g.,
"He drinks like a fish" or "He is as sober as a judge." Both popular similes, and both, incidentally, open to scientific doubt. A metaphor, on the other hand, is a comparison that dispenses with
such linking terms and goes right to the point, e.g., "What's going
on in the tinderbox of your mind?" Or just, "What's going on in
your tinderbox?" Metaphor is more daring than simile, but also
more difficult to handle.

In a sense, even an ordinary word is a metaphor, because *dog* is
not actually a barking and tail-wagging creature but a combination of letters or phonemes symbolizing man's best friend, the
latter being a periphrasis or circumlocution that constitutes a type
of—often wordy or windy—metaphor. Bona fide metaphors have
become a very considerable ingredient of everyday speech. If we
say, "What's eating her?," we are using *eat* metaphorically for
*worry* or *bother*, without even realizing that we are using a metaphor, just as Molière's bourgeois gentleman spoke *prose* without
knowing it. Such metaphors are usually known as fossilized—

deeply embedded in the language, sometimes slangy, and often smacking of cliché.

At the other end of the scale from these demotic metaphors are others that likewise have public currency but require a certain erudition. Thus one must know some history to recognize that "the sick man of Europe" was, or (depending on one's outlook) is, Turkey, or that the "nation of shopkeepers" were the English, as Adam Smith defined them to the delight of their French enemies, not so unshopkeeperish themselves. A good deal of slang is nothing but metaphor, e.g., *switch-hitter* or *AC-DC* for a bisexual, or *buying a pig in a poke* for an uninformed acquisition. But the metaphors that concern me here are the ones we make up in our daily speaking and writing. To a very large extent, they make our conversation and correspondence alive with our personality, or dead from the lack of it.

I. A. Richards has conveniently named the thing that is being compared to something else in a trope (or image) the "tenor," and the thing that does the comparing the "vehicle." So in Francis Thompson's "The Hound of Heaven," God is the tenor; and the heavenly hound, the vehicle. Nothing makes a metaphor or simile more effective than when tenor and vehicle come from points far apart yet unite into a perfectly fitting whole. You would not ordinarily think of God as a canine, but the way he pursues, clings to, and insists on rescuing the sinner, even against the unfortunate's errant will, makes God into a perfect Saint Bernard or good German shepherd. That is a much more powerful image than, say, "the honey of her lips" for a kiss. A kiss is experienced as sweet, which conjures up sugar or honey to the most plodding mind. Tenor and vehicle are too proximate to come together with the wonder of the unexpected and the pleasure of the appropriate. For a trope must be both astonishing and apt—must make sense. When Sylvia Plath writes in "The Stones," "Love is the uniform of my bald nurse," we are not quite sure, even in context, who this nurse is and why she suffers from alopecia.

One can, in fact, make a perfect ass of oneself with metaphors and similes. Thus a current radio commercial begins: "Dance is taking the country by storm, and the eye of the storm is American Ballet Theatre." Now, the eye of the storm—or, more properly, hurricane, for your ordinary storm is eyeless—is a place of great calm, where nothing at all is happening. Surely that is not what

ABT wished its ad agency to convey. Yet it is the very thing that ignoramuses keep doing when blindly striving to be creative. So Rex Reed wrote about a musical based on *Gone With the Wind* that it "sank . . . like the *Hindenburg.*" This was written, of course, before the movies (one of his chief sources of learning) taught our scholar otherwise.

Among the great master abusers of the trope are the aforesaid Rex Reed and Clive Barnes, and it is always instructive and hilarious to learn from them how not to use metaphors and similes. I pick at random Reed's March 8, 1978, column about the movie versions of *A Little Night Music* and *A Doll's House.* Here we read about a count played "as a dragon with the vanity of a peacock and the brains of a pea." True, the progression from *peacock to pea* is aurally pleasing, but the image is wretched. "Vanity of a peacock" is to imagery what a twenty-times-used razor blade is to shaving; and "brain of a pea" is nonsense. *Pea-brained,* which Reed is dimly harking back to, makes sense as a hyperbole meaning a brain the size of a pea; it does not mean the brain of a pea, which is inconceivable.

Next we read (or should it be *reed?*) about "the regal aplomb of a dowager empress stoned on Ovaltine." Reed is exemplarily insensitive to the denotation (never mind the connotation) of words: *regal* as applied to an empress is at the very least a redundancy, at worst a comedown. But why would a regal empress be stoned on Ovaltine? And how would that affect her aplomb? It certainly wouldn't make it regal. Presently we are told that the way Liz Taylor plays a famous actress, "it is impossible to see why so many brigands drew so many swords and fought so many duels for her affections." Here one thinks at first that *brigands* is some sort of tricky metaphor, until one realizes—there being nobody like a brigand in the film's action or dialogue—that Reed takes the word to designate something glamorously military, like dragoons or brigadiers.

The movie is next described as "one of the few stage musicals to make a successful crossing to the more literal shores of film." This is the last word in infelicitous imagery. To begin with, adapting a stage show into a movie resembles a sea voyage no more than does any other hazardous undertaking; the metaphor is both vague and trite. But what about those "more literal shores"? If Reed had the rudiments of erudition, one might surmise that he is punning on *littoral*, i.e., pertaining to a shore. But that pun would land him in a flagrant pleonasm. So "literal shores" must have something to do with film being, for Reed, a more literal medium than theater, whatever that means. But, then, how does a shore get to be literal? To work properly, an image must make full sense on both levels—as tenor and as vehicle.

About *A Doll's House* we read: "Filmed in Norway, it has a Breughel snowscape where the white lie of Nora's life is reflected back at her in every wintry Scandinavian vista." Norway may be a bit far afield for a Fleming like Bruegel (Breughel, by the way, is a now rejected spelling), but let that pass. "Reflected back" is grossly redundant (the *re-* already means "again" or "back"), and it is unclear how that *one* snowscape can contain *every* Scandinavian vista. But to think that a Norwegian snowscape can be a metaphor for a "white lie" is simply absurd.

Finally, we are informed that women's lib has turned the actress Delphine Seyrig "from a lovely light into a homely grouse." We have here that common failing, mixed metaphor. Light can fade into shadow or darkness, but not into a grouse, which is what, say, a bird of paradise could do. The components of a metaphor have to function within the same frame of reference.

But enough of this unthinking Reed and on to an even grander master, Clive Barnes, and his first review upon accession to his new eminence as critic for the *New York Post*, which he declared to be the pinnacle of his career. Clearly he labored with special love and care on his debut piece. The opening sentence reads: "Neil Simon's *Chapter Two* stormed into the Imperial Theater last night on waves of applause that sounded like the clatter of massed celestial typewriters." This metaphor, simile, or whatever it is, is not only mixed—it is minced, scrambled, electrolyzed at the very least. The combination of *stormed* and *waves* is already an uneasy yoking; but why should applause sound like typewriters (which have a different rhythm), and why, above all, should there be massed typewriters in heaven—hardly the music of the spheres? Barnes must have gotten his misbegotten trope from the advertisement for *Chapter Two*, which depicts a typewriter—an apt source for someone whose criticism reads like advertising. Next we gather that Mr. Simon "is walking barefoot on the heart. The heart is his own." To walk barefoot on a heart sounds murderously sadistic, and unhygienic besides; to walk on one's own heart must give the giggles even to a contortionist, to say nothing of a prose stylist. And what does such a walk, barefoot or shod, mean? Bare-faced shoddiness?

"All artists, worth the digestion, are cannibals." I guess that *cannibals* refers to the artists' feeding on, making use of, the people they know; but what is that "worth the digestion"? Presumably "worth our digesting them"; but the shift from *our* digestion to *their* cannibalism, both eating metaphors, implies, confusingly, some sort of connection between audience and playwright that the sense does not bear out. A character who provides another with unsuitable women to go out with is said to be "supplying . . . dates that prove only too pitted." This ineptly punning image says exactly the opposite of what Barnes intends: a pitted date is actually preferable to an unpitted one; moreover, there is no way in which a date can be *too* pitted. But puns can lead Barnes even farther astray, as when he mentions Simon's "carefully ironed irony." We can hardly imagine a playwright taking an iron to his wit; if we can, however, it means that the wit will be flattened out and lie, or fall, flat.

And so it goes, bad metaphors combining naturally with bad grammar and usage—for example, *more importantly* for *more important.* Thus in a review (April 10, 1978), Barnes wrote of the "death of he [*sic*] who plays the king." Poor imagery is not unrelated to subliteracy; it is, on a higher level, what bad grammar, usage, and pronunciation are on a somewhat lower one.

# Film Fluffs

The Academy Awards radiate as much bad usage as they do bad taste. The 1979 Oscar telecast was no exception. I could not begin to get Jack Valenti's and Laurence Olivier's scrambled metaphors down on paper; for all I know, they may have been commercials for Mixmaster. But here is something from Gregory Peck, an ex-president of the Academy: "at a time when worldwide interest in films and filmmaking has never been higher." The construction is utterly illogical: "a time when" refers to this time, now, whereas "never been higher" takes us, contradictorily, back to the past. Instead of hanging together, the statement hangs itself.

Peck should have said, "at a time when interest is higher than ever."

Leo Jaffe, the chairman of Columbia Pictures, was heard to say, "All segments of the industry are responsible people." Not when it comes to language. A *segment* is at best an abstraction, at worst a thing, whereas *people* are living beings, acting in this statement as responsible individuals. Hence one should say, doubtful as the proposition may be, that all segments of the industry "are staffed with" responsible people or "comprise" them, which would not reduce those worthies to fragments of something inanimate. Conversely, Walter Lanz referred to "Universal Pictures, with whom I have been associated," although a corporation, however warm the feelings it inspires, is an *it* with *which* one is associated.

Michael Cimino, the director of the vastly overrated *The Deer Hunter*, thanked somebody "most especially." Now, *especial*, a somewhat old-fashioned but still usable synonym for *special* (its sonorousness is certainly seductive), resembles such adjectives as *unique* and *perfect* in not having a superlative. Can you imagine sending a letter by most special delivery? Maureen Stapleton spoke about "striving to improve the media"; she meant film, which is a *medium.* Robin Williams perpetrated a gross error in "about he and Betty Boop."

But even speaking about the awards from the outside seems to bring out the worst in people. Thus the *New York Times* of April 12 quoted the following from Andrew Young, our strong man at the UN, in reference to *Coming Home* and *The Deer Hunter:* "These motion pictures help to assure political feasibility of an aggressive diplomatic policy that shuns warfare." "Motion pictures" is a trifle grand for what we now call movies, films, or just pictures, but "help to assure political feasibility" is grandiose jargon that means nothing more than *make possible.* And what on earth is "an aggressive diplomatic policy that shuns warfare" ? Surely not economic sanctions and not, I should hope, threats of military intervention. Such saber rattling is risible when it is not actually dangerous. How, in any case, do those movies achieve any such thing? For *Coming Home,* you could say, at best, that it makes war look unattractive; the superman hero of *The Deer Hunter* emerges even more glorious and noble from the most unspeakable (and preposterous) horrors. What aggressive but war-shunning policy does this film help to assure? Note, by the way, that "help assure" would have been quite sufficient but, of course, less orotund.

Those who write about movies seem particularly accident-prone when it comes to using words. I don't know whether there is a causal relationship here—whether prolonged staring at large screens blinds one to the needs of little words or whether only persons who have withdrawn from (or been abandoned by) language devote themselves to film and writing about film. Consider, for example, two specimens from a recent column (April 16, 1979) by Andrew Sarris, a film critic of the *Village Voice* and an associate professor in the film department of Columbia University. He writes about "need[ing] no encouragement to enthuse" about Greta Garbo. But how about some discouragement for the verb *enthuse*, a back-formation from the noun *enthusiasm* that should never have been formed and should certainly not be backed?

Sarris also writes that the echoes of *Sunset Boulevard* in *Fedora* are "enough to keep [him] reasonably entranced." This manages to be both infelicitous and inept: infelicitous because *reasonably* comes from *reason*, which differs vastly from an emotional experience, of which entrancement is a prime example; inept because entrancement is something so sweeping and all-encompassing that to limit it in any way is stylistically absurd. To be sure, one can figure out how Sarris fell into this trap: he must have begun with something like "sufficiently entranced" and then started looking for a livelier adverb with which to perk up the phrase. But a sort of linguistic tone-deafness led him to this catachresis.

Our critic might, conceivably, argue that "reasonably entranced" is an oxymoron, a two-word paradox like "the absent present" or "the living dead." But it isn't: though *reasonably* and *entranced* diverge considerably, they are not true opposites; more important, their conjunction does not yield a powerful image like "the living dead." It is simply unsuccessful straining after originality of the kind that can come off resoundingly, as when John Gregory Dunne speaks of "implacable ignorance" in one of the pieces in his collection, *Quintana & Friends.* At first, one assumes that ignorance cannot be implacable—that is to say, inexorable or unalterable. The ignorant person can be enlightened except if he is totally stupid or demented. The Catholic Church has the beautiful hypallage (or transferred epithet) "invincible ignorance," referring to a state of paganism that is forgivable because the word of Christ was not available to it; Dunne, a Catholic, must know and may have been inspired by that phrase. But his is just as good; on closer inspection, it suggests the kind of stubborn refusal to learn that is common even among sane people, as saneness is adjudicated nowadays.

But this same John Gregory Dunne, who often writes perceptively and elegantly about film, is also capable of some remarkable lapses. Take the essay from which I just quoted, "Pauline," an evaluation of Pauline Kael's film criticism, in the course of which several other film critics, myself included, have to take their lumps. (The charges are more amusing than just, but that need not concern us here.) In a mere seven pages, we find a number of linguistic or stylistic flaws, of which I adduce the most flagrant.

Says Dunne of Kael: "At times she seems less a critic than a den mother, swatting her favorites gently when they get out of line, lavishing them with attention, smothering them with superlatives for their successes." What happened here? Dunne was aiming for a triple-decker parallel, in which Kael is "swatting her favorites," "lavishing them," and "smothering them." But rhetorical afflatus lulled grammatical vigilance: you "lavish attention on someone" rather than (as might have been possible a few centuries ago) "lavish someone with attention." To maintain the parallelism, "indulging them with attention," for instance, would have served.

Next, Dunne castigates Kael for "her search for cosmology in the entertaining rubbish of *Jaws* and *The Godfathers* [sic]," but surely *cosmology* is not the right word here. The closest definition to what Dunne has in mind would be "a branch of philosophy dealing with the origin, processes, and structure of the universe." Now, it is obvious that hyperbole is intended, but even hyperbole is subject to appropriateness. What Pauline Kael reads into such potboilers is excessive moral, social, or aesthetic significance, for which *cosmology* is too scientific or insufficiently metaphysical. Dunne probably started out with "cosmic significance," where *cosmic* has the sense of universal pertinence, but found it a trifle hackneyed; so he made a leap into metonymy that ended in a pratfall.

Similarly, Dunne accuses Kael's "Raising Kane" of being "suffused with that protocol of banality that flourishes west of Central Park—Hollywood the Destroyer." "West of Central Park" is very clever: it is where Kael and many of her adherents used to live, yet this *west* is nowhere near far enough to bring one within seeing distance of what happens in Hollywood. But why *protocol*? The most relevant definition would be "ceremony and etiquette observed by diplomats, heads of state," and the like; and though the Kaelites can be mocked as self-appointed potentates, Hollywood baiting is more a sport or a pastime—at worst a passion or an aberration—than ceremony or etiquette. I would guess that Dunne first wrote "prototypical banality," then found that too obvious, and that he liked the absurdity of "ceremonial banality." Unfortunately for him, though, *protocol* suggests certain procedures and obeisances that conjure up irrelevant bureaucratic or courtly scenes and blunt his barb.

"The flaw was in them, not the community" is merely careless for "not *in* the community"; "cinema verite" for *cinéma vérité*, like "manqué litterateur" for *littérateur manqué*, is bad French, and not much better in an English context. "Scenarist Penelope Gilliatt" is inferior to *"the* scenarist Penelope Gilliatt"; "verb tense" is redundant for *tense*, which only a verb can have.

The most unpleasant grammatical error (about which I wrote in my last column) is "one of those film buffs who has seen everything and understood nothing." Obviously, the omnivorous incomprehension characterizes all "those film buffs," of whom Kael is only one; hence the verb must be in the plural: "who have seen everything."

Yet lest I be the only film critic who comes out innocent, let me cite an error from my critique of *The Innocent,* in my *National Review* column of March 16, 1979, as spotted by the perspicacious Rabbi Lyle Kamlet, who writes: " 'Among richly homoerotic overtones, Visconti's slender talent registers for the last time with a lurid, evanescent flicker.' . . . Shouldn't that first word be *amid*, not *among?"* Quite so.

# LINGUISTS AND OTHER ACADEMICS

# The Waning of O'Neil

One of the serious threats to the future of English comes from certain college and university professors who undermine the teaching of the language from within. One such professor is Wayne O'Neil, who, after the "Dick Cavett" show of December 20, 1978, on which we both appeared, rebuked me for wasting this column on unimportant matters. Heeding his warning, I address myself to a more suitable target: Wayne O'Neil.

Professor O'Neil, of MIT and Harvard, perceives Standard English as a tool by means of which the ruling capitalist middle class (as he sees it) keeps the lower orders subjugated in their lowly station. Accordingly, Standard English is merely a shibboleth, a linguistic method of identifying an outsider. As O'Neil puts it, "The enterprise of making lower-class speakers over into middle-class speakers was never meant to be successful except insofar as it has been necessary from time to time to recruit some few of them into the middle class." As you can see, this is the conspiracy theory of American education, and it is, I believe, a grievous insult to a good many hardworking English teachers who struggle against overwhelming odds to teach their pupils Standard English, which is simply the language that evolved from diverse sources into a norm. This norm enables people of goodwill and average or better intelligence to communicate more effectively, sometimes even beautifully.

As O'Neil indicated in answer to an inquiry, he corrects only the spelling and punctuation of his students. This raises the immediate question: Why a standardized spelling and punctuation without standardized grammar and syntax? Surely intelligibility depends equally on all four. Besides, how can you expect a student to punctuate correctly without knowing the syntax that dictates punctuation? Third, does O'Neil himself know how to punctuate? I quote from "Properly Literate" (*Harvard Educational Review*, May 1970): "Schools can build on not destroy a child's native literacy."

It would be nice if people like O'Neil had first learned what they set about to disparage. The very next sentence of the essay I first quoted from ("The Politics of Bidialectalism," in *The Politics of*

*Literature*, Kampf and Lauter, editors) declares: "The main purpose was indeed part of the main purpose of popular education,
i.e., to render school children skilled enough to be exploited but
finally uneducated, used to failure, and alienated enough to oppose their exploitation. . . ." Note that Professor O'Neil means *too
alienated to oppose their exploitation* or *alienated enough to be unable to
oppose their exploitation*; but he writes the exact opposite.

Consider now the following sentence from "Why *Newsweek*
Can't Explain Things," an article O'Neil published in the *Radical
Teacher*, June 1976: "More significantly—and this should be noted
at the outset before we list them—none of the explanations or
even the pieces of them has a shred of scientific or statistical
support in the [*Newsweek*] article or in fact." Observe that the first
"them," brought in rather too early for us to make much sense of
it, is plural and implies that the subject of the sentence is "explanations," but the predicate "has" is singular and implies that the
subject is "none." And the sentence should begin *More significant*,
not "More significantly," the former being the correct ellipsis for
*what is more significant*. "Or even the pieces of them" is unclear.

Take another sentence from the same article: "Let us suppose—
for the sake of discussion—that students at all levels are in fact
writing worse—presuming for the moment that we can character-
ize 'worse' in a nontrivial way—than they used to and that it is
getting worse and worse." You will note, if you are not too
dazzled by those dashes (with which O'Neil litters his prose as
schoolgirls of a bygone era used to litter their postcards), that the
"it" has absolutely no antecedent; if "writing" was meant to be
that antecedent, it would have had to be used as a noun.

Professor O'Neil's English tends to be sloppy, faddish, jargon-
ridden, and just plain bad. In an essay contributed to W. Feinberg's *Equality and Social Policy*, and ostensibly advocating Kro-
potkinian anarchism, O'Neil (who, curiously enough, changed his
name from Knudsen) commits atrocities such as "the overall well-
being of all" (for *universal well-being*), "the species character and the
species environment," "at any point in time" (this from an anti-
Nixon radical; but, then, he also uses the obsolescent, slightly
fuddy-duddy "learnt" for *learned*), "to correctly legitimate" (split
infinitive and redundancy; *to legitimate* is quite enough).

In his report on the Dartmouth Seminar of 1966 (*Harvard Educational Review*, Spring 1969), O'Neil mentions the "squalor that the

American Indian has been forced to" (either *forced into* or *reduced to*), "audial things" (no such word), "the reader or beholder have" (the "or" demands the singular *has*; were there an *and* in its place, the plural would, of course, be correct); he also, as usual, commits glaring errors of punctuation. In an article entitled "Comes the Revolution"—a revolution that O'Neil tries to hasten as best he can even in the brackish backwaters of the *Harvard Graduate School of Education Association Bulletin*, where the piece was printed—we find things like "where they're at"; "intriguing" for *fascinating*; "we do not understand at all well," which must read either *at all* or *well*, but not both. Well, at least O'Neil makes clear in "Properly Literate" that "you needn't be able to read to be properly literate."

Again, in his screed against *Newsweek*'s piece on student illiteracy, O'Neil writes of American education that "the trap has closed in again," the trap being the reaction to Kropotkin in the classroom. Now, whereas people can close *in* on someone or something, a trap closes *on* its victim, or is simply *sprung*. And bad usage has a way of going hand in hand with faulty logic; in the same essay, O'Neil writes that "it has become important for the ruling class to exclude the potentially radicalizing elements of higher education from the colleges. Thus everywhere along the scale of education there is a relentless march toward the basics." Aside from the mixed metaphor (a march along a scale is precarious indeed), why should a return to basics disqualify radicals from success in higher education? Can the brilliant minds that will transform society be unable to learn the three R's?

One reason, then, for O'Neil's eagerness to dispense with grammar, syntax, and such is, I dare say, his own inability to cope with them; charity, clearly, begins at home. Consider, too, that most learned journals, even (or especially) in these sorry times, practice some editing, which accounts for some improvement of their contributors' English. It would be instructive to see what the unedited manuscripts of our writers and academics look like—but I digress. What I want to get to is a probably even more compelling reason for O'Neil's approach to the English language.

From his writings and utterances, I conclude that Professor O'Neil considers language in general a political act, and he has certainly turned, or tried to turn, the classroom into a political battleground. As he puts it in his essay in the Feinberg volume, "The American educational system is rotten because the society from which it comes is rotten, built as it is on basic principles that lead people to exploit the labor and talents of others, indeed demand that exploitation, that celebrate the profit motive above all others, and that require the overwhelming and increasing majority of people to work at jobs destructive of mind and of body," and so, unsyntactically, on and on, along lines that turn out to be, on closer inspection, not Marxist or Socialist but downright anarchic. "Let them learn to read," he writes about young students in "Properly Literate." "Don't teach them. Let it emerge as they go about talking and telling of the riches they already possess." To listen to O'Neil and his likes, students are so full of wisdom as they enter school that they really don't need any schooling; after all, their reading skills will emerge while they're talking and telling. The riches they already possess will bring them to a pretty pass—alas, will account for all those "educated" people who today go around saying things like "between you and I," a usage that O'Neil wholeheartedly condones.

What is at work here is a kind of moral cowardice. If you haven't the guts to fight on the political barricades, where the stakes are high and you might pay with your hide, you cravenly undermine the teaching of Standard English in the classroom, all the while pretending that you are on those barricades. Every ungrammatical usage you endorse, every bit of syntax you don't require, every rule of rational communication you flout is a blow struck for the liberation of the masses—or so you imagine. Unfortunately, there is no evidence that organized and cosseted ignorance leads to human liberation; it does, however, lead to diminished communication, increased confusion, and lost confidence. O'Neil claims that asking a student to learn Standard English is like asking someone who knows how to walk to learn to hop because he'll be richer for it. Anyone who can seriously come up with such an invidious, misleading analogy is the worst kind of political hophead.

## Pressure From Below

**W**e are all in the gutter, but some of us are looking at the stars," wrote Oscar Wilde about life. The same applies to language: we all make mistakes (somebody just wrote in to point out a badly constructed sentence in one of my columns), but some of us at least try to maintain standards. It is not easy, and the best may stumble. Thus the worthy Irving Howe writes, on the front page of the *New York Times Book Review* (April 9, 1978), about "main protagonists." Now, the protagonist is the main actor in something and has, since Greek times, always been used in the singular. "Protagonists" is incorrect (unless you are referring to the protagonists of two or more dramas), and "main protagonists" (main main actors) is redundant to boot. A double-barreled error, but even the ablest among us, harried by the exigencies of rapid-fire journalism, are not immune to lapses.

What worries me more is abysmal illiteracy: in the gutter and looking at the sewers. David Sheff of *New West* sent me a good-sized National Airlines poster the other day, depicting a charming flight attendant (formerly stewardess) and bearing this caption emblazoned in mighty letters: "Watch us shine with more flight's to Houston." Be honest: did your jaw drop when you read that "flight's"? I showed the poster to a couple of civilized friends, and it took them some time and quite a bit of prodding to notice the howler. So there you have it: half the population (I guess) thinks that any plural ending in *s* requires an apostrophe, and the other half stands idly by without squirming, if, in fact, it even notices.

Where does it all come from? Who is the chief culprit? Surely the schools, both lower and higher, and the distemper of the times, which influences them. Let me give you some horrible examples. Jim Deutsch of Greenville, Mississippi, has just sent me a Xerox copy of a letter published in *American Studies International* (Winter 1977), in which Toby Fulwiler protests what seems to be a fairly obvious plagiarism of a paper he wrote. But he twice misspells "plagiarize" as *plagerize*, which the editors duly note with a *sic.* If Mr. Fulwiler is that concerned with plagiarism, he might at least ascertain how it is spelled, especially since he is the director of freshman English at Michigan Technological University. It is clear, furthermore, that he knows neither Latin *(pla-giārius:* a kidnapper) nor any major modern language in which the spelling of the word is made manifest by the pronunciation, e.g., French *(plagiat)* or German *(Plagiat).* But it may be asking too much of a contemporary director of freshman English that he know other languages; English should be part of his competence.

Or need it be? Two readers, no less (Hortense Berman and Thomas A. Long), have sent me identical clippings from *UC This Week*, a University of Cincinnati faculty and staff newspaper. The May 21, 1978, issue summarizes a talk by William Lasher, an associate professor of English, chairman of the committee on linguistics, and director of undergraduate studies in English. Professor Lasher adduced two sentences—"we was at the ball game last night " and "Mary had five card"—that he called clear and logical attempts to simplify the language.

I quote: "In the first example, Lasher says, the speaker has decided that the distinction between 'was' and 'were' is insignificant and has chosen 'was,' no matter if the subject is singular or plural." Note the assumption that the speaker consciously "decided" to make a simplifying choice. How about the supposition that the speaker was an illiterate ignoramus who neither knew nor cared to know better? But to go on: "The second example is what Lasher calls Black English, a social dialect of American English. In it the speaker drops the 's' from 'cards' because the five already indicates more than one." And Lasher proceeded, at least by strong implication, to belittle those who would consider the above speakers ungrammatical just because they violate what he patronizingly called "the experts' rule." For Lasher, "The people who say 'was' for 'were' or drop the 's' have a grammar that describes the relationship between sound and meaning in their cultures."

Why should we consider some, usually poorly educated, subculture's notion of the relationship between sound and meaning? And how could a grammar—any grammar—possibly describe that relationship? Grammar exists mainly to clarify meaning. *Five* does indeed indicate plurality, but the final *s* confirms it. After all, the speaker may have said "a fine card" or "a five card," and it is the final *s* that ensures that we have not misheard him. So, too, we may be uncertain whether we heard, say, *he* or *we* until the *were* dispels our doubt concerning who was at the ball game.

There is more to it, though. Maintaining these alleged niceties links our language to that of the giants of the English tongue who preceded us, all those great writers and speakers who were—not was—in the ball game that counts: the great struggle to use English as clearly and beautifully as possible. We do not wish to dissociate ourselves from them, lose familiarity with their mode of utterance on account of ignorant, misguided, or merely lazy creatures for whom making distinctions is an unnecessary effort. When Professor Lasher invokes the lofty principle of "making things easier," he serves up a typically disingenuous historical example: the shifting of *inpossible* to *impossible* from circa 1300 on. Yes, *inp* is harder to say than *imp*; but is *were* a greater strain on the tongue than *was*? Or, to put it differently: should we destroy a beautiful old building because it has decorative elements on its facade and replace it with a square box because the box is a simpler structure? Of course, there are people who tear down architectural masterpieces for just such reasons; but whatever they call themselves, *we* should call them barbarians and fight their vandalism in every way we can.

What this is, masquerading under the euphemism "descriptive linguistics" (and Lasher is far from being an isolated promulgator of it—in fact, he is part of a growing majority), is a benighted and despicable catering to mass ignorance under the supposed aegis of democracy, of being fair to underprivileged minorities—in other words, an irruption of politics where it has no business being.

Black English, for example, has a perfect right to exist; it just hasn't the right to change Standard English. The Lashers of this world are being illogical. Either Black English is something different from Standard English, in which case it is no more entitled to interfere with it than Portuguese is, or it is—or means to be—part of Standard English, in which case it has to espouse the latter's rules. And it will not do for the Lashers to say that they do not pass judgment, that they merely record changes in the language that may actually make the language "better" as it "adapts to

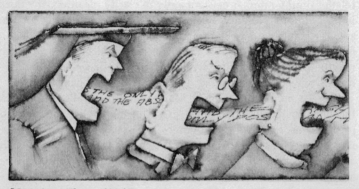

PRESSURE FROM ABOVE

cultural needs." What kind of cultural need is it that demands *we was* for *we were?* An uncultured, indeed anticultural, need, for the supporting of which Lasher deserves five kick in the pant.

There is, I believe, a morality of language: an obligation to preserve and nurture the niceties, the fine distinctions, that have been handed down to us. And the Lashers cannot wash their dainty hands and pretend that anyone who uses the term "language deterioration" displays "ignorance of the facts of language change." Well, there may actually be some ignorance at work in that, though not as Lasher perceives it: "deterioration of language" would be better than "language deterioration."

The pressure on language to deteriorate does not, however, come merely from below, from the "democratic" levelers. It comes also from above, from the fancy jargonmongers, idle game players, fashionable coteries for second-rate intellectuals. But more about them next time.

## Pressure From Above

Last time, I discussed corrupting pressures on language from below—from misguidedly democratizing sources. This time, let us consider the attack on language from above: obfuscation in the name of some supposedly higher philosophy, academicism, linguistic or literary arcanum being foisted on language by allegedly

exalted authorities. Here I do not mean simply mistakes—as when William Safire, in his commencement address at Syracuse University ("The Decline of the Written Word," May 13, 1978), declares: "We need not degenerate further from written English to verbal signals to sign language." Safire means *oral*, i.e., spoken, signals; verbal means anything pertaining to words, written or spoken—hence "written English" is also a series of "verbal signals."

No, I refer to the so-called superior wisdom destructively inflicted on language in an effort to rise above what "lesser" people consider correct, straightforward, and self-evident. A typical and highly offensive example of this was submitted to me by Philippe Perebinossoff of Plattsburgh, New York. It is a prospectus for a summer seminar being given at Brown University under the sponsorship of the National Endowment for the Humanities. These seminars, as my correspondent quotes, are "for college teachers . . . who are concerned primarily with increasing their knowledge of the subjects they teach."

The case in point is a seminar entitled "Theories of Reading: Fiction and Film," offered by Robert Scholes and Michael Silverman, both members of the Brown faculty. Scholes instructs "in the semiotics of fiction, in semiotic theory [etc.]—all for undergraduate students." Silverman teaches courses in "visual theory and film." The bibliography for the seminar, replete with texts by structuralists and semiologists, also features movies by Robert Altman, Bernardo Bertolucci, and Nick Ray. Lacking space for the whole prospectus, I quote its essence:

The engagement of reader, text, and culture in the act of reading points to the constant play of two elements over the face of the third; and this play of movement we would see as semiotic activity.

We intend the seminar members to read a number of examples of current theory, to read some prose passages and to see some films. . . . We do not want them to come up with "readings" of stories and films in the traditional sense; the substantive notion of "a reading" is opposed to our more participial sense of reading. . . . We will at all times read a "primary" text *through* a theoretical text. We hope in this to avoid the notion that the theory of reading and the practice of reading can be divorced. [Surely, what Professors Scholes and Silverman have joined together, no man would be rash enough to put asunder!] Those not conversant with recent theory of reading will not

acquire it in isolation from texts, but will at the very least be led to
posit a dialectical relationship between texts. Thus a Lawrence story
will be read through Todorov's *Poetics of Prose*, Bertolucci's *Before the
Revolution* will be read ["Read any good movies lately?" "No, but I've
seen the books."] through Althusser on Brecht.

Now, it may be that this playing of two elements over the face
of the third comes down to not much more than viewing films,
reading fiction, and also consulting some critical works. But note
the horrible obfuscation of this "reading through other readings,"
these "positings of dialectical relationships between texts." Amid
all that "semiotic activity" and the embargo on "readings in the
traditional sense" will anyone see *through* to the books and
movies? But to go on:

> The aim is not to make the theoretical text a transparent gloss or aid
> [no danger of that, I dare say] to the understanding of the "primary"
> text (thus inevitably producing new "readings" of the primary text),
> but to help us situate the text (both theoretical and "primary") within
> the area of something that can be read, while simultaneously under-
> taking to question the relationship between texts and our relation to
> them. Ideally, we would like at the end of eight weeks to have reached
> the point in our work in which a seminar member might undertake to
> read Todorov through Lawrence, or to theorize his own position as a
> reader through an examination of *Before the Revolution*.

Just as there are some people from whom I would not buy a
used car, there are certain professors from whom I refuse to buy
this secondhand semiology—not that it would be much better
new. Even without being able to make sense out of all this taut-
ologizing, highfalutin jargon, obnubilation, and deadwood, I am
dead certain that I have nothing to gain from reading Todorov
through Todorov, much less through D. H. Lawrence. And
whereas I would be happy to assess the artistic value of Bertolucci's second film (in my opinion, minimal), I would not, while
in the possession of a shred of sanity, wish to theorize my own
position on it as a reader through Althusser. Rather than that, I
would even watch the movie through a bunch of women refusing
to take off their hats.

Now for a few further caveats from our pundits: "We must
stress that we do intend, in any case, to stress the differences
between fiction and film . . . there is a clear difference, for exam-

ple, in [sic] reading a novel in one's study and viewing a film in a public place." O profundity! Could one have arrived at this wisdom without viewing it through Todorov and Althusser? I seriously doubt it. But onward with Scholes and Silverman: "Since one of us is a specialist in prose narrative, the other a specialist in film, our approach to the material will not be fully congruent (this would seem to us a distinct advantage)." Perish the thought of anything so unstructuralist as congruence, so unsemiotic as clarity! Rather, the students will be expected to read Scholes through Silverman, and ideally, if one dare hope it after a mere eight weeks, even Silverman through Scholes. Note also that wonderful "We must stress that we do intend . . . to stress." I wonder: do two stresses equal one distress?

And here at last, as stressed by Scholes and Silverman, is the promised end:

> (1) To establish that the reader of fiction must himself be activated in dramatistic terms, set into motion and theorized; (2) that the cinematic viewer must give over his passivity, undertake the more strenuous activity of reading, while analyzing what this does to his relation to the text; (3) that the use of a by now widespread body of semiotic material on the place [sic] of the reader-viewer will facilitate a re-thinking of old critical positions.

So in order to view (I mean, read) an Altman movie or a Hemingway story (pardon me, a "primary" text) I must be dramatistically activated, set into motion, and theorized; I must read while analyzing my relationship to the text (a bit onerous for someone already spinning like a top from all that activation); and I must use a widespread body of semiotic material while dramatistically whirling about in one place—the place allotted to the reader-viewer. All this will immeasurably facilitate my rethinking (with or without a hyphen) and is sure to jolt me out of any old position as a sitter-reader or sitter-viewer that I might have eased myself into in my outmoded and benighted, dramatistically unactivated state.

If I consecrate all this space to Scholes and Silverman, it is because the woods are full of them, various endowments sponsor them, and your tax dollars and the English language have to pay for them. In the place of the three R's, the new education has posited the three S's: structuralism, semiotics, stultification.

Look now at a more obvious disaster wrought by the new higher philosophizing. Mrs. M. C. (I am deeply sorry that legal reasons forbid my naming names), of a Dade County, Florida, college, has sent me a Xerox copy of the memo from her division director that lists his reasons for denying her tenure as an instructor of freshman composition. I quote:

> She holds some tenets regarding her role as an English teacher which . . . does [sic] not lend itself to freedom of thought and exchange [of what?] for students because students are too busy looking for the right answers, i.e. the truth. For example: "Language (English) is precise. . . . I want my students to be precise when they write. They should not use one word when there is a better (more precise) word to say what they mean." This principle ignores two basic considerations: A. Denotative definitions of English words can vary from one to ten (10) or more definitions. Very few English words, usually nouns, have less [correctly: *fewer*] than two meanings. [Actually, quite a few leap to mind; for example, nincompoop, numskull, ignoramus, cretin, division director.] B. Connotative definitions are as many as there are people. They are functions of our perceptual field, our view of the world, and are based on our experiences and our psychological imprinting. Hardly precise. This belief is a major guiding principle for Mrs. C.

When you get into the higher reaches of semantics, epistemology, textual explication, and semiology, seven or more types of ambiguity doubtless creep into almost every statement. But while you are writing a simple freshman English composition in Dade County, there is no reason for not hitting your simple point Dade center. A teacher must be propaedeutic before turning heuristic; a student must learn precise, unambiguous expression before he can start comtemplating the relativity of the universe and all its components. Or, as they used to say in my school days, you must know the rules before you can break them. Breaking them, in any case, is for shrewd and sophisticated writers, usually of fiction. Otherwise, the rules are still the most practical solution.

So, you see, the language is being attacked from above by the relativists and overcomplicators, from below by the democratic levelers. And, of course, there is overlapping: demotic ignorance plays into the hands of pseudoscientific mumbo jumbo, and structural linguistics rushes to the defense of every popular distortion or misconception. Can the beleaguered middle survive? Perhaps, if you will reject the trends, and yield neither to ignorance nor to obfuscation.

# Compact With Computers

**H**ardly do I get through telling you about the dangerous shenanigans of one influential academic when my mail is bulging with matching horror stories contributed by readers. It seems that on the surface, the raving academics can be divided into the political maniacs and the technological fanatics. Underneath, the two species are closely related, as will be seen.

To start with one of the latter, let me quote from an article in the *Futurist* (August 1978), contributed by Gary Groth, of Riverdale, Maryland. "Illiterates with Doctorates: The Future of Education in an Electronic Age" was written by Peter H. Wagschal, director of the future-studies program at the University of Massachusetts at Amherst; currently, he is editing a collection of speeches from the "Learning Tomorrows" conference, to be published by Praeger. Wagschal argues that everyone concedes that student performance in the three R's is declining; the solution, however, is not "back to the basics." In the past, the print media (lovely phrase!) may have been needed for the achievement of "knowledge, communication and maybe even wisdom." Now "computers and video-cassettes have clearly put an end to all that." The written word has been superseded: "The present generation of computers can store more information in less space and communicate more quickly and reliably than any form of printed matter." Consider that the ultimate space in which information must be stored and processed is the inside of the skull. How are computers going to make craniums smaller—unless, of course, they turn the brain into a recessive organ.

Notice also the sneaking in of that unscientific phrase "more

COMPACT WITH COMPUTERS

... reliably." Why is it assumed that computers are more reliable than print? Presumably because a human writer may spread misinformation. But who feeds the computer its data? Or is it, like Kubrick's Hal, taking over thinking and decision making? Sure enough, Wagschal speaks of "generations" of computers, a term previously reserved for human beings—albeit also, you may recall, for vipers.

By the time Wagschal's four-year-old son grows up, the proud dad tells us, "there will be hardly any compelling reason for him to be able to read, write, and do arithmetic." Computers will "call up information instantly in response to the spoken word." Of course, in Wagschal's computerized dystopia even the spoken word may be in serious trouble; moreover, what questions does an illiterate ask of his computer? What is the big bang theory of the universe? What were the consequences of the Counter Reformation? What was James Joyce's contribution to the novel? How, if I needed to, would I spell "cat"?

Observe that when it comes down to the new "basics," what the computer dispenses is "information" rather than education. Let us assume that the computer is a faster working, more compact library. But just as today's students don't know how to use the library, tomorrow's will be helpless when confronting their tiny, unexercised, hopelessly sluggish minds. For information is *not* knowledge and wisdom, which are the ability to put the raw material of information to good use. Yet Wagschal is benighted enough to write that "books can offer only words and still photographs. . . . How much more would we know of Freud's thought and work if we had videotapes of his therapy sessions instead of only his books."

Well now, since Freud's sessions, alas, have not been taped, are we going to make tapes in which an actor or a computer impersonates Freud? And assuming even that a later generation of computers can, if not resurrect, at least reenact Sigmund Freud in mid-therapy, what good would watching this do the future ignoramus—say, young Wagschal, Jr.—playing with his mini- or microcomputer? Someone has to interpret for him what is happening, and that is just what books have been doing all along. But, his pop tells us, the printed word has "serious flaws"; a "book is inherently passive: You can ask it all the questions you want, but it simply cannot respond." But how much response can you get from a computer to the complicated questions that you simply cannot *ask*?

And now it all comes out: "Reading and writing are inherently solitary activities. You can't read or write a book and talk about it at the same time." Nothing, apparently, mixes more democratically than information and conversation. Relegate reading and writing with that other well-known solitary vice; like it, they are sure to make you go blind. But imagine now the democratic bliss of riding on a bus on which, aside from the usual creep with his tape deck blaring away, there will be a chap to your left studying loudly and chattily his veterinary science, while the woman to your right will be gleaning information on Tennessee Williams for her "Drama for Illiterates" course and periodically asking you what some word of two or three syllables means—unfortunately she left her language minicomputer at home.

And what according to Wagschal explains global illiteracy? That "the three R's are, by their very nature, tools of the affluent and elite [sic]. . . . Only a minority of the globe's population can afford the time and resources required to learn and use the three R's." But, of course, your Egyptian fellah, your Iranian shepherd, your Nicaraguan peon will have a wide variety of computers and videocassettes: the next generation of computers, between supplying the global illiterates with information, will also see to it that affluent elitism the world over be abolished and the millennium inaugurated. The timetable is already at hand: "audio technologies" are already competitive with the printed word; "video technologies are sure to be within a decade; and computer technologies will be within two decades."

At that time, "electronic media will make everything there is to know *universally* accessible to all people of the globe." Hang in there, young Wagschal: you may be a total illiterate until you get to be twenty-four, but what glories await you then! You will become an illiterate with universal knowledge.

Down with print, which, as Wagschal informs us, is *"inherently* centralized and elitist," and let us look forward to "21st-century America . . . a society in which knowledge, ability, and wisdom [will be] exceedingly widespread in a population that is substantially illiterate." If this were better—more pungently—written, you would think it was the modest proposal of some latter-day Swift; but no, it is the utter, pedestrian earnest of Professor Peter Wagschal of the University of Massachusetts at Amherst.

To equate potential knowledge (not even *actual*—for who will guarantee that our computerized illiterates will actually help themselves to the available technologies?) with wisdom is one of the most egregious enthymemes in the history of Western thought. Wisdom, I repeat, is the ability to put information to good use. But unfortunates like Wagschal make the democratic—or, rather, populist—error of assuming that anything that takes time and effort, intelligence and discrimination is ipso facto elitist and *"inherently* centralized." Yet isn't the computer the most centralized source of information? Whereas books can afford to be pluralistic and in disagreement with one another because they deal in opinions as much as in facts, the data banks of computers must be identical. If facts begin to differ according to whose computer they are on, they are no longer facts.

"Widespread wisdom" in a "substantially illiterate" society is possible if you mean by wisdom tradition, experience, laws, and moral codes. But the kind of wisdom Wagschal intends cannot exist without thought, and the one thing that computers do not foster any more than television does is the ratiocinative process. How, for example, are you going to teach poetry to illiterates with cassettes and microcomputers? How can you reduce the study of any art or philosophy to push-button facts? A good book can lead to a dialogue far more involving and exhaustive than can any of Wagschal's technologies. It allows you time to reflect; it also obliges the mind to make the effort known as thinking. But in a democracy, if the majority does not want to think—is perhaps incapable of thought—thinking becomes undemocratic, obsolete, and finally rejected, if not actually outlawed.

Several readers have sent me a UPI story on Stanley Berne and Arlene Zekowski, associate professors of English at Eastern New Mexico University, who, having published fifteen volumes between them (fiction, drama, poetry, criticism), have now come out with a book against English grammar and will soon tape their gospel of "grammarless language" for public television, which will then offer it to stations across the nation. Declares Berne: "We are concerned with the idea of expressing feelings. Arbitrary rules of grammar prohibit that." Pity the great writers of all time whose feelings were strangled in the cradle by grammar! And note also the sloppiness of Professor Berne's utterance: "the idea of" is sheer deadwood. Then comes the usual radical politics of language: "Grammar and spelling are the property of a once privileged minority class imposing its order on a willing majority," and so forth, ad nauseam.

"Arbitrary sentence structure is logical," chimes in Zekowski. If it is logical, how can it be arbitrary, I wonder. "But the brain isn't logical. You don't think in sentences." So which do you throw out? The incompetent or lazy brain that does not learn the grammar people everywhere have been fruitfully acquiring for centuries, or the grammar? Obviously, if logic is too hard for a soft brain, you throw out logic. Berne makes it quite clear: "The arbitrary rules are the cause of the decline . . . in English." And is it not written: if thy grammatical rule offend thee, pluck it out? To think that I always assumed that those arbitrary rules were created by consensus!

Now Zekowski posits advertisements, with their ungrammatical English, as models for all of us to emulate. She explains: "They are successful." Ah, there it is: if you have been unsuccessful with fifteen published volumes (fiction, drama, poetry, criticism), you can always try for celebrity by making obsolete the great imaginative works of the past. *Flectere si nequeo superos, Acheronta movebo.* But note that it is all done in grammatical English; without that, one could not even get on public television to jeer at grammar. Well, you can make almost as good a compact with a compact computer as with the devil; but will it be acceptable for future Faustuses to make, in blood, a mere cross?

# CERTIFIED INFERIORITY

PLAYING TENNIS WITHOUT A NET

# Playing Tennis Without a Net

The National Council of Teachers of English is about to debate once again at its 1979 annual meeting in New York a resolution passed in a 1974 business meeting of the Conference on College Composition and Communication that accepted as valid "all the regional, ethnic, and social dialects of American English." The C.C.C.C. voted, in other words, to make acceptable in schools and colleges any kind of English that until recently was called substandard, although the N.C.T.E. then added an equivocal codicil stating that there was "a distinction between spoken and written English." The document justifying this resolution is a special issue of the journal *College Composition and Communication* entitled "Students' Right to Their Own Language."

The first and most obvious flaw in all this is the N.C.T.E.'s jesuitical assumption that one can differentiate between spoken and written English—that one can tell students that "I be baaad" (meaning "I am good") is acceptable when spoken but inadequate when written. There is enough schizophrenia on the rampage in the world without nurturing further forms of it in the classroom. But the very ideas behind the resolution and the brochure that is meant to proselytize for them strike me as not a little absurd and, ultimately, pernicious.

The committee to which we owe the C.C.C.C. language statement consists of a baker's dozen of academics, apparently carefully chosen to represent both renowned and obscure institutions and to include women, blacks, Hispanics, and teachers at community colleges. Nothing could be more democratic. In the introduction to the eighteen-page double-column statement, the committee permits itself a rare irony: "Lack of reliable information . . . seldom prevents people from discussing language questions with an air of absolute authority." To prove their own authoritativeness, the committee members helped one of their number, Jenefer Giannasi (whose Christian name reads rather as if she didn't know how to spell it), compile a thirteen-page single-column bibliography, containing mostly items on sociolinguistics, descriptive linguistics, and such—my favorite being "Davis, Philip W.: *Modern Theories of Language*," which deals with "the theories of

Saussure, Hjelmslev, Bloomfield, the Post-Bloomfieldians, and the Prague School; tagmemics; Firthian linguistics; stratificational grammar; transformational generative grammar." Nevertheless, Miss Giannasi and her colleagues write things like "a controversy which must be faced before staff can react to students' needs," which is rather like what you hear from medical receptionists: "Doctor will see you now." Clearly, there are cases where neither Bloomfield nor the Post-Bloomfieldians, to say nothing of tagmemics, prove to be of much help.

But right at the beginning, our committee commits an error in logic that is considerable for such valiant structural linguists. The committee bemoans the fact that all kinds of people—"businessmen, politicians, parents, and the students themselves"—insist "that the values taught by the schools must reflect the prejudices held by the public." It soon becomes apparent that what these people want and agitate for through their representatives on various boards is nothing more or less than what has generally been called Standard English, which the committee prefers to call edited written English or edited American English (E.A.E.). In its democratic, pluralistic zeal, the committee obviously reprehends what I am still quite happy to call Standard English for being "Anglo" and ignoring, indeed affronting, the customs and needs of "the people," many of whom belong to black, Latin-American, or other ethnic groups. Yet, clearly, businessmen, politicians, parents, and students themselves (not to mention the historians, mathematicians, and nurses adduced earlier in the pamphlet) include a lot of people, probably at least as many as there are members of various ethnic groups. Why then should *their* traditions and demands be ignored?

The point, of course, is that everyone has a right to his ignorance and no one is compelled to become educated. But everyone is then also entitled to suffer the consequences of choosing not to become educated. This is very different, needless to say, from having been discouraged from becoming educated or from, worse yet, having been deliberately prevented from so becoming. But when I read our supposed educators' statement that "we need to discover whether our attitudes toward 'educated English' are based on some inherent superiority of the dialect itself or on the social prestige of those who use it," I begin to despair. Could anything be sadder than the fact that those quotation marks around educated English come from the pen of an educator—someone who ought to be proud of the fact that generations of educators have labored to develop and codify that English? Yet now the C.C.C.C.'ers act as if there were something fishy and indecent about all this, something to condescend to with quotation marks, because, as they later put it, it is merely the dialect of the middle class. The poor old middle class, by the way, gets it coming and going. After centuries of kicks from above, it can now look forward to centuries of kicks from below.

And we read on: "We need to ask ourselves whether our rejection of students who do not adopt the dialect most familiar to us is based on any real merit in our dialect or whether we are actually rejecting the students themselves, rejecting them because of their racial, social, and cultural origins." Not only is ignorance going to be defended on the sacred ground of the right to nonconformity, but also it will be upheld on the still more sacred grounds of antiracism and antielitism. Under the circumstances, it is not surprising to find our committee arguing forthwith that "Mary daddy home" is just as comprehensible and good as "Mary's daddy is at home" and that "the grammar of one American dialect may require 'he is' in the third person singular present tense; the grammar of another dialect may require 'he be' in that slot."

Of course, what is the use of arguing with English teachers who pronounce "Mary daddy home" equally clear as "Mary's daddy is at home"? The former concatenation of words (it would be preposterous to call it a construction) could just as easily mean "the home of Mary's daddy" or "Mary's daddy has gone home" or "Mary and daddy are at home" or God only knows what else. (Or perhaps I should write "Don't nobody but God know that," which our authors find "just as clear" and "in certain circum- stances [unspecified] more emphatic.") It may be true that we can gradually figure out from the context what was meant, but why should we have to make such an effort? And suppose the speaker were trying to discuss more complicated matters with that kind of grammar. Where would *that* conversation lead?

As for "I be," "you be," "he be," etc., which should give us all the heebie-jeebies, these may indeed be comprehensible, but they go against all accepted classical and modern grammars and are the product not of a language with roots in history but of ignorance of how language works. It may be a regrettable ignorance, innocent and touching, one that unjust past social conditions cruelly imposed on people. But it *is* ignorance, and bowing down to it, accepting it as correct and perhaps even better than established usage, is not going to help matters. On the contrary, that way lies chaos. The point is that if you allow this or that departure from traditional grammar, everything becomes permissible—as, indeed, it has become, which is why we are in the present pickle.

Here is what our C.C.C.C.'ers have to say about this: "Once a teacher understands the arbitrary nature of the oral and written forms, the pronunciation or spelling of a word becomes less important than whether it communicates what the student wants to say. In speech, *PO*lice communicates as well as po*LICE*, and in writing, 'pollice' is no insurmountable barrier to communication, although all three variations might momentarily distract a person unfamiliar with the variant." One difficulty with addressing oneself thoroughly to the absurdity of this pamphlet is that where every sentence, like the above, pullulates with logical and moral errors, one doesn't know where to begin with a rebuttal.

To start with, what does the crucial but glided-over term "less important" mean to the committee? Should pronunciation and spelling mistakes be ignored entirely? Almost entirely? On alternate Tuesdays only? Should they be punished with merely one stroke of the ferule, as opposed to two for physical assault on the teacher? Furthermore, why should people have to be distracted even momentarily by having to figure out what other people are saying? There are situations in which these could cause serious damage. But, above all, language is not just a matter of communication. It is a way of expressing one's fastidiousness, elegance, and imaginativeness; it is also a way of displaying one's control over a medium, just as a fine horseman displays his horsemanship by the way he sits in the saddle and handles his horse. Even a person who desperately hangs on to the mane of his mount might make it from point A to point B, but that doesn't make him an equestrian.

The basic contradiction in which the committee wallows is this: on the one hand, we are told that blacks and Chicanos and other minorities cannot be expected to know and speak the "dialect" of the established "Anglo" middle class and that we must have sympathy and respect for their dialects; on the other hand, we are told that these youngsters are just as bright as anybody else and can learn correct E.A.E. as easily as anyone. I am willing to give credence to either of these assertions, but I find it difficult to accept *both*. Thus we find our C.C.C.C.'ers declaring on page 7 that "dialect itself is not an impediment to reading" and "cannot be posited as a reason for a student's failure to be able to read E.A.E." But on page 12 we read: "Standardized tests depend on verbal fluency, both in reading the directions and in giving the answers, so even slight variations in dialect may penalize students by slowing them down." Well now, which will it be?

Again, we are told on page 6 that "dialect switching . . . becomes progressively more difficult as the speaker grows older." But on page 16 we read that "it is unreasonable for teachers to insist that students make phonemic shifts, which we as adults have difficulty in making." Well, if it's so much easier for young people to learn, why can't their elders expect them to do so? It is, however, useless to expect anything resembling logic from people who could write the following: "All languages are the product of the same instrument, namely, the human brain. It follows, then, that all languages and all dialects are essentially the same in their deep structure, regardless of how varied the surface structure might be. [This is equal to saying that the human brain is the human brain.]" And with this, the committee thinks that it has proved that all dialects are equally good.

But they are not—just as all human brains are not equally good, a simple fact that in their democratic, egalitarian frenzy the C.C.C.C.'ers cannot admit. Indeed, they will go so far as to assert that "if speakers of a great variety of American dialects do master E.A.E.—from Senator Sam Ervin to Senator Edward Kennedy, from Ernest Hemingway to William Faulkner—there is no reason to assume that dialects such as urban black and Chicano impede the child's ability to learn to write E.A.E. while countless others do not." Notice the choice of people of outstanding intellectual gifts or at least of privileged background from earliest childhood: these are not typical cases and so prove nothing. And just as individual situations vary, so do the circumstances behind dialects. For instance, the kinds of English that blacks and Chicanos speak are based on underlying thought structures that are not native and idiomatic but derived from African languages and from Spanish—and not the best Spanish at that—and so are not germane to the English language at all.

The disingenuousness of the committee is downright insidious.

It argues that "just as most Americans added 'sputnik' to their vocabularies a decade or more ago, so speakers of other dialects can add such words as 'periostitis' or 'interosculate' whenever their interests demand it." Consider: "Sputnik" was at that time in every headline, in every news broadcast everywhere. The other two terms will always be abstruse for the average citizen, and "interosculate" is almost ridiculous—no doubt deliberately chosen for that reason.

With similar dishonesty, the committee perceives an analogy between fighting "he be" and "he don't" and the alleged efforts of yesteryear's teachers to prevent accreditation of "jazz," "lariat," and "kosher." But, clearly, there are no more proper ways of saying "lariat" or "jazz" or "kosher," whereas there are such things as "he is" and "he doesn't." In fact, one wonders why people who believe so fanatically in the rights, if not indeed the superiority, of other dialects chose to cast their tract in E.A.E., especially since they are not particularly good at it. They write "alternate approaches" for "alternative approaches"; "because 'Johnny can't read' doesn't mean that Johnny is immature" for "that 'Johnny can't read,'" etc.; "different than" for "different from"; "equally as willing" for "equally willing"; and are capable of writing sentences like "Classroom reading materials can be employed to further our students' reading ability and, at the same time, can familiarize them with other varieties of English." Who would want to familiarize reading materials ("them") with varieties of English? Or take this alleged sentence: "For example, an unfamiliar speech rhythm and resulting pronunciation while ignoring the content of the message." And in the very next sentence (page 4) there is a "they" for which there is no antecedent.

"E.A.E. allows much less variety than the spoken forms," the C.C.C.C.'ers pronounce. But that is just the point: to speak correctly yet with individualism and variety is, to adapt Frost's old trope, to play a good game of tennis with the net up; without a net, anyone can perform all kinds of meaningless prodigies. In any case, the point of language is not simply to communicate but to communicate with originality and imaginativeness—within the bounds of propriety. Otherwise, as Stéphane Mallarmé so wisely observed, "it might suffice by way of exchanging human thought to take or put into another's hand silently a coin." When language becomes a mere convenience, like the mute passing of money from hand to hand, it ceases to have any aesthetic or, indeed, humanistic value. And when accepted language begins to model itself on what a culturally underprivileged group or individual says, it becomes a parochialism. This is the very opposite of an ecumenical language, which is perhaps difficult to master, but which, once mastered, unites all its initiates in a common pursuit and a shared beauty.

# Teacher, Heal Thyself

For us language watchers this has been the winter of our discontent. We heard about a number of New York high-school principals who were dismissed for illiteracy; samples of their prose, reproduced in the press, were truly hair-raising. Even more frightening, though, was the statement from the principals' union to the effect that the delinquent principals were fired not *just* for illiteracy but for graver offenses! Then came the sensational story about President Carter's official interpreter in Poland, who grossly mistranslated Carter's first salute to the Poles. This may seem to have nothing to do with the state of the English language, but consider the following from the *New York Times* of December 31, 1978: " [The interpreter] did very well on the difficult qualifying examinations for both Polish and Russian. . . . He was judged excellent in both languages." Note that "excellent" for someone who proceeded to translate "when I left the U.S." as "when I abandoned the U.S.," "your desires for the future" as "your lusts for the future," "Pulasky County" as "Pulasky Duchy," and so on. A curious concept of linguistic excellence, whether in Polish or in any other language.

Previously, in late November 1978, the National Council of Teachers of English held its sixty-seventh convention in New York, and there were some rather extraordinary topics. One entire session was devoted to the "Literature and Lore of Bituminous Mining," with a chair (ghastly coinage for chairman!), an associate chair (a lesser piece of furniture?), a recorder, and two speakers

with identical topics ("Literature and Lore of Bituminous Mining—For Classroom Use")—all from the Penn State Fayette campus. Why, one wonders, was this session held in New York City rather than on Pennsylvania State's Fayette campus?

There were any number of sessions on teaching science fiction and sports writing (the N.C.T.E. membership, by the way, comprises elementary-school, secondary-school, and university

teachers); there were several sessions for lesbian and gay (an unfortunate neologism deplored by most civilized homosexuals)
teachers and about gay literature; and there was, moreover, a great
deal of jargon in the very titles of sessions and individual presen-
tations, e.g., "mainstreamed students," "curriculum modules,"
"visual literacy," and so on.

Among my favorite speech titles were: "Multiple Meaning of
Words, or Magic Found on the Sports Pages of Newspapers,"
" 'Ya! Ya! Yawm! Now Hear This!' Out Far and in Deep: A Re-
sponse-Centered Approach to Science Fiction," "Significance and
Impact of Haley's *Roots* in American Culture," "Same-Sex Relationships in the Contemporary Novel for Adolescents," "The Future Application of Television Reading," "Ageism—Literature for
Youth That Provides a Positive Portrayal of Senior Citizens" (this
paper, by a college professor, employs the illiterate term "ageism"
[What does it mean? Adherence to the writings of James Agee?]
on top of the unsavory euphemism "senior citizen"), "Being Open
and Creative with Gayness in High-School Classes," and "Today's
Tragedy as Strategy" ("strategy" seems to have become the leading vogue word of our educators, suggesting that the classroom
has become a battlefield; perhaps a more appropriate title would
have been "Today's 'Strategy' as Tragedy").

What would Carlyle and Arnold (to pull two great names out of
the hat) have made of "Developing Language Arts/Communica-
tion Skills Through Interarts Strategies"? A good many titles were
scarcely better than gibberish. But, I suppose, the most revealing
and awesome session must have been the one entitled "Teaching
Reading to College Students," where, I assume, "reading" meant
nothing fanciful, such as "close reading" (i.e., textual explication),
but simply one of the three R's.

Yet why should college students know English when their
teachers don't? In the particular session I audited the first speaker
was Professor Marianna W. Davis of Benedict College (a Boston
University Ph.D.), one of whose first utterances (she had just returned from the women's conference in Houston) was "We were
really into an exciting experience in Houston"; the rest of her talk
was on the same level of literacy. The next speaker, Dr. Jerrie
Cobb Scott of the Detroit public-school system (a Michigan
Ph.D.), began with the statement "I really pondered with that

problem." Presently she referred to "the language of whatever group that is represented." And so it went. In a piece of black rabble-rousing from the floor, the militant Professor Geneva Smitherman of Wayne State University said, among other things, "the mainstream looks at most disfavorably" and "that sample type of elitism effect"; the point of her tirade was that so-called correct English is merely a capitalist maneuver to keep the underprivileged in their place, and I must admit that her English showed few, if any, traces of such capitalist intimidation.

Harvard has to take some credit for the literacy—or illiteracy—of Geneva Smitherman (a former Harvard instructor), and it is in the January-February issue of *Harvard Magazine* that I find one Josh Rubins writing as follows: "What *have* [italics his] surfaced are similes, viscous streams of them. . . ." Now, it is bad enough not to know that "What, as subject, takes the singular verb, whether the complementary noun be singular or plural" (Eric Partridge, *Usage and Abusage*), but ignorance italicized is considerably worse yet.

Then there was the December 11 issue of the *New York Times Magazine* (the most heavily edited section of the Sunday paper), where we read in the cover story on José Quintero by Barbara Gelb, the wife of one of the editors, that Quintero "sometimes behaves as though he is a character in an O'Neill play." I do not wish to raise here the whole vexed question of the subjunctive in English, so let me merely cite Fowler's example: *"It is not as though there has been cruelty and injustice. Had,* in place of *has,* is the only right English."* "As if" and "as though" take the subjunctive, not the present indicative. What, I wonder, has become of that useful bit of wisdom formerly inculcated in all high-school students: "A statement contrary to fact takes the subjunctive"? Of course, it is fashionable these days to proclaim the death of the subjunctive; still, it requires fairly porcine ears not to be jarred by "as though he is a character."

But what am I talking about? Grammar in high school? Ridiculous! Consider, after all, what is happening in colleges and universities. Take the case of Dr. Campbell Tatham, a tenured professor of English at the University of Wisconsin–Milwaukee. He declares: "It seems pretty clear that the students can't write—or speak, in some cases. Sometimes they are illiterate in writing and incoherent in talking. But those are not areas that I stress very much." What are the areas he stresses? (All that follows derives from Joel McNally's fine article in the *Milwaukee Journal* of October 24, 1978, sent to me by a reader, John M. Olson.)

It seems that a typical class in a Tatham English course addresses itself to a Joan Baez album. Everything from the photograph of Baez to the liner notes is scrutinized. Then the song "Caruso" is subjected to *explication de texte* with regard to Baez's relationship with Bob Dylan. Other required texts include albums by Jackson Browne, Joni Mitchell, Cat Stevens, Leonard Cohen, Paul Simon, Buffy Sainte-Marie, and Dylan. Besides this course, entitled "The Poetry of Contemporary Song Lyrics," Tatham offers one on the literature of the occult, and another called "Masculinism," which is an examination of male stereotypes. He says that he seldom teaches the same course twice, because he'd rather teach things he doesn't know about. And he has "simply no self-doubts" about these courses. A few "suspicious" souls in the English department "see it as pandering. But," says Tatham, "I've got tenure. People are less likely to hassle me."

He wouldn't use the term "method." "It sounds like [sic] I know what I am talking about. I don't. I think confusion is a very healthy state." The approach is random; the unexpected, always welcome. Thus the class will discuss Dylan's relationships with women (mostly unsuccessful) as described in the songs. Abandoned by his wife, the mother-and-nurture-craving Dylan will "have to confront the woman in himself." That is the ultimate goal in class, too: "for every student to confront the masculine and feminine sides in themselves [sic]." A picture accompanying the *Journal* story shows Dr. Tatham, a soft-faced young man with lots of hard, multidirectional hair. His pudgy, bejeweled fingers curl exquisitely around a cigarette held nonchalantly aloft as his soulful eyes, through modified granny glasses, contemplatively confront his other, masculine or feminine, side—it is hard to say which.

Campbell Tatham dislikes grades and doesn't care if students don't know about iambic pentameter. His aim is to "hurt" and "shock" them into thinking: "My own goal is to change them rather than teach them how to write a complete sentence." But is there a better and more radical way of changing most of them, I wonder, than teaching them how to write a complete sentence? As Dr. Tatham sees it, however, "I don't think anything is essential. If people are interested in *Beowulf*, it will be taught. These things matter so long as there are students who want them. That's the criteria [*sic*]." What would have become of Western culture long ago, I ask, if the students' desires had governed the curriculum? More to the point, what will happen now that the students' desires do increasingly govern it? Dr. Tatham doesn't even notice a major self-contradiction: how can you really change students by giving them what they already know or will pick up on their own—Baez, Dylan, and the rest? Can you imagine what will become of students trained (if that is the word) in such Mickey—sorry, Mickey and Minnie (the feminine side must be confronted)—Mouse courses, taught by someone whose own language is subliterate? Campbell Tatham may become the boor that made Milwaukee infamous.

We used to deplore the passing of the striving for excellence from the American scene. But who even remembers how excellence tasted? After all, Carter's Polish interpreter was judged "excellent" by his superiors. Excellence pretty much died out when, under the pejorative "elitism," it became hateful. It was replaced by competence. But, as Professor William A. Stewart, a linguist at C.U.N.Y., writes me, the present lowering of intellectual and aesthetic standards constitutes "a unified attack on *competence*." What has become odious is no longer excellence, merely competence. Even in hatred standards have been lowered.

# A Dud by Any Other Name

Some of you may have been as ignorant as I was about competency testing in our high schools. I assumed that standards these days were pitifully low—that in order to accommodate the socially or ethnically underprivileged (despite numerous scholastic programs for the elimination of such inequalities), it had become far too easy to obtain a high-school diploma. Only quite recently was it brought home to me that high-school diplomas were being handed out to total incompetents (enabling them to go on to college, where, again out of misguided liberalism or academic inertia, they would be carried along to undeserved graduation), so that even our lax educational authorities were obliged to take steps.

Florida and Arizona, it appears, are the only states in which a competency test in English and mathematics has for a couple of years been a prerequisite of graduation from high school. Now seventeen states are proposing similar tests, to be phased in with greater or lesser delay. In New York, the test is to be a requirement by this June (1979), and it has—shockingly, albeit unsurprisingly—elicited tremendous opposition. Even though its demands seem to me very far from draconian, it is being denounced as a fiendish tool for depriving countless innocent young people of advancement in life. The *New York Times* of February 8, 1979, reprinted a few sample questions from the math test. One ran: "Lou's marks on three tests were 90, 80, and 88. What was Lou's average for the three tests?" There follow four answers from which to choose. In the same issue of the *Times*, we read about a high-school student's taking a test in which he couldn't solve the equation $2x + 3 = 11$. And this after completing a course in algebra!

Although I have not seen the reading test, I can imagine what it must be like if it is the equivalent of the math test, in which another question reads: "On a map, if 1 inch represents 10 miles, how many inches will represent 50 miles?" The New York Board of Regents has set aside three days, from February 28 to March 2, 1979, for debate and voting on a proposal by Gordon M. Ambach, the state education commissioner, that "certificates of achievement" be given those students who fail to pass the test and thus to obtain diplomas. Whereas these certificates would probably not get you into college, they would tell potential employers that you have gone through all your high-school courses. The attitude represents that of a student, quoted in the *Times*, who declared that he had attended school "in blizzards and other things"—although even he proposes to retake the competency test until he passes it.

Some of the fifteen members of the Board of Regents have already voiced their opinions. Said Dr. Kenneth L. Clark (the *Times*, February 7): "We might as well give students certificates for being born." Another regent, who (and this is indicative) refused to be identified, commented: "It's a ridiculous recommendation. It's a cop-out to make the kids happy." The certificate would entitle a student to continue getting free public education up to the age of twenty-one and to keep trying to pass the competency test and earn a diploma. Particularly interesting is the reaction of Dr. Frank J. Macchiarola, the New York City schools chancellor: "The Commissioner appears to be responding to the need to treat children fairly. We should be interested in challenging the system to do a better job rather than in frustrating the students." This is an almost Pavlovian response, typical of all politically—or demagogically—oriented educators: it is always the system, never the student, that is at fault. It means, in effect, "Keep voting for me, folks, and I'll see to it that your children get ahead, whether they deserve to or not" and "keep pouring tax money into education and, coincidentally, into my salary."

It is especially instructive to note that even one of the regents who are (not is!) opposed to the test is (obviously, not are!) putting it this way: " [The certificate is a] sellout to professional educational interests, which do not want to confront their own failures in student performance." This is the typical bleeding-heart-liberal position: *Nothing is ever the dear students' fault; it is the quality of instruction, the System, that is to blame for any failure.* Once again I am reminded of that great cartoon in *The Saturday Evening Post* of yesteryear in which a psychiatrist tells his supine patient: "You don't have an inferiority complex, Miss Jones. You *are* inferior." Where are the good old days when such an idea could be expressed even as a joke in a popular magazine? Today, nobody is inferior in any way whatsoever.

And yet here we are, with roughly 15 percent of young Americans functionally illiterate and 20 percent of adult Americans (23 million people) functional illiterates. The term "functional illiterate" designates someone who, although he can technically read and write, cannot do it well enough to be a fully functioning member of our society. In other words, you cannot read road signs or the instructions on a medicine jar and draw the correct inferences. Yet even these frequently adduced examples of functional illiteracy ought to point to an inescapable conclusion: what good is reading and writing to people who cannot think?

There is, it seems to me, a great discovery for which our democratic, populist, egalitarian society is waiting: that of human inequality. By this I do not mean definition two in the *American Heritage Dictionary:* "Social or economic disparity"—although there is plenty of that around, too. I mean extending definition one to

"the condition of being unequal *intellectually.*" Officially, every citizen of this Jeffersonian democracy is proclaimed—in a travesty of
Jefferson's own concept of democracy—the equal of every other
citizen in *every* way, which naturally includes *mentally.* If he is not,
someone or something else—capitalism, the government, white
supremacy, the System—is to blame. And yet we live in a society
clearly based on competition, that is, on someone's outsmarting
someone, or everyone, else. Which, in turn, means that people are
not equally smart.

What this signifies in the field of language is that some people
simply are not bright enough to become fully literate and articulate, no matter how good the instruction they receive. Let me
recapitulate three recent changes in attitude toward language as
noted by Arn and Charlene Tibbetts in their important and useful
book *What's Happening to American English?* "First," write the authors, "there is a tendency toward treating all opinions as equal.
They need not be sensible, well put, or coherent. Degrees of authority are hardly taken into account." The second basic change
lies in the fact that "few people today ask, Does it mean anything?
We have lost the simple urge to ask, for example, Just what is a
*quality education* anyway? " And, last, "Now almost every part of
our lives has been invaded by the verbal fads of politics."

The authors observe: "A college freshman can write of the
*power structure* in his university and of his family. Battles between
the second and third sexes bring on cries of *fag* and *straight. Honky*
and *whitey* are still available to those who wish to make race relations more wretched than they are. Husbands are *sexist* or *chau-
vinist.* . . . The world is full of greasers, *WASPs, elitists, bourgeois,
far-outs, New Lefts,* and *Maoists,* all of them resisting or accepting
the labels without clear notions of what they mean." When
Jacques Barzun predicted during the student rebellion of 1968—
and in view of the knuckling under of the academy—that our
colleges and universities would not recover from this capitulation
for a very, very long time, he was, if anything, overoptimistic.
*Never* might have been a perfectly plausible estimate.

Let us consider, however, what the three points made by the
Tibbettses really mean. First, the "democratic" sleight of hand,
whereby differences in intellect, understanding, *mind,* are dismissed tacitly, theoretically, or on principle. Next, the abandon-
ment of intellectual discrimination in practice: the end of all

questioning, discussion, or analysis—either because it is no longer
socially and politically safe or because the ability to make qual-
itative distinctions has been lost. Finally, hitting upon an easy
substitute for thought, indeed for basic intelligence, in political
name-calling: the indiscriminate reliance on slogans and formulas
as a surrogate for cerebration. In other words, the use of the verbal arm of brute force. What all three of these steps represent is
the march of stupidity into power, supported by a genuine sense
of social and political inequality carried to morbid or cowardly
extremes.

I doubt whether there is any solution to this problem—indeed, I
doubt whether there is any thoroughly acceptable solution to any
major human problem. But I think that some headway could be
made by promulgating, at the very latest in high school, the tenet
that intellectual differences exist, which means no more and no
less than that some minds are better, or worse, than others. And
we must not be intimidated by the hue and cry denouncing this as
elitist, racist, defeatist, or whatever. A Bartók or an Einstein may
come out of the ghetto, and Park Avenue and Harvard may produce their quota of incompetents. Nevertheless, every ghetto child
is not a potential Bartók or Einstein—or even passable musician or
physicist—any more than every Park Avenue child is. There are
limits to everyone's abilities, and some limits are more limiting
than others. Learn this, and you are already a little wiser.

Of course, intellect isn't everything. For many jobs, from garbage collecting to acting, it is not only not needed, it may even be
a hindrance. Besides, goodness and beauty matter just as much.
Fail in the intellectual world, and there are still the moral and
aesthetic worlds at your disposal. And even if you are a flop in all
three realms, there is still hope for you. Proclaim yourself intellectually inferior; instead of a certificate of achievement, acquire a
certificate in inferiority. You will ipso facto become something
rarer and more precious than oil, gold, or uranium. You will be
lionized by guilt-ridden liberals, militant populists, power-mad
politicians and academics—maybe even by high society. In short,
you will have it made.

CHAPTER TEN

# BAD NEWS FROM ALL OVER

# Readers, Writers, and Rotters

One of my great joys in writing "The Language" column has been the mail from readers. Most of it is favorable, which is gratifying; much of it, favorable or unfavorable, is thought-provoking and often enlightening, which is delightful; almost all of it is literate and acutely concerned with the state of the language, which is truly exhilarating. This time I dedicate my column to the perceptive and enterprising readers who sent me the clippings and communications I shall quote. They are in no particular order, unless it be an aleatory one.

I must admit, however, that I am surprised at the literal-mindedness of certain otherwise perfectly literate correspondents. Some of them, for instance, have complained, like Dr. F. W. Rhinelander, of Little Rock, that *Esquire* in its logo is turning the word *fortnightly* into two words, *fort nightly*. Don't people understand the power of design (for good or ill) in our publishing world? If the art director wants the tail of the *Q* in *Esquire* to extend into the line below, *fortnightly*, like the Red Sea, will have to part to let the designer pass through. Even more astonishing is an otherwise sympathetic epistle, from a retired southwestern teacher, in which I am rebuked for using sentence fragments, a lapse for which his students would have been penalized. Now, students should indeed avoid an incomplete sentence if they don't know what they are doing. But experienced writers may take liberties legitimately. For effect. Sparingly used, the device can be very forceful. Downright compelling.

While we are on stylistic matters, P. J. Hertsgaard, of St. Louis, Missouri, wonders (in a very amiable letter) how I can refer to an "uninformed acquisition" when it is surely the buyer, not the thing bought, that is uninformed. In a similar vein, but in a rather unpleasant letter, Walter H. Mueller, of Indianapolis, claims that there is no such thing as a "grammatical error," only an "error in grammar." The first instance is a rhetorical device (for which the *terminus technicus* is *hypallage*) vaguely on the order of syllepsis and zeugma, in which the epithet normally modifying the subject is transferred to the object—as in "unwise decision" or "uneasy sleep." The second is a perfectly acceptable verbal shortcut; we say "hormonal deficiency," not "deficiency of hormones"; "technical fault," not "fault in technique"; and so on.

With like captiousness, Mr. Mueller proceeds to chastise me for writing "one of the most insidious pitfalls." He writes: "There is one 'most' and no more." Much more sympathetically, Dr. William Houston, of Bulawayo, Rhodesia, objects to the similar "even the ablest among us" and comments, "abler yes, but ablest, no." Well, the superlative need not be confined to one, though, of course, it should not be devaluated (avoid *devalued*): "the hundred best breakfast foods" would be quite ludicrous. But surely all those people who make ten-best lists are, grammatically at least, on safe ground. "The ten best movies of the year," though one may frown on the practice from the critical point of view (vastly preferable to *viewpoint*), would make less sense if labeled "the ten better movies of the year." The comparative always makes you worry about "Better than what?" and "How much better?" and "Was there no *best*?" It can even sound unpleasantly snobbish, as in those ads that end with "At better stores everywhere," or in the phrase "the better people," which sounds much nastier than "the best people."

Several readers have written more or less in the manner of Will Dix, of New Orleans, who mentions, apropos my objection to *most* as a synonym for *almost*, that the abbreviation '*most* may be what people have in mind, though he prudently adds, "Whether this makes it any better . . . I'm not sure." And Ray Russell, of Beverly Hills, notes that this is probably borrowed from southern dialect, with "an implied or invisible apostrophe . . . not that I approve of invisible apostrophes." That's just it! The absurd '*til* came in as an abbreviation of *until*, but at least it caused no oral (or aural) damage, because there is a perfectly good *till*, meaning the same thing. But in writing, '*til* is an abomination, as is '*most*, which, moreover, has the further drawback of being a homonym of *most* and thus a source of damnable confusion. Until apostrophes can be sounded—say, with a glottal stop (and I hope it never comes to that!)—let us not invent new ones. Or drop old ones, for that matter.

Readers are sending in examples of bad usage from various sources, including my own writings. Michael O'Boyle, from Jackson, Mississippi, notes that I erred in calling St. Bernards and German shepherds hounds, which are used for hunting, instead of *working dogs*. I stand corrected, or in the doghouse. Sandra Wilde, of Fredericton, Canada, questions my use of *blanch* instead of *blench* in the August 15, 1978, column: "Wouldn't one flinch or wince rather than turn pale?" In the words of Oscar Wilde's Lady Bracknell, "Both, if necessary."

Robert Chandler, of Beverly Hills, rightly objects to the trendy misuse of *chauvinism*. The word, derived from the French super-patriot Nicolas Chauvin, is, as Mr. Chandler notes, "a useful reference to overzealous nationalism," but it "has been trivialized so that it is now taken to be the short form of *male chauvinism*." This is, of course, yet another case of a minority or special-interest group—in this case the feminists—perverting the language to its own presumed benefit. I recently protested here against the misuse of the word *gay* to suit the whim of certain homosexual organizations—although many literate homosexuals abominate this usage. I got some interesting letters on this subject, but I have space to quote from only a couple of them. Professor James L. Lucas, of Chicago, angrily calling me "no better an English teacher than . . . a critic," writes, "Let your ill-directed complaint be levelled [in America, *leveled* is the preferred spelling, because the accent is *not* on the syllable before the participial ending; where it is, as in *preferred*, consonantal reduplication is in order] against [surely *at* would be better here] those who invented the terms which the word *gay* was adopted to counteract—queer, faggot, pansy, fruit, sissy, degenerate, pervert." To which I can only reply that one evil is no cure for another; I would similarly deplore the misuse of *queer*—except that it is on the decline, whereas *gay* is on the rise.

Now from a letter sent by Emmett Graybill, of Shippenville, Pennsylvania: "I recently was invited to my neighbors' house to meet their guests from Columbus, Ohio. . . . My neighbors also have a very earnest daughter, aged twelve. . . . I remarked to the visitors from Columbus that when I lived there, I always bought my liquor at a store on the corner of Gay and High streets, because it seemed the perfect place for a liquor store. They smiled politely. My neighbors' daughter told me I was 'discriminating' against 'gays.' It turned out the girl was 'studying gays' at school in something called 'civil rights.' I also learned the girl knew no meaning for 'gay' but 'homosexual,' which her teacher had told her was not a nice word."

Another reader (whose name I regrettably lost) sent me a poem by the fine British poet Vernon Scannell (from the *New Statesman* of June 9, 1978) called "Protest Poem," which contains the lines "All right. Then let's call heterosexuals *sad.* / *Dainty* for rapists, *shy* for busy flashers, / *Numinous* for necrophiles, *quaint* for stranglers." The poem ends, "A small innocence gone, a little Fall, / I grieve the loss. I am not gay at all." Lovely, despite the anacoluthon in the second line I quote.

Steve Sherry, of Berkeley, California, deplores an ugly trend that seems to be evolving and that he pinpoints on page 57 of *Time*, August 8, 1978: "PP could care less"—where, of course, "couldn't care less" is what is meant. Ghastly. M. O. Young, of Surry, Virginia, raises several interesting issues, but I have space only for the last: "And what is happening to the perfect tense? 'I ate already' has nearly driven out 'I've already eaten.' Whose idea was that?" Whose indeed? In what school nowadays can kids still learn the difference between the past perfect and imperfect tenses? In fact, how many college students today even know that such differences exist?

Rob and Helen Hardy, of Jackson, Mississippi, write: "In regard to what to call a chairman, our church now has a chairor. Rhymes with error." That's the feminists again; still, it's nice to see organized religion and—what shall I call it?—lay religion reaching out to each other. Gertrude de Silva, of Carlsbad, California, points to page 88 of *Esquire*, March 28, 1978, where one reads "There is absolutely no reason why," which is, as she says, a redundancy. That is an old and tenacious error and has, alas, been enshrined by good writers. It is possible that if Tennyson had not written "Theirs not to reason why" (even though, here, "reason" is not a noun but a verb, after which "why" is possible) and if Dickens had not put another beastly solecism into his title *Our Mutual Friend*, the two errors would not have become so popular.

But people aren't being taught anything any more (not *anymore*, please!). Thus Franklin R. Garfield, of Los Angeles, thinks that in referring to a lady (he actually means *woman*), one must use the relative pronoun *who*, not *that*. In fact, *that* is equally correct for people and things, whereas *who* is right only for people. Even more astounding, Joan Mastropaul, of Syracuse, New York (in a long, fascinating letter, from which I wish I could quote at greater length), reports her doctor's astonishment when she used the word *prone:* "How do you know what the word *prone* means—do you have a medical background?" I am afraid that when it comes to learning good English, most people are prone to be supine.

Eileen Maley, of West Tisbury, Massachusetts, sends in a full-page ad from *Vogue* for Friedricks Sport. The caption reads: "When others are called for cross-checking, who's timing is always right?" Miss Maley wonders about all the "professionals" who must have approved this copy of Friedricks, at the ad agency, and at *Vogue,* none of whom, apparently, knows the difference between *who's* and *whose.* David H. Jackson, of New York City, sends in an ad from *New York* magazine with the caption "Sooner or later you'll try on a Sasson jean / Then . . . you'd wished it was sooner." For one thing, *jeans* should always be plural, like *pants;* for another, the tenses should not have gone haywire here. "Then" obviously calls for the future, "Then you'll wish"; but the repentance refers to the past, ergo, "Then you'll wish it had been sooner."

From *Esquire* comes an ad passed on to me by Gould B. Hagler, of Atlanta; in it, the Bombay Company offers "an authentic reproduction of a fine old English antique." An authentic reproduction strikes me as not far removed from a genuine sham. Miss Diane Knox, of St. Louis, sends in a Budweiser coaster whose text begins: "Drink Budweiser. only for five days." (The period after Budweiser is probably a typo.) If this means we are to drink no water or beverage other than Bud for five days, it is correct. Otherwise *only* is misplaced. It belongs just before or just after the word or words it modifies; in this case, "for only five days" or "for five days only" would be correct. There are, however, exceptions to this rule (noted by Fowler and others) where, for the sake of emphasis or euphony, one may want to dislodge the *only.* Thus, "If only I could be sure!" is clearly more idiomatic than "If I could only be sure!"

An anonymous reader sends me a photocopy of a May 22, 1978, memo that went out over the signature of Wayne Teague, the Alabama State Superintendent for Education; in it, jargon, redundancy, and solecism abound. Particularly disturbing are "mutually beneficial to both agencies" and "distribution by currier service." The latter, as my correspondent notes, would mean service by people who curry leather; though, it occurs to me, they may also curry favor. Several readers have sent me a printed note from Bloomingdale's credit office concerning a previously dispatched credit card: "We wish to confirm whether it has been received." The sender can only *inquire;* it is up to the recipient to *confirm.*

Jerry Bradley, of Socorro, New Mexico, sends me the August 18, 1978, column by Mark Acuff, media columnist of the *New Mexico Independent,* in which Acuff defends a local radio station against "a couple of schoolmarm types" who complained about its English. Writes Acuff: "One biddy took certain broadcasters to task for saying 'where it's at' when 'where it is' is proper. Tough, lady—you perhaps have noticed that the former horrible phrase is much in vogue these days, in a cultural sense. Formerly it had considerable currency in the sense of spatial location, adding emphasis. It remains in wide use in that sense as well as in the new sense." Aside from its tautologies ("much in vogue" and "spatial location") and various dangling constructions, this is sheer nonsense. What is the *it* in "where it's at," and what does the *at* contribute that is not covered by "where it is"? And what culture is referred to in Acuff's "cultural sense"? So much for our self-appointed people's champions.

Now for an error that is very frequent even among civilized people. This particular example was sent in by the indefatigable Rabbi Lyle Kamlet and comes from Vincent Canby's review of *Joseph Andrews* in the April 14, 1978, *New York Times:* "It's one of the few movies around now that truly lifts the spirits." Clearly, *lift* must agree with *movies* and not with *one:* there are a few *movies* around that *lift* the spirits, and one of them is (in Canby's opinion, not mine) *Joseph Andrews.* It is astonishing how few people understand this perfectly logical rule. A senior lecturer from the University of Queensland, Australia, who quite rightly deplores an Op-Ed piece in the July 16, 1978, *New York Times* in which Richard Burt of the paper's Washington bureau misspells *consistent* and *insistent* as "consistant" and "insistant" is nevertheless guilty himself. The gentleman (I withhold his name) bemoans the "grammatical blunder of the first magnitude" allegedly committed by David Binder of the *Times* in "One of the blacks who have submitted their resignations," which, however, is perfectly correct. The error would have been to write "who has submitted"; there were several blacks who *have* resigned, and one of these is singled out and quoted by Binder. The verb must agree with the several who have submitted resignations.

Claire Lobel, of Toronto, takes me to task for an error in one of my *Hudson Review* drama chronicles, where I wrote about "Neil Simon and his ilk." Quoting Fowler, she points out that *ilk* "does not mean family or kind or set or name" but is reserved "for the case in which proprietor and property have the same name: *The Knockwinnocks of that ilk* means the Knockwinnocks of Knockwinnock." True enough, yet according to the *American Heritage Dictionary*, 65 percent of the usage panel will accept *ilk* in the sense of *type* or *kind* when used facetiously or disparagingly. Miss Lobel could, of course, argue that I have been known to disagree with my colleagues on the usage panel, and, indeed, I agree with them only when they agree with me. But that is the point about grammar: it does have gray areas where disagreement is possible and even useful in keeping interest in correct English alive.

A number of readers have sent in additional examples of verbal "sibling rivalry," as I dubbed it. Thus Thomas A. Stewart, a senior editor of Harcourt Brace Jovanovich, notes that in the very issue of *Esquire* in which I discussed this topic, "Arthur Schlesinger, Jr., quotes Robert Kennedy using 'forego' (to go before) when he meant 'forgo' (to go without)," and wonders whether the error is Kennedy's or Schlesinger's. In a similar vein, a reader whose name I stupidly lost sent in the following excerpt from *New Times* magazine (August 7, 1978): "[Norman] Lear was pouring over that day's *New York Times* when I walked in." My correspondent wonders whether it was coffee or orange juice that Lear was pouring. The correct word is *poring*. Another reader, Jerry Sutlef (if I read his signature correctly), sends me a Xerox copy of a decision of the Third Circuit Court of Appeals as reported in the NOSSA Safety Log; it contains a reference to the "knowing, conscious and deliberate flaunting of the Act." It is not clear which Act is flaunted; but it is perfectly plain that what is judicially *flouted* here is good English.

*Time* magazine comes in for its share of croppers. Benjamin Adler, of Plantation, Florida, submits a *Time* cover story (August 7, 1978) in which we read about a bill that "would have required the lobbyists to reveal . . . who they represent." Lyle Kamlet contributes a *Time* Essay (August 14, 1978) that rattles off in rapid succession "as though names are," "as if they expect," "as though names do," and "as though they have." Both the accusative *whom* and the subjunctive "as though names *were*" may die out of the English language (more's the pity if they do), but it ill behooves a supposedly reputable publication to play gravedigger to the refinements of our tongue.

It is not as if *Time* really knew better and were only indulging itself in a bit of linguistic slumming. William P. Cleere, of Oakland, sends in this gem (again from the August 7 issue): "Washington remained hopeful that Secretary of State Cyrus Vance might breech [*sic*] the gap on his trip to the Middle East." When *Time* can no longer spell *breach* or distinguish between it and its antonym, bridge, it is not surprising that, as Mr. Cleere also reports, some months ago one could read "just desserts" in *Time*—which is just yummy.

Still, *Time* does have its uses, as in a May 15, 1978, item about a bizarre federal grant to Professor E. D. Hirsch, Jr., of the University of Virginia, who "received $137,935 from the National Endowment for the Humanities to develop a standard for judging the 'relative readability' of writing." And how does Professor Hirsch define readability, or "intrinsic effectiveness," as he calls it? "A text's intrinsic effectiveness is the proportion between its effectiveness and that of a synonymous version which is optimally effective." There! Roland Barthes could not have put it better! My thanks to James W. Gaynor, of Grosset & Dunlap, for passing this on. With such optimal effectiveness of expression in our university English departments, what can we expect from ordinary tongue waggers?

Erica Bard Riley, of Louisville, kindly mailed me a copy of the disclaimer she found preceding the text of the novel *Fairytales* (Arbor House, 1977), by Cynthia Freeman: "With the exception of a few historical events, this story is purely fictional and has no relevance to any one [*sic*] living or otherwise. If one sees themself in the characters depicted herein, it is strictly a figment of their own imagination." Miss Freeman's English clearly has no relevance to anyone living and belongs in the great Otherwise. Miss Riley adds that she returned the book, unread, to the library.

Finally, for all those among you for whom language is a constantly growing organism ready for accretions from everywhere, here is a happy note. Gene Shalit, of NBC, forwards a letter from the letters column of the May issue of *Ms.* It begins: "I protest the use of the word 'testimony' when referring to a woman's statements, because its root is 'testes' which has nothing to do with being a female. Why not use 'ovarimony'?" Shalit wonders

whether the writer is serious and concludes that she is—as is her
condition. And as, I add regretfully, is the condition of the English
language.

# Attack and Counterattack

Some of the letters that come in point out my errors. I am
grateful for that: nobody is perfect, and with a subject as fascinat-
ingly tricky as language in general and the English tongue in particular, nobody is even as near perfection as a few headwaiters,
masseurs, and hairdressers still manage to be. I have valued no
less the letters of general sympathy and encouragement and the
letters that called my attention to abuses of the language as yet
unknown to me.

Inevitably, there have also been attacks, two of which I shall
advert to now. They appear in two columns: "A Spitball for
Teacher's Pet," by Patrick Owens in *Newsday* (April 29, 1977),
which names me outright, and David Mehegan's "Shut Up, You
Carping Nitpicking Wordsmiths" in the *Boston Globe* (September
2, 1977), which does not name me, but contains a sufficient number of oblique references to make it clear that I am one such
wordsmith and had better nitpick up my carpbag and scram
before Mr. Mehegan, to use his own elegant turn of phrase,
"beat[s me] senseless with an unparaphrased *Canterbury Tales*."
This would, of course, put the fear of the Lord into me if I weren't
confident that Mr. Mehegan wouldn't begin to know where to
find the particular weapon with which he threatens me.

It is interesting to note that the defenders of impure English
have one thing in common: violence. Mr. Owens, somewhat less
fiercely, would be content with "a committee . . . appointed to
frog-march critic John Simon [that should be "the critic"] into a
mud puddle, there to splash his velveteen knickers." What with
the cost of dry cleaning these days, and velveteen knickers being
even harder to come by than an unparaphrased *Canterbury Tales*,
this seems to be a bit outré. To be sure, Mr. Owens is apt to get

carried away with his own wordsmithery, as when he suggests that I am as out of place in *Esquire*, "that citadel of real language," as a "rabbi on the sanitation truck at Mecca." Quite a masterly insult, that: against me, obviously; against the Jews, whose priests are consigned to a garbage truck; and against the Arabs, whose holy city is reduced to having one piddling instrument of cleanliness, "*the* sanitation truck at Mecca." It is not given to everyone to wield such a triple-edged sword, one that even Sultan Saladin (to stay in the world of Owens's trope), for all his Toledo blades, might have envied.

With violence always comes some kind of hatred, whether of a minority, a group, or a class. Thus Owens describes me as a "teacher's pet" who thrives on "her beams of approval and on her . . . acceptance . . . into the sorority of the . . . semantically pure." You'll note that "teacher" becomes automatically female, as if there were not a great many male teachers, and that what one gets into is labeled, with obvious contempt, a sorority. Later on, Owens refers to my "teacher's-pet hysteria," hysteria being, traditionally, a female complaint. Still later, one of my mentors, Jacques Barzun, is described sneeringly as a "schoolmarm." I need hardly point out what kind of hatred is—probably unconsciously— at work here.

From Mehegan, on the other hand, we learn of a class conspiracy, of "educated snobs" or, sarcastically, "Higher Orders," who would foist on the world the nonsensical notion "that the English language is a work of art." Now, nobody in his right mind would claim that any language is a work of art. What I would claim is that the correct, effective, and beautiful use of language is an artistic pursuit that, in some exceptional cases, can be heightened into poetry, fiction, drama, et cetera, and so become a work of art. The artistic use of language, whether in conversation, correspondence, speechmaking, or whatever, is worth striving for, as is the artistic treatment of such disparate things as a love letter, a movie, a home-cooked meal—and all benefit from the effort. But there is no compulsion. According to Mehegan, "Johnny will get along fine without being able to write if he can do something else well." Why then, one wonders, has English been taught in schools all along? Why not just teach plumbing or pottery or podiatry? Those are all very good professions if practiced efficaciously—and that is precisely where language does come in. For language is, minimally, a tool, a tool in communication and expression, and just as a potter or plumber, an astronomer or yachtsman, is judged according to how well he uses his tools, a speaker (and everyone is a speaker) is also judged by others (who may or may not include Owens and Mehegan) according to his use of his tools: vocabulary, grammar, syntax, and style.

Perhaps it shouldn't be so; certainly, we are likely to buy a well-turned pot from someone incapable of a well-turned phrase. But a very large segment of society still values correct and imaginative use of language, and for a good many important jobs, like it or not, that is still a prerequisite. Having good language may not be a work of art, but it is an act of decency, just like good taste, good manners, good elocution—all of them, I sadly concede, endangered species. There is a joy in beholding a person whose clothes form a harmonious ensemble, just as there is delight in seeing a carpenter's work neatly executed; similarly, to hear somebody's sentence fall tidily into place, with the sort of click that the knowing ear can actually register, is a civilized pleasure available to anyone, regardless of social class. If he doesn't trouble to acquire that pleasure, he may still be an effective candlestick maker, but he is also a less cultivated human being.

But, of course, it is culture that the Mehegans overtly and the Owenses covertly have it in for. "If you can't quote Byron or Shakespeare," writes Mehegan sneeringly, "you can always find some less graceful writer or speaker than yourself [where *you* would be more graceful—and correct] to wince at." Notice that Mehegan is making fun here of grace, or gracefulness; or is, by clear implication, writing in praise of its opposite, boorishness. It may be, however, that he is not aware of what he is doing, as he may be unaware, too, of the implication of this statement: "You can [properly, *may*] be a pauper, but if you can remember how to use 'whom' [comma missing] your reputation is assured." Well, who wouldn't want an assured reputation? Having that, he might not even remain a pauper for long.

Here let me quote a letter from a reader who told me my columns helped her stand up to her psychiatrist, who accused her of pretentiousness and of hiding behind masks by "using any but the most common words, phrases, and grammatical constructions." "I was beginning to entertain the thought," she writes, "that an inarticulate slide into the vernacular might be a sign of

mental health, after all." And now comes a sentence leagues beyond anything Mehegan or Owens has come up with: "I am a
poor woman and language is one of the few wealths available to
me." I hope you will share my admiration not only for the content
of this sentence, but also for the comeliness of that phrase, "one
of the few wealths." No fancy words or construction here, but
what originality and daring in using the plural "wealths": with
one simple stroke the world has been enlarged and enriched. It is
now a place where there is not merely one obvious, often unat-
tainable, even more often vulgar, wealth, but a choice of wealths,
one being, as this writer compellingly demonstrates, language itself.

Owens is somewhat more sophisticated than Mehegan. He
speaks of the fascination of the "words of poor and working people," which may or may not be a patronizing term. "More recently," he continues, "I have started to listen closely to the
language of psychotics. Craziness turns out to be an extraordinary
purifier of human speech; schizophrenia does more than John Simon ever will to bring beauty from the mouths of plain folk." I'll
pass over that cliché "plain folk" and the feeble "bring," where
something like "wrest," "elicit," or "coax" would be more to the
point; but, my God, what nonsense! *Pace* R. D. Laing, schizophrenia is no guarantor of beautiful, let alone purified, speech—except,
obviously, in the case of people who are both schizophrenic and
linguistically gifted: the crazed Hölderlin, Nerval, Christopher
Smart, and John Clare were poets and masters of language first;
madmen only second. But read Nijinsky's journals and, if you can
maintain any kind of unsentimental objectivity, you will see how
little madness did for this inarticulate artist, whose poetry, while
he was sane, was of the wordless sort. As for me, I have known a
good many advanced neurotics and even, perhaps, a psychotic or
two in my day; some spoke with purity and beauty, some not—
just as was the case with cartographers, contractors, and columnists.

I wonder, furthermore, whether Owens realizes the implications of a statement like "Except for 'hopefully,' a word I cheerfully misuse because I like the sound of it, I do not recall
committing any of the four locutions that [Simon] finds definitive
of gibberish." Here's a pretty kettle of fishiness! (My four examples, by the way, were the impersonal "hopefully," staunchly

championed by Mr. Mehegan, and "oh, wow," "like, I mean," and "mind-blowing.") First of all, even Mr. Owens's arithmetic is off: once you confess to "hopefully," only *three* locutions are left for you to be innocent of. Consider, however, the style of our defender of language from the mouths of plain folk: "committing . . . locutions . . . definitive of gibberish." Why, this is grandiloquent fustian; soon, however, Mr. Owens lapses into such things as "quote marks" for "quotation marks" and "us literary virtuosi" for "we literary virtuosos"—which makes me wonder whether his study of schizophrenia was conducted in front of a mirror.

But to return to the quoted sentence and its gleeful assertion that misuse can be justified by liking the sound of it. Naturally, with a man of Mr. Owens's relative sophistication, this means only the misuse of "hopefully," but what happens when a more advanced miscreant cheerfully says "irregardless," "heinious," or "aggravating" (for "annoying") because he likes the sound of such a manifest piece of linguistic ignorance and nonsense? And why stop at that; every grotesque mangling of English sounds good to *some* ears. Mehegan, for instance, writes, "Robert Wood no longer speaks North Florida and Walter Cronkite no longer talks Texas." Obviously, that should be "North Floridian" and "Texan": one does not speak England but English. But I am sure it is music to the Mehegan ear.

Owens, in line with his greater *raffinement*, avers that I am a "remorseless and fatuous nitpicker [that word again—pretty soon I'll have to join the nitpickers' union], able to spot a dangling participle at fifty paces, and quite incompetent to distinguish the virtuoso dangle from your usual graceless blunder." Well, I'm glad to note that in Mr. Owens's book, unlike in Mr. Mehegan's, "graceless" is still a pejorative, but I am left in the dark about when a misplaced participle is a blunder and when a virtuoso dangle. Perhaps when it performs on the high wire without a net. But, then, I am not a master tergiversator like Mr. Owens, who begins by assuring us that, like me, he has never used "mind-blowing," and promptly proceeds to wonder: "What is the *correct* equivalent of 'mind-blowing'? The essence of English as prudery is the denial of the validity of concepts that cannot be expressed in received language. That minds are sometimes blown, and that people who have had the experience want to tell about it, is irrelevant to Simon."

There are, needless to say, countless ways of saying "mind-blowing" in a civilized way. In fact, they are all more precise: astounding, staggering, devastating, dumbfounding, breathtaking, stupefying—I could go on—have each the virtue of describing the nature and intensity of the experience a little more evocatively. We know exactly how our breathing can stop for a moment, how our voice may fail us, or how we may find ourselves stuporous; but how does a mind get blown? Perhaps Mr. Owens, erudite Latinist that he no doubt is, is merely confusing *mens* and *mentula*, blowable organs of rather different sorts. A person who claims to have experienced the blowing of his mind has, I am afraid, nothing up there to be blown.

Speaking of Latin, incidentally, Mr. Mehegan informs us with solemn contempt that "the Higher Orders before Chaucer's time wouldn't stoop to the peasant's tongue—they communicated with each other in Latin." This is typical pseudolearned rubbish: certainly Latin was the learned language of the day, a very useful lingua franca in which the educated people of all European nations could communicate with one another—one can only wish that there were such a language today, whether called English or Esperanto or Volapük. And Chaucer's time, obviously, was not when this practice stopped. On the other hand, even the Highest Orders (whoever they might have been) spoke their native language on all ordinary occasions among themselves. Furthermore, Dante, almost a century before Chaucer, had already composed one of the world's most elevated poems in the "peasant's tongue," which had also served the troubadours for their exalted lyricism a couple of centuries earlier still.

Then, says our historian, the Higher Orders "confiscated" the language that the people had invented "and told the rest of us that . . . we couldn't use it without asking them how." Well now, Mr. Mehegan has no more accurate information than anyone else about who invented what part of the language. But it is certain that some very good minds whose names are known to us spent centuries tracking down and codifying English speech and deriving a number of rules from it. Once these rules were fully categorized and disseminated, it became possible for virtually everyone to learn them and abide by them. That is the way to combat chaos and shame the devil. That is the way in which meanings could be made unambiguous and communication instantaneous and elegant.

Yes, language is a living thing. But all that means is that as new concepts and inventions crop up, names have to be created for them. As other notions and institutions become obsolete, the words designating them can be laid to rest. There is also a juiciness and validity in regional speech and in slang, both of which deserve to exist as secondary languages on which the primary one can draw for needed replenishment. But there is no need for all the absurd changes—really corruptions based on ignorance. Thus, for example, because the ignoramuses cannot tell the difference between "fortunate" and "fortuitous" or "disinterested" and "uninterested," are we all, with the blessing of the structural linguists, to accept ignorance as the norm and allow language to ooze into a confused, confusing blur? Nothing that stems from enthroned, systematized ignorance has ever proved a blessing.

On one point, alas, Mehegan is right, or almost so. He boasts that "hopefully" and "hung" (for "hanged") will be accepted in time, because "the Higher Orders . . . always follow the peasant's lead eventually." I don't know whether it is possible *not* to follow the peasants' lead, but it is a noble experiment worth trying. Especially when you consider how unlovely the peasants are—Mr. Mehegan, who wants to use Chaucer's masterpiece as a club, and Mr. Owens, who accuses me (and anyone else who stands for standards) of "puritanic ranting . . . shrilly brainless resort to authority," of being a "fidgety, sour-lipped savant" and "more Catholic than your average pope." Now, unlike Mr. Mehegan, Mr. Owens does not reveal to us the state of his historical erudition, but if he is taking the long view he will descry a number of popes who could have used a little more Catholicism or, at any rate, Christianity.

## Stop Compromise Now!

Not another tiresome sermon on standards!" you exclaim in horror of homiletics. Yet whether we like it or not, the time has come to reexamine—or perhaps examine properly for the first time—the premises of this column. The urgent need for reassessment dawned on me after reading the letters of two school teachers in response to my article "Just Between Us" (see page 17).

One teacher, from Redwood City, California, writes: "You are right, of course, about the use of *him* and *me*, but I will bet that you lost everyone but English purists and students of romance [*sic*] languages when you brought up the accusative, nominative, parts of speech, and prepositions. [Are prepositions, then, not parts of speech?] A simpler way of teaching those who know nothing about this esoteric vocabulary follows."

The teacher then lists a number of prepositions in "Column One" and all the personal pronouns in the accusative in "Column Two." A caption reads: "The words in Column One must be followed by the words in Column Two."

This strikes me as worthless to students of English, though probably helpful to those wishing to learn how to order in Chinese restaurants. There follows a set of "Further Simplifications" pertaining to compound objects and then the conclusion: "This method avoids reference to parts of speech or case, and requires comparatively little memorization. I'm not sure I have all the prepositions. Some are also adverbs or adverbial prepositions but again nobody needs to know that if he memorizes the list." All this seems to me a paradigm of wrongheadedness, the very thing that ails most of our basic education in English.

In the first place, this teacher's technique is nothing but brute mnemonics—memorization as a substitute for thought—precisely the approach the good woman shies away from. But her deludedness goes much deeper. Not to teach students grammar qua grammar is as bad as teaching mathematics unmathematically, by memorization. A student would have to memorize, for example, the multiplication table up to, say, a million so as to obviate learning how to multiply. That way, I am afraid, lies madness. But English as a subject is so hated by students and so apologized for by teachers (imagine burdening young people's minds with things like parts of speech!) that this kind of nonsense thrives. Surely it is easier to learn what sort of thing a preposition or an adverb is than to commit to memory all extant prepositions and adverbs.

Take another example: the difference between *lay* and *lie*, a problem I once dismissed here as too elementary for *Esquire* readers. Since then I have received half a dozen letters complaining about how widespread the misuse of these siblings is even among schooled speakers. Now, you can try to make students memorize a long list: you lay a pencil on the table, you lay your hands on a rascal, you lay your head to rest, you lay an egg; you lie down, lie in bed, lie in state, and let sleeping dogs lie. But if you can say to a student that *lay* is transitive and *lie* intransitive, he gets it easily and indelibly—provided only that those grammatical terms are known to him.

A much more sophisticated letter comes from a teacher in Yuma, Arizona; yet it, too, profoundly disturbs me. It reads in part: "So many . . . of us who teach . . . tend to forget that the children we instruct have rushed schedules . . . and fragmented areas of responsibility (seven classes, extracurricular activities, unpredictable and sometimes uncontrollable homelives) which we too often dismiss as irrelevant or not a good enough excuse for incomplete or careless work. . . . If some fundamental changes alone could be accomplished in general usage, a great victory could be hailed. Something as seemingly insignificant as proving . . . that the expression 'The injury wasn't that bad' needs a comparison would go a long way to improving everyday abuse of English. [The man is saying, in effect, that abuse would become bigger and better abuse. He should have written 'improving everyday use' or 'alleviating everyday abuse.'] As a compromise, we, the experts (or 'they' as we are called) should let up a little . . . because there aren't enough of us to stop them [I thought *them* was *us,* but never mind!] if they decide the hell with us."

Again, what confusion! Students have always had rushed schedules, extracurricular activities, less than perfect home lives, seven classes or more. But few people—and no teachers—considered this an excuse for not learning the basics of English or any other required subject. Of course, the poor dears may have had neither television sets with which to fragment their areas of responsibility nor parents who, ignorant themselves, were ready to do battle against schools demanding Standard English from their pupils.

Yet the real horror in these remarks lies in the supine willingness to compromise with sloth, ignorance, and anti-intellectualism. If a man threatens to beat me to a pulp, I don't offer, by way of compromise, to let him beat me black-and-blue; rather, I defend myself with might and main. Then, if he still trounces me, too bad; but at least I put up a good defense, and the rest was inevitable. One does not intentionally compromise with any sort of evil; what happens in most cases is that a compromise takes place of itself. In other words, things level off somewhere between the purism of the intellect and the erosions of the world. But such, as it were, unavoidable historical compromise should not be pandered to and accelerated—otherwise the natural order of things, which is less good than an ideal order but better than a natural disorder, is disrupted, to our peril.

A frightening specimen of compromise run amok, again concerning the use of *lay* and *lie*, was submitted to me by Clyde Lee, of Austin, Texas. She had been teaching English to Turkish businessmen in Ankara when she discovered on the day's work sheet the sentence "The dog is laying under the tree." She informed her class that this was a typographcal error and properly substituted *lying* for *laying*. In her own words: "I was called to a meeting which included the (then) director of the Georgetown University Language Group, who happened to be 'visiting the field' from Washington, and he explained that it was not an error and it was to be taught so people would understand a New York cab driver when they arrived in our country. Or, he continued, 'English as she is spoke.' Our students were 30- to 40-year-old men, well-educated and intelligent, who were going to America to study highly technical postgraduate subjects and I could see no excuse for that excuse."

That, I think, is well thought out and well expressed. But notice now what this cultivated woman's solution is: "Better to do away with [*lay* and *lie*] altogether. You can, after all, describe a shotgun *on* the front seat, or the importance of *resting* after lunch. . . ." Because the New York cabdriver says *lay* for *lie*, everyone must be mistaught his English. The New York cabby becomes the measure of all things, in the name of either pragmatism or democracy. And if the cabby cannot learn the difference between two words, we must drop them altogether. So runs the opinion of a civilized person not even cursed with being a high-school teacher.

Well, like E. M. Forster, I am willing to give two cheers for democracy, and, on occasion, one for pragmatism, but for maintaining good and useful English words I'll give three cheers at any time, along with my lifeblood. Neither the New York hackie nor the upper-crust ignoramus who graduated from Groton and Harvard nor yet the black-English-speaking hordes shall dictate what good English is to those of us who adhere to an enlightened and serviceable tradition—though, in the end, they may prevail over our dead bodies. Meanwhile, the distinction between *lay* and *lie* is worth fighting for.

The trouble is that we live in an age of cultural compromise. Take the word *lingerie*. Why should even such an estimable dictionary as the *American Heritage* (forget about *Webster's Third* and the *Random House*) give as the first pronunciation the equivalent of lahn-zher-ray—in other words, the illiterate's notion of how this French word is pronounced by the French. Conversely, the *Oxford English Dictionary* gives the equivalent of lan-zhree, with the first syllable nasalized, which is a decent approximation of what the French say. So the best American dictionary espouses the pronunciation of people not only uncultivated (otherwise they would have some notion of how French sounds) but also benighted enough to compound their deficiency by pretentiously faking something they know nothing about.

Why, then, does *Heritage* go along with a combination of ignorance and imposture? Presumably because the unholy alliance reflects the ways of the majority. And because, in a broader context, democracy encourages the majority to decide things about which the majority is blissfully ignorant. Of course, matters of social, political, and economic well-being are for the majority to determine; cultural, artistic, scientific, and intellectual matters are not. Even the greatest English dictionary maker, Samuel Johnson, felt obliged to concede:

> Pronunciation will be varied by levity or ignorance . . . illiterate writers will at one time or other, by publick infatuation, rise into renown, who, not knowing the original import of words, will use them with colloquial licentiousness, confound distinction, and forget propriety. . . .But if the changes that we fear be thus irresistible . . . it remains that we retard what we cannot repel, that we palliate what we cannot cure.

One problem is that a good many intellectuals simply throw up their hands. Thus Israel Shenker, in *Harmless Drudges*, a book mainly about dictionary makers, quotes this statement from Lionel Trilling: "I find righteous denunciations of the present state of the language no less dismaying than the present state of the language"—a remark all the more dispiriting for having been made in response to a questionnaire by the editors of the *Harper Dictionary of Contemporary Usage.*

I propose herewith a new dictionary, to be compiled by the best and least trendy Anglo-American authorities. This dictionary would list under one heading the refined, educated, elitist usage; under another, the popular, demotic, uneducated usage. It would then be up to every one of us to decide what he wants to be, to choose the parlance suited to his aspirations. Do not fear that this procedure would polarize our society; it would merely confirm a polarization that has already taken place and enable people to become more conscious of where they stand and what they are fighting for. Verbally, of course.

# CHAPTER ELEVEN

# A PARTING WORD

# Why Good English Is Good for You *

**W**hat's good English to you that, though it may be subjected to as many grievances as were Hecuba and Niobe combined, you should grieve for it? What good is correct speech and writing, you may ask, in an age in which hardly anyone seems to know, and no one seems to care? Why shouldn't you just fling bloopers, bloopers riotously with the throng, and not stick out from the rest like a sore thumb by using the language correctly? Isn't grammar really a thing of the past, and isn't the new idea to communicate in *any* way as long as you can make yourself understood?

Let us, for a moment, go back into the past, or, to be as nearly exact as I can, to the early 1630s, when Etienne Pascal was teaching his barely teenaged son, Blaise, about languages. As Blaise's elder sister, Gilberte, was to report in a memoir later on, the father was making "him [Blaise] perceive in general what languages were about; he showed him how they were reduced to grammars subject to certain rules; that these rules had yet some exceptions that had been carefully noted; and that means had thus been found to make languages communicable from country to country. This general idea disentangled his mind"—or, as some of you today might put it, *blew* his mind; in the original, "lui débrouillait l'esprit." All this Etienne taught Blaise *before* he was twelve, at which time he started him out on his first foreign language, which was Latin.

Let us now take an even longer step back, to 1511, in which year Erasmus's *The Praise of Folly* was published. In this facetious, satirical work, Folly herself is speaking (I quote only brief excerpts, in H. H. Hudson's translation): "Among those who maintain . . . an appearance of wisdom," she declares, "the grammarians hold first place." Their schools are "knowledge factories . . . mills . . . even . . . shambles." "Yet thanks to me," Folly continues, "they see themselves as the first among men," beating the living daylights out of their wretched students, whom "they cram . . . with utter nonsense." The grammarians are particularly delighted when they "can drag out of some worm-eaten man-

---

* This is the text of a talk originally delivered to a college audience.

uscript . . . some word not generally known," or some other trivial information; they also form mutual admiration societies, "scratching each other's itch. Yet if one commits a lapse in a single word, and another . . . lights on it . . . what a stir presently, what scufflings, what insults." Then Folly cites a certain polymath who laid aside all other pursuits to hurl himself into the study of grammar so as to settle at last issues that "none of the Greeks or Latins succeeded in doing definitively. It becomes a matter to be put to the test of battle when someone makes a conjunction of a word which belongs in the bailiwick of adverbs. Thanks to him, there are as many grammars as there are grammarians—nay, more," and Folly names the great printer Aldus, who published at least five different books on grammar.

Here we have the two extremes: in Erasmus, grammar ridiculed as the ultimate waste of both students' and teachers' time; in Gilberte Pascal's memoir of her brother, the principles of grammar shown as the abolishers of boundaries between countries and the clearers of a young mind. I think both statements are as true today as they were then, but both, of course, are to some extent oversimplifications. The virtues of grammar—or, in our case, of good English—are not quite so monolithically manifest as all that; nor is the pigheaded, despotic nitpicking of the perfectionists, elitists, or fuddy-duddies (call them what you will) entirely misguided and ludicrous.

The usual, basic defense of good English (and here, again, let us not worry about nomenclature—for all I care, you may call it "Standard English," "correct American," or anything else) is that it helps communication, that it is perhaps even a *sine qua non* of mutual understanding. Although this is a crude truth of sorts, it strikes me as, in some ways, both more and less than the truth. Suppose you say, "Everyone in their right mind would cross on the green light" or "Hopefully, it won't rain tomorrow," chances are very good that the person you say this to will understand you, even though you are committing obvious solecisms or creating needless ambiguities. Similarly, if you write in a letter, "The baby has finally ceased it's howling" (spelling *its* as *it's*), the recipient will be able to figure out what was meant. But "figuring out" is precisely what a listener or reader should not have to do. There is, of course, the fundamental matter of courtesy to the other person, but it goes beyond that: why waste time on unscrambling simple meaning when there are more complex questions that should receive our undivided attention? If the many cooks had to worry first about which out of a large number of pots had no leak in it, the broth, whether spoiled or not, would take forever to be ready.

It is, I repeat, only initially a matter of clarity. It is also a matter of concision. Space today is as limited as time. If you have only a thousand words in which to convey an important message it helps to know that "overcomplicated" is correct and "overly complicated" is incorrect. Never mind the grammatical explanations; the two extra characters and one space between words are reason enough. But what about the more advanced forms of word-mongering that hold sway nowadays? Take redundancy, like the "hopes and aspirations" of Jimmy Carter, quoted by Edwin Newman as having "a deeply profound religious experience"; or elaborate jargon, as when Charles G. Walcutt, a graduate professor of English at CUNY, writes (again as quoted by Newman): "The colleges, trying to remediate increasing numbers of . . . illiterates up to college levels, are being highschoolized"; or just obfuscatory verbiage of the pretentious sort, such as this fragment from a letter I received: "It is my impression that effective interpersonal verbal communication depends on prior effective intra-personal verbal communication." What this means is that if you think clearly, you can speak and write clearly—except if you are a "certified speech and language pathologist," like the writer of the letter I quote. (By the way, she adds the letters Ph.D. after her name, though she is not even from Germany, where *Herr* and *Frau Doktor* are in common, not to say vulgar, use.)

But except for her ghastly verbiage, our certified language pathologist (whatever that means) is perfectly right: there is a close connection between the ability to think and the ability to use English correctly. After all, we think in words, we conceptualize in words, we work out our problems inwardly with words, and using them correctly is comparable to a craftsman's treating his tools with care, keeping his materials in good shape. Would you trust a weaver who hangs her wet laundry on her loom, or lets her cats bed down in her yarn? The person who does not respect words and their proper relationships cannot have much respect for ideas—very possibly cannot have ideas at all. My quarrel is not so much with minor errors that we all fall into from time to time even if we know better as it is with basic sloppiness or ignorance or defiance of good English.

Training yourself to speak and write correctly—and I say "training yourself" because nowadays, unfortunately, you cannot depend on other people or on institutions to give you the proper training, for reasons I shall discuss later—training yourself, then, in language, means developing at the very least two extremely useful faculties: your sense of discipline and your memory. Discipline because language is with us always, as nothing else is: it follows us much as, in the old morality play, Good Deeds followed Everyman, all the way to the grave; and, if the language is written, even beyond. Let me explain: if you can keep an orderly apartment, if you can see to it that your correspondence and bill-paying are attended to regularly, if your diet and wardrobe are maintained with the necessary care—good enough; you are a disciplined person.

But the preliminary discipline underlying all others is nevertheless your speech: the words that come out of you almost as frequently and—if you are tidy—as regularly as your breath. I would go so far as to say that, immediately after your bodily functions, language is first, unless you happen to be an ascetic, an anchorite, or a stylite; but unless you are a styl*ite*, you had better be a styl*ist*.

Most of us—almost all—must take in and give out language as we do breath, and we had better consider the seriousness of language pollution as second only to air pollution. For the linguistically disciplined, to misuse or mispronounce a word is an unnecessary and unhealthy contribution to the surrounding smog. To have taught ourselves not to do this, or—being human and thus also imperfect—to do it as little as possible, means deriving from every speaking moment the satisfaction we get from a cap that snaps on to a container perfectly, an elevator that stops flush with the landing, a roulette ball that comes to rest exactly on the number on which we have placed our bet. It gives us the pleasure of hearing or seeing our words—because they are abiding by the rules—snapping, sliding, falling precisely into place, expressing with perfect lucidity and symmetry just what we wanted them to express. This is comparable to the satisfaction of the athlete or ballet dancer or pianist finding his body or legs or fingers doing his bidding with unimpeachable accuracy.

And if someone now says that "in George Eliot's lesser novels, she is not completely in command" is perfectly comprehensible even if it is ungrammatical, "she" having no antecedent that is a substantive (*Eliot's* is a modifier), I say, "Comprehensible, perhaps, but lopsided," for the civilized and orderly mind does not feel comfortable with that "she"—does not hear that desired and satisfying click of correctness—unless the sentence is restructured as "George Eliot, in her lesser novels, is not . . ." or in some similar way. In fact, the fully literate ear can be thrown by this error in syntax; it may look for the antecedent of that "she" elsewhere than in the preceding possessive case. Be that as it may, playing without rules and winning—in this instance, managing to communicate without using good English—is no more satisfactory than winning in a sport or game by accident or by disregarding the rules: which is really cheating.

The second faculty good speech develops is, as I have mentioned before, our memory. Grammar and syntax are partly logical—and to that extent they are also good exercisers and developers of our logical faculty—but they are also partly arbitrary, conventional, irrational. For example, the correct "compared to" and "contrasted with" could, from the logical point of view, just as well be "contrasted to" and "compared with" ("compared with," of course, is correct, but in a different sense from the one that concerns us here, namely, the antithesis of "contrasted with"). And, apropos *different*, logic would have to strain desperately to explain the exclusive correctness of "different from," given the exclusive correctness of "other than," which would seem to justify "different than," jarring though that is to the cultivated ear.

But there it is: some things are so because tradition, usage, the best speakers and writers, the grammar books and dictionaries have made them so. There may even exist some hidden historical explanation: something, perhaps, in the Sanskrit, Greek, Latin, or other origins of a word or construction that you and I may very easily never know. We can, however, memorize; and memorization can be a wonderfully useful thing—surely the Greeks were right to consider Mnemosyne (memory) the mother of the Muses, for without her there would be no art and no science. And what better place to practice one's mnemonic skills than in the study of one's language?

There is something particularly useful about speaking correctly and precisely because language is always there as a foundation—or, if you prefer a more fluid image, an undercurrent—beneath what is going on. Now, it seems to me that the great difficulty of life lies in the fact that we must almost always do two things at a time. If, for example, we are walking and conversing, we must keep our mouths as well as feet from stumbling. If we are driving while listening to music, we must not allow the siren song of the cassette to prevent us from watching the road and the speedometer (otherwise the less endearing siren of the police car or the ambulance will follow apace). Well, it is just this sort of bifurcation of attention that care for precise, clear expression fosters in us. By learning early in life to pay attention both to what we are saying and to how we are saying it, we develop the much-needed life skill of doing two things simultaneously.

Put another way, we foster our awareness of, and ability to deal with, form and content. If there is any verity that modern criticism has fought for, it is the recognition of the indissolubility of content and form. Criticism won the battle, won it so resoundingly that this oneness has become a contemporary commonplace. And shall the fact that form *is* content be a platitude in all the arts but go unrecognized in the art of self-expression, whether in conversation or correspondence, or whatever form of spoken or written utterance a human being resorts to? Accordingly, you are going to be judged, whether you like it or not, by the correctness of your English as much as by the correctness of your thinking; there are some people to whose ear bad English is as offensive as gibberish, or as your picking your nose in public would be to their eyes and stomachs. The fact that people of linguistic sensibilities may be a dying breed does not mean that they are wholly extinct, and it is best not to take any unnecessary chances.

To be sure, if you are a member of a currently favored minority, many of your linguistic failings may be forgiven you—whether rightly or wrongly is not my concern here. But if you cannot change your sex or color to the one that is getting preferential treatment—Bakke case or no Bakke case—you might as well learn good English and profit by it in your career, your social relations, perhaps even in your basic self-confidence. That, if you will, is the ultimate practical application of good English; but now let me tell you about the ultimate impractical one, which strikes me as being possibly even more important.

Somewhere in the prose writings of Charles Péguy, who was a very fine poet and prose writer—and, what is perhaps even more remarkable, as good a human being as he was an artist—somewhere in those writings is a passage about the decline of pride in workmanship among French artisans, which, as you can deduce, set in even before World War I, wherein Péguy was killed. In the passage I refer to, Péguy bemoans the fact that cabinetmakers no longer finish the backs of furniture—the sides that go against the wall—in the same way as they do the exposed sides. What is not seen was just as important to the old artisans as what is seen—it was a moral issue with them. And so, I think, it ought to be with language. Even if no one else notices the niceties, the precision, the impeccable sense of grammar and syntax you deploy in your utterances, you yourself should be aware of them and take pride in them as in pieces of work well done.

Now, I realize that there are two possible reactions among you to what I have said up to this point. Some of you will say to yourselves: what utter nonsense! Language is a flexible, changing, living organism that belongs to the people who speak it. It has always been changed according to the ways in which people chose to speak it, and the dictionaries and books on grammar had to, and will have to, adjust themselves to the people and not the other way around. For isn't it the glory of language that it keeps throwing up new inventions as surf tosses out differently polished pebbles and bits of bottle glass onto the shore, and that in this inexhaustible variety, in this refusal to kowtow to dry-as-dust scholars, lies its vitality, its beauty?

Others among you, perhaps fewer in number, will say to yourselves: quite so, there is such a thing as Standard English, or purity of speech, or correctness of expression—something worth safeguarding and fostering; but how the devil is one to accomplish that under the prevailing conditions: in a democratic society full of minorities that have their own dialects or linguistic preferences, and in a world in which television, advertising, and other mass media manage daily to corrupt the language a little further? Let me try to answer the first group first, and then come back to the questions of the second.

Of course language is, and must be, a living organism to the extent that new inventions, discoveries, ideas enter the scene and clamor rightfully for designations. Political, social, and psychological changes may also affect our mode of expression, and new words or phrases may have to be found to reflect what we might call historical changes. It is also quite natural for slang terms to be invented, become popular, and, in some cases, remain permanently in the language. It is perhaps equally inevitable (though here we are on more speculative ground) for certain words to become obsolescent and obsolete, and drop out of the language. But does that mean that grammar and syntax have to keep changing, that pronunciations and meanings of words must shift, that more complex or elegant forms are obliged to yield to simpler or cruder ones that often are not fully synonymous with them and not capable of expressing certain fine distinctions? Should, for instance, "terrestrial" disappear entirely in favor of "earthly," or are there shades of meaning involved that need to remain available to us? Must we sacrifice "notwithstanding" because we have "in spite of" or "despite"? Need we forfeit "jettison" just because we have "throw overboard"? And what about "disinterested," which is becoming a synonym for "uninterested," even though that means something else, and though we have no other word for "disinterested"?

"Language has *always* changed," say these people, and they might with equal justice say that there has always been war or sickness or insanity. But the truth is that some sicknesses that formerly killed millions have been eliminated, that some so-called insanity can today be treated, and that just because there have always been wars does not mean that someday a cure cannot be found even for that scourge. And if it cannot, it is only by striving to put an absolute end to war, by pretending that it can be licked, that we can at least partly control it. Without such assumptions and efforts, the evil would be so widespread that, given our current weaponry, we would no longer be here to worry about the future of language.

But we are here, and having evolved linguistically this far, and having the means—books of grammar, dictionaries, education for all—to arrest unnecessary change, why not endeavor with might and main to arrest it? Certain cataclysms cannot be prevented: earthquakes and droughts, for example, can scarcely, if at all, be controlled; but we can prevent floods, for which purpose we have invented dams. And dams are precisely what we can construct to prevent floods of ignorance from eroding our language, and, beyond that, to provide irrigation for areas that would otherwise remain linguistically arid.

For consider that what some people are pleased to call linguistic evolution was almost always a matter of ignorance prevailing over knowledge. There is no valid reason, for example, for the word *nice* to have changed its meaning so many times—except ignorance of its exact definition. Had the change never occurred, or had it been stopped at any intermediate stage, we would have had just as good a word as we have now and saved some people a heap of confusion along the way. But if *nice* means what it does today—and it has two principal meanings, one of them, as in "nice distinction," alas, obsolescent—let us, for heaven's sake, keep it where it is, now that we have the means with which to hold it there.

If, for instance, we lose the accusative case *whom*—and we are in great danger of losing it—our language will be the poorer for it. Obviously, "The man, whom I had never known, was a thief" means something other than "The man who I had never known was a thief." Now, you can object that it would be just as easy in the first instance to use some other construction; but what happens if *this* one is used incorrectly? Ambiguity and confusion. And why should we lose this useful distinction? Just because a million or ten million or a billion people less educated than we are cannot master the difference? Surely it behooves us to try to educate the ignorant up to our level rather than to stultify ourselves down to theirs. Yes, you say, but suppose they refuse to or are unable to learn? In that case, I say, there is a doubly good reason for not going along with them. Ah, you reply, but they are the majority, and we must accept their way or, if the revolution is merely linguistic, lose our "credibility" (as the current parlance, rather confusingly, has it) or, if the revolution is political, lose our heads. Well, I consider a sufficient number of people to be educable enough to be capable of using *who* and *whom* correctly, and to derive satisfaction from this capability—a sufficient number, I mean, to enable us to preserve *whom*, and not to have to ask "for who the bell tolls."

The main problem with education, actually, is not those who need it and cannot get it, but those who should impart it and, for various reasons, do not. In short, the enemies of education are the educators themselves: miseducated, underpaid, overburdened, and intimidated teachers (frightened because, though the pen is supposed to be mightier than the sword, the switchblade is surely more powerful than the ferule), and professors who—because they are structural linguists, democratic respecters of alleged minority rights, or otherwise misguided folk—believe in the sacrosanct privilege of any culturally underprivileged minority or majority to dictate its ignorance to the rest of the world. For, I submit, an

English improvised by slaves and other strangers to the culture—
to whom my heart goes out in every human way—under dread-
fully deprived conditions can nowise equal an English that the
best literary and linguistic talents have, over the centuries, perceptively and painstakingly brought to a high level of excellence.

So my answer to the scoffers in this or any audience is, in
simplest terms, the following: contrary to popular misconception,
language does not belong to the people, or at least not in the sense
in which *belong* is usually construed. For things can rightfully belong only to those who invent or earn them. But we do not know
who invented language: is it the people who first made up the
words for *father* and *mother*, for *I* and *thou*, for *hand* and *foot*; or is it
the people who evolved the subtler shadings of language, its po-
etic variety and suggestiveness, but also its unambiguousness, its
accurate and telling details? Those are two very different groups
of people and two very different languages, and I, as you must
have guessed by now, consider the latter group at least as important as the former. As for *earning* language, it has surely been
earned by those who have striven to learn it properly, and here
even economic and social circumstances are but an imperfect excuse for bad usage; history is full of examples of people rising
from humble origins to learn, against all kinds of odds, to speak
and write correctly—even brilliantly.

*Belong*, then, should be construed in the sense that parks, national forests, monuments, and public utilities are said to belong
to the people: available for properly respectful use but not for
defacement and destruction. And all that we propose to teach is
how to use and enjoy the gardens of language to their utmost
aesthetic and salubrious potential. Still, I must now address myself to the group that, while agreeing with my aims, despairs of
finding practical methods for their implementation.

True enough, after a certain age speakers not aware of Standard
English or not exceptionally gifted will find it hard or impossible
to change their ways. Nevertheless, if there were available funds
for advanced methods in teaching; if teachers themselves were
better trained and paid, and had smaller classes and more as-
sistants; if, furthermore, college entrance requirements were
heightened and the motivation of students accordingly strength-
ened; if there were no structural linguists and National Councils
of Teachers of English filling instructors' heads with notions about

"Students' Rights to Their Own Language" (they have every right to it as a *second* language, but none as a *first*); if teachers in all disciplines, including the sciences and social sciences, graded on English usage as well as on specific proficiencies; if aptitude tests for various jobs stressed good English more than they do; and, above all, if parents were better educated and more aware of the need to set a good example to their children, and to encourage them to learn correct usage, the situation could improve enormously.

Clearly, to expect all this to come to pass is utopian; some of it, however, is well within the realm of possibility. For example, even if parents do not speak very good English, many of them at least can manage an English that is good enough to correct a very young child's mistakes; in other words, most adults can speak a good enough four-year-old's idiom. They would thus start kids out on the right path; the rest could be done by the schools.

But the problem is what to do in the most underprivileged homes: those of blacks, Hispanics, immigrants from various Asian and European countries. This is where day-care centers could come in. If the fathers and mothers could be gainfully employed, their small children would be looked after by day-care centers where—is this asking too much?—good English could be inculcated in them. The difficulty, of course, is what to do about the discrepancy the little ones would note between the speech of the day-care people and that of their parents. Now, it seems to me that small children have a far greater ability to learn things, including languages, than some people give them credit for. Much of it is indeed rote learning, but, where languages are concerned, that is one of the basic learning methods even for adults. There is no reason for not teaching kids another language, to wit, Standard English, and turning this, if desirable, into a game: "At home you speak one way; here we have another language," at which point the instructor can make up names and explanations for Standard English that would appeal to pupils of that particular place, time, and background.

At this stage of the game, as well as later on in school, care should be exercised to avoid insulting the language spoken in the youngsters' homes. There must be ways to convey that both home and school languages have their validity and uses and that knowing both enables one to accomplish more in life. This would be hard to achieve if the children's parents were, say, militant blacks of the Geneva Smitherman sort, who execrate Standard English as a weapon of capitalist oppression against the poor of all races, colors, and religions. But, happily, there is evidence that most black, Hispanic, and other non-Standard English-speaking parents want their children to learn correct English so as to get ahead in the world.

Yet how do we defend ourselves against the charge that we are old fogeys who cannot emotionally adjust to the new directions an ever-living and changing language must inevitably take? Here I would want to redefine or, at any rate, clarify, what "living and changing" means, and also explain where we old fogeys stand. Misinformed attacks on Old Fogeydom, I have noticed, invariably represent us as people who shudder at a split infinitive and would sooner kill or be killed than tolerate a sentence that ends with a preposition. Actually, despite all my travels through Old Fogeydom, I have yet to meet one inhabitant who would not stick a preposition onto the tail of a sentence; as for splitting infinitives, most of us O.F.'s are perfectly willing to do that, too, but tactfully and sparingly, where it feels right. There is no earthly reason, for example, for saying "to dangerously live," when "to live dangerously" sounds so much better; but it does seem right to say (and write) "What a delight to sweetly breathe in your sleeping lover's breath"; that sounds smoother, indeed sweeter, than "to breathe in sweetly" or "sweetly to breathe in." But infinitives begging to be split are relatively rare; a sensitive ear, a good eye for shades of meaning will alert you whenever the need to split arises; without that ear and eye, you had better stick to the rules.

About the sense in which language is, and must be, alive, let me speak while donning another of my several hats—actually it is not a hat but a cap, for there exists in Greenwich Village an inscription on a factory that reads "CRITIC CAPS." So with my drama critic's cap on, let me present you with an analogy. The world theater today is full of directors who wreak havoc on classic plays to demonstrate their own ingenuity, their superiority, as it were, to the author. These directors—aborted playwrights, for the most part—will stage productions of *Hamlet* in which the prince is a woman, a flaming homosexual, or a one-eyed hunchback.

Well, it seems to me that the same spirit prevails in our approach to linguistics, with every newfangled, ill-informed, know-nothing construction, definition, pronunciation enshrined by the joint efforts of structural linguists, permissive dictionaries, and allegedly democratic but actually demagogic educators. What really makes a production of, say, *Hamlet* different, and therefore alive, is that the director, while trying to get as faithfully as possible at Shakespeare's meanings, nevertheless ends up stressing things in the play that strike him most forcefully; and the same individuality in production design and performances (the Hamlet of Gielgud versus the Hamlet of Olivier, for instance—what a world of difference!) further differentiates one production from another, and bestows on each its particular vitality. So, too, language remains alive because each speaker (or writer) can and must, *within the framework of accepted grammar, syntax, and pronunciation*, produce a style that is his very own, that is as personal as his posture, way of walking, mode of dress, and so on. It is such stylistic differences that make a person's—or a nation's—language flavorous, pungent, alive, and all this without having to play fast and loose with the existing rules.

But to have this, we need, among other things, good teachers and, beyond them, enlightened educators. I shudder when I read in the *Birmingham* (Alabama) *Post-Herald* of October 6, 1978, an account of a talk given to eight hundred English teachers by Dr. Alan C. Purves, vice-president of the National Council of Teachers of English. Dr. Purves is quoted as saying things like "We are in a situation with respect to reading where . . . ," and culminating in the following truly horrifying sentence: "I am going to suggest that when we go back to the basics, I think what we should be dealing with is our charge to help students to be more proficient in producing meaningful language—language that says what it means." Notice all the deadwood, the tautology, the anacoluthon in the first part of that sentence; but notice especially the absurdity of the latter part, in which the dubious word "meaningful"—a poor relation of "significant"—is thought to require explaining to an audience of English teachers.

Given such leadership from the N.C.T.E., the time must be at hand when we shall hear—not just "Don't ask for who the bell rings" (*ask not* and *tolls* being, of course, archaic, elitist language), but also "It rings for you and I."

# Index

Aaron, Daniel, 91
Abbott and Costello, 72
academy of Anglo-American language, proposal for, 6-7, 12
"AC-DC," 132
"acquacentric," 90-91
Action, Harold, 110
Acuff, Mark, 185
"adaptizing," 100
adjectives, 15-17, 81-83, 84-85, 88, 94, 128-129, 136
"adultery," 64-65
adverbs, 3-4, 15, 47, 57, 94, 181, 184, 195, 204
"aggravate," 47
Albee, Edward, 105
Aldridge, John W., 105, 106
"almost, most," 15, 181
Alpert, Don, 8
"also," 4-5, 98
ambiguity, 46, 58, 100, 153, 203, 210
*American Film*, 105
*American Heritage Dictionary*, 6, 16, 19, 46, 55, 83, 176-177, 186, 198
*American Studies International*, 146
Amis, Kingsley, xv
"among, amid," 14, 139
"among, between," 112
anacoluthon, 183
Anderson, Maxwell, xii-xiii
antecedents, 90, 111, 143, 205-206
"antelucan," 82-83
"any more," 46, 115, 183
"anyone," 40-41
apostrophes, 42, 56, 184, 203
  omitted letters replaced by, 8-9, 181
  in possessive forms, 11, 42, 88
Arnold, Matthew, 107
*Ars Poetica*, 81
*Art Education*, 59
"as, like," 46, 56
"aspersions," 54
"as to," 45-46
*Atlantic Monthly*, 9-10
Atlas, James, 75
Auden, W. H., 55, 56

Barnes, Clive, 99-100, 133, 134-135
Barth, John, 109
Barthelme, Donald, 108-109
Barthes, Roland, 109, 187
Barzun, Jacques, 4, 55-58, 177, 189
Beittel, Kenneth R., 59
"belong," 211
Bergen, Candice, 65-66
Berne, Stanley, 158-159
Bernstein, Theodore, 101
"between, among," 112
"bimonthly," xvi
Binder, David, 185
Bird, Caroline, 118, 120
*Birmingham Post-Herald*, 214
"black," 28
Black English, 147, 148-149, 165-167
Bolinger, Dwight, xvii
*Boston Globe*, 188
"breech, breach," 187
Breslin, Jimmy, 118, 120
Brooks-Baker, H. B., 28
Browne, Sir Thomas, 61
Brustein, Robert, 98-99, 106-107
Buckle, Richard, 31, 32
Buckley, William F., 105
Burchfield, Robert, xvi
Burgess, Anthony, 89-99, 100
Burroughs, Edgar Rice, xi
Burt, Richard, 185
"buying a pig in a poke," 132

Califano, Joseph A., 41-42
Calisher, Hortense, 118, 120
"can, may," 40-41, 54, 190
Canby, Vincent, 64, 185
"cannibals," 135
Capote, Truman, 110
Carter, Jimmy, 92, 94, 95, 97, 169, 174, 204
Casson, Stanley, 78
catch phrases, 75, 76-80
  defined, 76
"cavalry," 55-56
*Celebrations and Attacks*, 44
"chairperson," 27-28